McCoy POTTERY

REFERENCE & VALUE GUIDE

Bob Hanson
Craig Nissen
Margaret Hanson

Flower bowl values can be found on page 78.

COLLECTOR BOOKS
A Division of Schroeder Publishing Co., Inc.

The current values in this book should be used only as a guide. They are not intended to set prices, which vary from one section of the country to another. Auction prices as well as dealer prices vary greatly and are affected by condition as well as demand. Neither the Authors nor the Publisher assumes responsibility for any losses that might be incurred as a result of consulting this guide.

SEARCHING FOR A PUBLISHER?

We are always looking for knowledgeable people considered to be experts within their fields. If you feel that there is a real need for a book on your collectible subject and have a large comprehensive collection, contact Collector Books.

Book design by: Karen Long
Cover design by: Beth Summers

On the Cover: Information and values for items pictured on the cover are located on the following pages: 44, 46, 57, 59, 62, 66, 76, 80, 91, 97, 176, and 240.

Oil jar information and value is located on page 17.

COLLECTOR BOOKS
P.O. Box 3009
Paducah, KY 42002-3009

Craig Nissen   Bob and Margaret Hanson
P.O. Box 223   P.O. Box 1945
Grafton, WI 53024   Woodinville, WA 98072

Copyright © 1997 by Bob and Margaret Hanson, Craig Nissen

CONTENTS

Bob, Craig and Margaret are long time collectors of Nelson McCoy Pottery. Their collecting began when McCoy was usually the pottery on the floor at an antique show or in the grass at a flea market. It was one of the "other" potteries. However, part of the attraction to McCoy then was that you could find it as well as afford it. These factors are major reasons that the collections of the Hansons and Nissens have grown to a combined total of more than 5,000 pieces.

Bob and Margaret are interested in a variety of collections in addition to McCoy, including Brush-McCoy, and J.W. McCoy as well as many pieces from the "Arts & Crafts Era." In addition to pottery, they collect reverse paintings and trays, silhouette pictures, vintage whimsical plastic pins and electric novelty clocks. Bob and Margaret have four children and live in the Seattle,

Washington, area.

Craig, and his wife Pat, also enjoy collecting a number of other things in addition to the Nelson McCoy pottery. They have a modest collection of Van Briggle and Roseville pottery. They also collect Aladdin electric lamps, beaded "sugar" shade lamps from the '20s, cupid photos, rug and pillow beaters, "Chandler" pastels and fruit and vegetable wall pockets. Craig and Pat have one daughter and are located in the greater Milwaukee area of Wisconsin.

Vintage items included in many photographs throughout the book are used to enhance a piece or to demonstrate a particular way of displaying pieces and are part of the authors' collections. Both the Hansons and the Nissens have a primary "obsession" of collecting McCoy pottery.

Margaret Hanson (holding Fergie), Craig Nissen, and Bob Hanson

DEDICATION

This book is dedicated to all the past, present, and future collectors of Nelson McCoy Pottery.

*May you have as much fun and enjoyment
as we have had in our collecting.*

PREFACE

This reference book is exclusively about the pottery made by the Nelson McCoy Pottery Company from 1910 through the Lancaster years of ownership in the 1980s. We have purposely not included the subject of cookie jars. This area of McCoy pottery collecting has already been appropriately handled as a separate topic, published by more than one author.

We have tried to present the information in a sequential format from a collector's perspective. Being collectors ourselves, we have hopefully been successful in that goal. We have also included brief facts and/or opinions about some of the individual pieces that are bits of information we have picked up during our period of collecting. We hope you enjoy this information and will find it very useful as you add to your own collections.

ACKNOWLEDGMENTS

We want to say thank you to all of our friends in the McCoy Pottery collecting family who have so generously helped us, from sharing information, shipping pieces with risk of loss or damage, allowing us to come into their homes to photograph pieces or simply giving important moral support. All of these efforts have been greatly appreciated and have meant a great deal to all of us.

We include the names of those collectors who shared some of their treasured pieces with us and /or related reference information. Again, thank you!

We would also like to extend a special thank you to Chiquita Prestwood of North Carolina for packing and shipping literally dozens of her pieces for us to photograph. This put some fine pieces at risk and we want to thank her again for her generosity and significant effort.

Jean Bushnell – Colorado

Lillian Conesa – Florida

Mark and Marilyn Cooley – Wisconsin

Louie and Eleanore Geissel, Silver Parrot Antiques – Washington

Stan Gracyalny – Wisconsin

Bob and Sharon Huxford – Indiana

DeWayne and Audrey Imsand – Alabama

Bill Jensen – Nevada

Sharon and Herb Klaviter – Oregon

Kathy Lynch – Missouri

Bob and Dorothy MacIntyre – Ohio

Billie and Nelson McCoy – Ohio

Chiquita and Dewey Prestwood – North Carolina

John Sweetman – Delaware

Fred and Sarah Wolfe – Mississippi

The history of "McCoy" pottery is actually a bit complex. Four generations of McCoy family members were involved in the business of manufacturing pottery for several different companies. The following information is presented with the hope of simplifying the history of "McCoy" pottery and eliminating any confusion that may exist with some collectors.

- In 1848 W. Nelson McCoy and W.F. McCoy, great-grandfather and great-great-uncle respectively of Nelson McCoy, started a pottery business which made stoneware crocks and jars. The business was located in the present Zanesville, Ohio area. These products were mainly sold through general stores. Although most pieces were not marked, some did carry stenciling on the side of the ware with "W.F. McCoy" included in the lettering.

- In 1899, the son of W. Nelson McCoy, J.W. McCoy, organized the J.W. McCoy Pottery company in Roseville, Ohio (close to Zanesville). In addition to crock-type products made in the initial years, the J.W. McCoy Pottery company made several lines of art pottery. One of the earliest was the Loy-Nel-Art line which was named after his three sons, Lloyd, Nelson, and Arthur. In 1909, George Brush became general manager. In 1911, J.W. McCoy Pottery merged with other small pottery companies and became known as the Brush-McCoy Pottery Company. W.R. Baker was president and George Brush remained as the general manager. J.W. McCoy continued with the company as a principal stockholder. In 1925, after the McCoy family sold their interest in the company, Brush-McCoy Pottery was renamed Brush Pottery.

- In 1910 Nelson McCoy, one of three sons of J.W. McCoy, started the Nelson McCoy Sanitary Stoneware Company in Roseville, Ohio, with the financial help of his father. This company was in direct competition with the Brush-McCoy company, making stoneware churns, jars, and jugs. These earlier pieces were marked only on the side with a stencil of a clover pattern in a shield with an "M" above it. In the 1920s, they began marking some pieces on the bottom, inside the pottery, usually with a number inside a shield pattern.

- In 1933, the company reorganized to become The Nelson McCoy Pottery Company and Nelson McCoy changed the design of their products to a more artware type pottery. The early pottery of the Nelson McCoy Stoneware Company was designed mainly by Walter Bauer, including the leaves and berries pattern. In 1934, McCoy hired Sidney Cope, an Englishman, who ultimately replaced Mr. Bauer as designer. Cope held this position until his death in 1961. Many of the popular pieces today were his design, including the hunting dog planter, the Liberty Bell planter and the wishing well planter. After his death, his son Leslie became the designer until 1966 when Billie McCoy, the wife of Nelson, took over as head of the design group on a full-time basis.

- Nelson McCoy Pottery flourished in the 1940s. Some of the floral vases were released with great success. The wishing well and spinning wheel planters were also great contributors to a very profitable time for the company. In 1945, Nelson McCoy died and was replaced as president by his nephew, Nelson McCoy Melick, who had been with the company since 1924. In 1950, all the manufacturing buildings were destroyed by fire. The McCoy family decided to rebuild with the latest technology which helped position the company for the years ahead. They were the largest producer of pottery in the United States and by the end of the decade were shipping millions of pieces per year. Melick remained as president until his death in 1954 when Nelson McCoy Jr., who had joined the company in 1948 after his tour of duty in WW II, became president at the age of 29, a position he would hold for almost three decades.

- In 1967, the company was sold to David Chase of the Mount Clemens Pottery Company. Some pieces from this era can be identified by an "MCP" on the bottom. In 1974, Chase sold the company to Lancaster Colony Corporation who also added a logo marking to the bottom. Throughout this entire period, Nelson McCoy Jr. remained as president and the pottery continued to carry the McCoy name. In 1981, Nelson McCoy left the company after more than 30 years of service. Four years later, after significant losses, Lancaster sold the company to Designer Accents, a company which was unsuccessful and closed the doors around 1990.

The art pottery produced by J.W. McCoy Pottery and Brush-McCoy Pottery is often confused with the pottery produced by Nelson McCoy Pottery. Although it is certainly true that all of it is "McCoy" pottery, it is equally important to recognize which era of "McCoy" pottery is represented.

If you want additional details on the history of McCoy Pottery, a good reference is The Collector's Encyclopedia of McCoy Pottery by Sharon & Bob Huxford, first published in 1978 by Collector Books.

A recent "prize" found by Billie in Columbus, Ohio. A beautiful blended glaze pedestal and jardiniere set from the 1920s. The jardiniere is 10½"–11" and the pedestal is about 18½" tall. $400.00 – 450.00.

Billie and Nelson McCoy Jr. We would like to thank them for all of their support and generous offering of information.

PRICING INFORMATION

The price values throughout the book are based on undamaged pieces; no hairlines, chips, cracks, crazing or flakes. Some collectors actually feel that, depending on the defect, pieces damaged in the manufacturing process can actually be more valuable. For example, a piece with a chip glazed over when originally made has added character as well as a degree of rarity and may therefore be more valuable. We leave such judgments to the individual collector.

While photos may show pieces either individually or in groups, if items are typically found as individual pieces, they are priced as such; if they are typically found in pairs or sets, such as pairs of bookends and candleholders or ashtray sets, they are priced accordingly also.

The price range accounts for variation in prices throughout the country. It also considers that one particular piece may have a sharper look than another sample of the same piece due to the color of the same glaze or the crispness of the piece out of the mold. When a piece has a pattern in the greenware, the sharpness of the pattern starts to fade as the mold is used over and over. This is how you can

tell if a particular piece was "early" out of the mold or made near the end of the mold's life. The number of years of manufacture of many of the pieces will also affect the value. This, of course, also adds to the probability of finding a particular piece.

There are several pieces that are not known to be cataloged. However, in most cases, one or more of these has been found by collectors. The lack of factual information is why we have not used the "not produced" designation at all. Where few have been found, we have indicated as such by describing the piece as "rare." What is very important to the collector is that these pieces have been found by collectors and therefore can be found again.

There are a number of pieces that were made for several years but with a variety of glazes. In some of these examples, the marking of the piece may also have changed. This is especially true of several pieces made initially in the late '20s to early '30s. They were available in one or more of the glazes of that era and then were also manufactured in the pastels glazes of the late '30s and '40s. A few were still being made in

the early '50s. One example is the lower sand butterfly porch jar. The early pieces were not marked and had matte glazes. The later pieces had gloss finishes and were marked McCoy. The tall 20" sand butterfly piece is another example which, although never marked, can have its year of manufacture estimated best by the glaze on the piece. Other later examples of these glaze differences are some of the turtle and frog pieces that were originally made in the same green color but were produced with other glazes several years later. The values of these types of pieces will vary greatly. We have considered these issues in assigning price values to these types of pieces; however, some of these issues can be subtle and thought should be given to this area before making a purchase.

Several pieces were hand decorated over the glaze with a paint commonly described as "cold paint." This paint was not very durable and pieces are commonly found with much, if not all, of the paint missing. A piece with all of the original cold paint will command a premium price over one with no paint at all. The price ranges in the book account for this variation. However, it again is a topic that relates to the personal preference of the individual collector in terms of the amount of additional value "cold paint" should add to a piece.

Several paper labels were used on a number of lines and were usually attached to the side of the piece. If a piece in the book has a label, this has *not* been considered in the value. If the label is in good condition, you should add from $5.00 to $15.00 to the value of the piece. This range covers slight variations in acceptable condition as well as the rarity of the label.

See the Marks and Labels section for photo examples of most of these labels. A few examples of where labels can be found:

• The Blossom Time and Wild Rose lines of the '40s and '50s respectively, as well as several of the floral vases, frequently had a "Hand Painted by McCoy" label. A few rarer styles of "McCoy" labels can also be found on these same pieces.

• The Capri and Garden Club lines can be found with labels specific to each. (Capri by McCoy; Garden Club by McCoy)

• The Golden Brocade pieces sometimes had a label specific to their line.

• A few "general" McCoy labels were also used, not specific to a line (see Labels section).

• The turtle sprinkler can be found with a "sprinkler" label on the bottom (photo in Labels section).

Throughout the book, we have included additional information on all pieces such as size information of a particular piece pictured as well as other sizes that were sold of that same style piece. Generally, jardinieres are sized by the width of the opening, vases by their height. We have also included information on other glazes that were offered on a piece. The difference between cataloged glazes and others found by collectors is noted where that information was available. An estimate of the original year of manufacture is also included.

Finally, we have included an indication of whether or not a piece is usually marked. We have listed the types of marking styles in the Marks and Labels section. Also, we have noted when pieces have been found both with and without marks.

MARKS AND LABELS

The following are examples of some of the marks used on the bottom of the pottery throughout the history of the Nelson McCoy Pottery Company. There are many different styles of these marks. Variations exist on letter style, and position of the "USA" or "Made in USA" mark in respect to the McCoy name, location of mark, etc., but the content should be similar. The following examples provide a range of those styles so that you can make an identification. As

we indicate the presence or absence of a mark, you will see that we do it by general style. In addition to a "no mark" indication, we will use either "old mark" for the first style group shown, "NM" for any variation of that mark and "McCoy," if any style of "McCoy" is used. For Floraline, we will indicate as such. We have also included photo examples of labels as reviewed in the **Pricing Information Section.**

Old Stoneware Marks (1920s)

  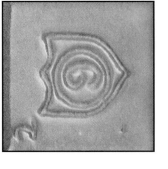 

"NM" Marks (Late '30s and '40s) – Small "NM" mark shown on bottom side of piece is typical of the mark used on many of the smaller pieces of this era.

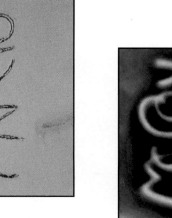 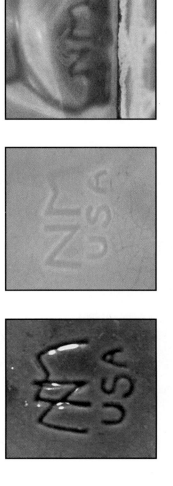

"McCoy" Marks ('40s through the late '60s)

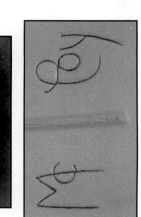 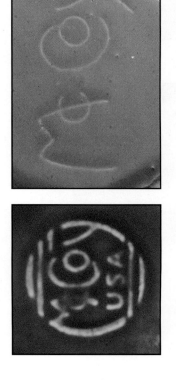

Later Marks ('70s and '80s)

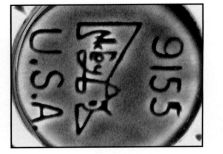

Floraline Marks ('40s through the late '70s)

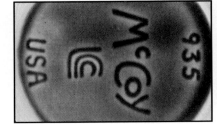

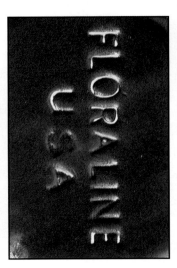

Labels

EARLY STONEWARE

These pieces were marked with stenciling on the side. No other marks are present. The "M" in the stenciling stands for McCoy.

#3 jar, $90.00 – 100.00 and #2 jug, $60.00 – 75.00.

#12 Jar, $90.00 – 100.00.

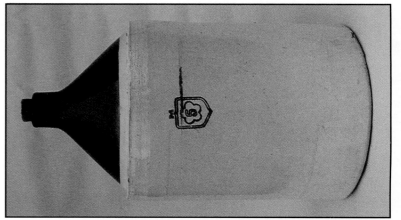

#5 jug, $75.00 – 85.00.

See description of top row 1 below.

Mixing bowls were a very popular product. They were sold in the '20s and well into the '30s, and are usually marked with one of the old style marks. Glaze colors varied from green to yellow to a cream color as pictured. Left to right sizes, 10", 7", and 5½". In similar condition, the value of the bowl usually increases with the size, $35.00 – 75.00.

PAGE 13

	Year	Description	Size	Mark	Available Colors	Value
Top						
Row 1	1926	Pitcher	5¼"	Old Mark	Green, Yellow	$25.00 – 35.00
	1926	Lamp	9"	V2	Green, Yellow	$75.00 – 100.00
Row 2	1935	Pitcher	5"	No Mark	Several	$25.00 – 35.00
	1935	Pitcher	6½"	No Mark	Several	$35.00 – 45.00
	1935	Pitcher	5"	No Mark	Several	$25.00 – 35.00
Bottom						
Row 1	1935	Teapot	5"	No Mark	Several	$40.00 – 50.00
	Same as left piece — opposite side shown.					
Row 2	1926	Tankard	8½"	Old Mark	Green	$50.00 – 60.00
	1926	Grape Cuspidor	5¼"	No Mark	Several	$30.00 – 50.00
	(Made many years)					

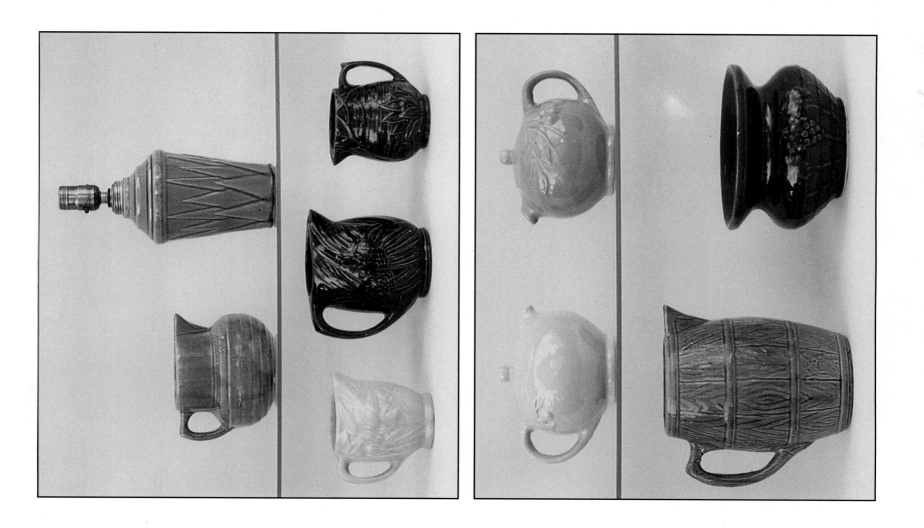

Year		Description	Size	Mark	Available Colors	Value
Row 1	1935	Pitcher	7"	No Mark	Several	$65.00 – 80.00
	1935	Pitcher	5½"	No Mark	Several	$40.00 – 55.00
		Same as left piece — opposite side shown.				
Row 2	1920s	Covered Casserole	7½"	No Mark	Several	$60.00 – 75.00
	1920s	Covered Butter	6"	No Mark	Several	$75.00 – 100.00
	1920s	Tobacco Humidor	7½"	No Mark	Several	$65.00 – 85.00

Year		Description	Size	Mark	Available Colors	Value
Row 1	1926	Mug	5"	No Mark	Green	$20.00 – 30.00
		Elephant Dish	8"	No Mark	Green	$40.00 – 55.00
	1926	Mug	4¾"	No Mark	Green, Brown	$20.00 – 30.00
Row 2	1926	Tankard	8½"	No Mark	Brown	$65.00 – 85.00
	1926	Tankard	8½"	Old Mark	Green, Brown	$60.00 – 75.00
	1926	Tankard	8½"	No Mark	Green	$60.00 – 75.00

BLENDED GLAZES

From the mid 1920s, a blended gloss glaze was used on many pieces. Solid color gloss glazes were also used. The pieces to the right are good examples of this glaze style from the later 1920s. As you can see, this jardiniere was offered in several sizes. Most of these pieces are not marked. A few of the very early pieces of this line of pottery can be found with the shield style mark typically used on pieces from the previous era.

Description	Size	Value
Left to right:		
Jardiniere	10"	$60.00 – 85.00
Jardiniere	4½"	$25.00 – 30.00
Jardiniere/Pedestal Set		$450.00 – 500.00
Jardiniere 10½", Pedestal 18" Tall *(This set has also been found with small handles on jardiniere.)*		
Jardiniere	7"	$45.00 – 60.00

Additional old "shield" marked pieces: Both pieces pictured are 7" jardinieres. Both were also sold in a smaller size. A jardiniere similar to the piece to the left was also sold by Brush-McCoy. The way to determine if it is a Nelson McCoy product or not is by the shield mark. Value on both jardinieres below: $40.00 – 55.00.

Description **Size** **Value**
Jardiniere 7½" $45.00 – 60.00
Jardiniere/Pedestal Set, Jardiniere 9", Pedestal 13" $250.00 – 500.00
Jardiniere—Same as left, different color

Jardiniere/pedestal set, $500.00 – 550.00; jardiniere 9½"; pedestal 19".

To the right are two styles of umbrella stands. The smaller size was made only during the early part of this era in these two glazes. The taller stand was made in this glaze as well as a blended glaze pictured on page 40. This stand was also made later in the pastel glaze era.

Description **Size** **Value**
Left to right:
Umbrella Stand 18" $300.00 – 350.00
Umbrella Stand 21" $350.00 – 400.00
Umbrella Stand Same as pictured on left with different glaze.

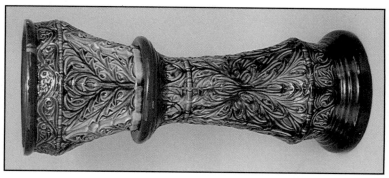

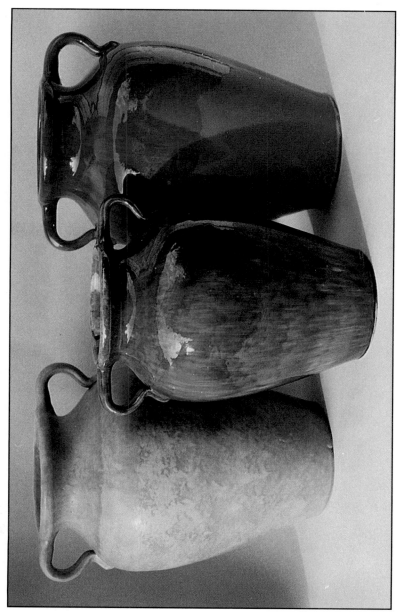

Above are two sizes of oil jars. These jars were made in a variety of glaze colors for a number of years and are not marked.

Left to right:

Description	Size	Value
Oil Jar	18"	$300.00 – 400.00
Oil Jar	15"	$250.00 – 300.00
Oil Jar		Same as pictured on left with different glaze.

Left:
Same as 18" size oil jar above. $300.00 – 400.00.

Right:
Jardiniere/pedestal set, $450.00 – 550.00. Jardiniere 10", pedestal 18½". Similar to set on page 20.

Right and below:
Same jardiniere and pedestal set shown in two different glaze combinations.

Jardiniere   8½"
Pedestal   12½"
Set Value: $250.00 – 350.00

Also cataloged in a 10½"/18½" combination size but none known to have been found. $450.00 – 500.00.

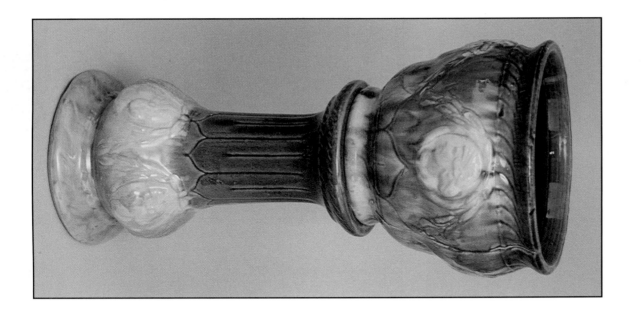

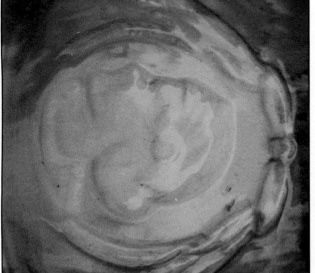

Close-up of cameo design.

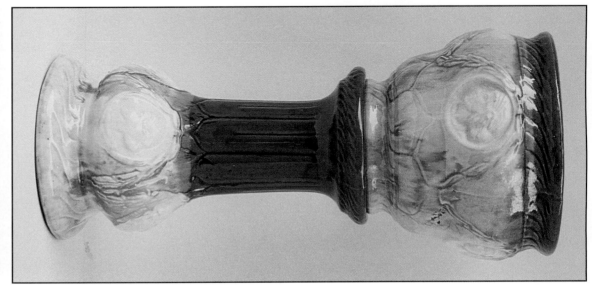

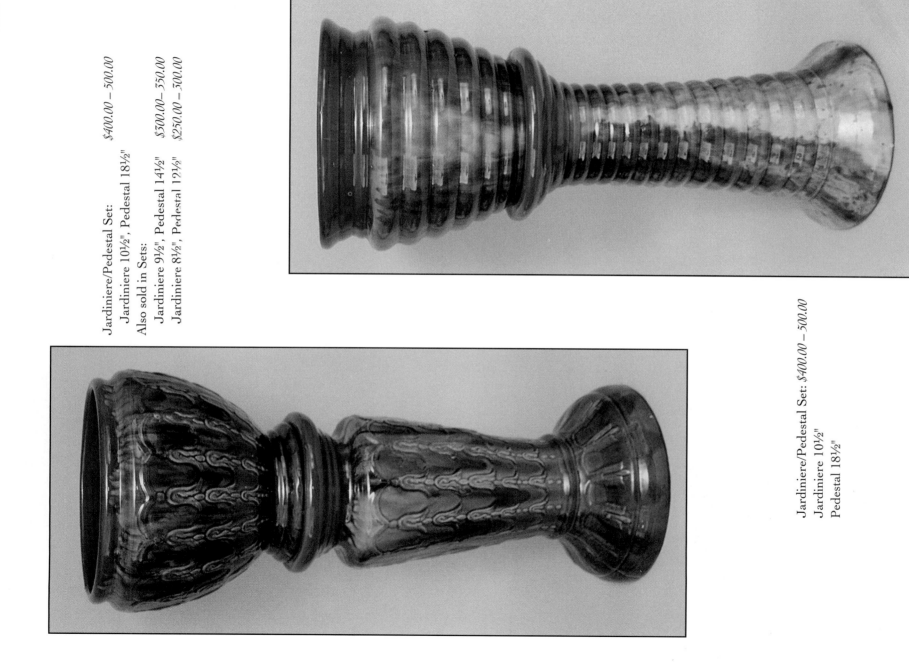

Jardiniere/Pedestal Set: *$400.00 – 500.00*
   Jardiniere 10½", Pedestal 18½"
Also sold in Sets:
   Jardiniere 9½", Pedestal 14½"   *$300.00 – 550.00*
   Jardiniere 8½", Pedestal 12½"   *$250.00 – 500.00*

Jardiniere/Pedestal Set: *$400.00 – 500.00*
Jardiniere 10½"
Pedestal 18½"

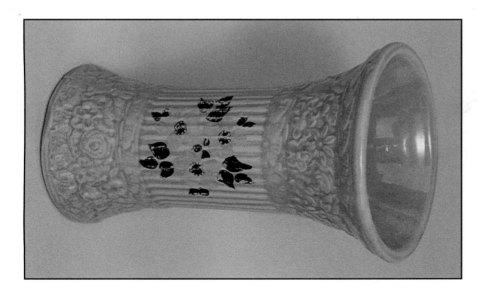

The pedestal and jardiniere set is from the late 1920s. The jardiniere is 11" and the pedestal is 18½" tall. No mark. This pattern was offered in a couple shapes of pedestal and jardiniere and also in a blended gloss glaze. $400.00 – 500.00.

Top photo same as 7" urn piece on following page, only with handles, same value. Lower right photo same vase as listed on following page, pictured in 10½" size, same value range. Floral decoration is original.

Top pieces, clockwise left to right:

Year	Description	Size	Mark	Available Colors	Value
1926	Urn	4½"	No Mark	Blended & Solid	$25.00 – 35.00
1920s	Jardiniere	4½"	No Mark	Natural	$25.00 – 35.00
1926	Jardiniere	4½"	No Mark	Natural	$25.00 – 35.00
1926	Urn		Same as first piece.		

Lower pieces:

Year	Description	Size	Mark	Available Colors	Value
1926	Urn	7"	No Mark	Blended	$40.00 – 60.00
1920s	Vase	8½"	No Mark	Green or Blended	$85.00 – 110.00

Same pattern as pedestal shown on page 7.

In addition to the blended gloss glazes used in the late '20s and '30s, standard matte glazes in white, dark green, and a combination of brown and green were regularly used. The combination of brown and green color glaze was offered in a very dull matte brown and green color glaze was offered in a very dull matte as well as a more brilliant, somewhat glossy combination. To a much lesser extent, pieces were sold in other glazes including matte blues and gloss and matte yellows. Examples of these glazes are included throughout the section. Some of the pieces from this period were produced into the early '40s, being offered in some of the pastel glazes of that period.

Left to right:
Pedestal/jardiniere set (white), 1930s, matte glazes. $250.00 – 350.00. Jardiniere, 8½"; pedestal, 12½". Also sold in 10½" / 18½". Set $450.00 – 500.00. Pedestal/jardiniere set (blended), 1930s. Also matte glazes. Final set shown in white is same. $250.00 – 350.00. Jardiniere – 8½", Pedestal – 12½".

PAGE 23

	Year	Description	Size	Mark	Available Glazes	Value
Top						
Row 1	1930s	Lamp		No Mark	Matte Colors	$75.00 – 100.00
	1930s	Urn	4"	No Mark	Matte Colors	$25.00 – 40.00
Row 2	1930s	Urn – Same as middle piece this row, different glaze.		No Mark		
	1930s	Vase	7"	No Mark	Matte Colors	$40.00 – 100.00

All three vases on this row are the same pattern with different glazes pictured. Wide range in values due to glaze. Plain green and white are most common, blue is not very common.

	Year	Description	Size	Mark	Available Glazes	Value
Bottom						
Row 1	1935	Jardiniere (Acorn)	4½"	No Mark	Matte Colors	$25.00 – 35.00
	1920s	Jardiniere	4½"	Old Mark	As Shown	$35.00 – 45.00
		Jardiniere – Same as middle piece this row, different glaze. See page 15 for larger size.				
Row 2	1926	Jardiniere (Acorn)	7"	No Mark	Matte Colors	$60.00 – 85.00
		Same pattern as in row above.				
	1926	Low Planter	6"	No Mark	Matte Colors	$30.00 – 40.00
		Also sold as a hanging basket with holes.				

Holly pattern pedestal and jardiniere sets. Smaller sizes shown are 8½" jardinieres with 12½" pedestals. The larger size is a 10½" jardiniere with an 18½" pedestal. Both sizes were available in all color matte glazes. 8½" / 12½", $250.00 – 350.00; 10½" / 18½", $450.00 – 500.00.

Holly pattern jardiniere/pedestal sets shown in brown/green glazes. Smaller size: 8½" jardiniere with 12½" pedestal. $250.00 – 500.00. Larger size is a 10½" jardiniere with 18½" pedestal. $450.00 – 500.00.

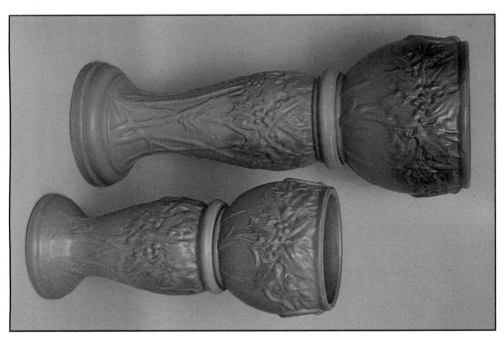

All pieces are the Basketweave pattern. The smallest jardiniere is 7½". The smaller pedestal and jardiniere set shown is a 8½" jardiniere with 12½" pedestal. The larger is a 10½" jardiniere with an 18½" pedestal. All samples shown are in blended glaze and were also sold later in pastel matte colors. Samples of these are included later in the book on pages 56–57. 7½", $60.00 – 75.00; 8½" / 12½", $250.00 – 350.00; 10½" / 18½", $450.00 – 550.00.

Same jardinieres as shown on page 25 only in the brown/green matte glaze. 7½", $75.00 – 100.00; 10½", $100.00 – 125.00.

Page 27

	Year	Description	Size	Mark	Available Glazes	Value
Top						
Row 1	1930s	Vase	8"	No Mark	Matte Colors	$60.00 – 85.00
		All three vases on this row are the same with different glazes. Also available in 9" size.				$85.00 – 100.00
Row 2	1930s	Vase	6"	No Mark	Matte Colors	$45.00 – 60.00
		Vase – Same as left this row.				
	1930s	Jardiniere	4"	No Mark	Matte Colors	$45.00 – 60.00
Bottom						
Row 1	1930s	Centerpiece Planter		No Mark	Matte Colors	$45.00 – 60.00
	1930s	Matching Candleholder		No Mark	Matte Colors	$30.00 – 40.00
	1930s	Jardiniere	7"	No Mark	Matte Colors	$75.00 – 100.00
		Same pattern as 4" piece above.				
Row 2	1930s	Vase	9"	No Mark	Matte Colors	$75.00 – 100.00
	1930s	Vase	8"	No Mark	Matte Colors	$65.00 – 85.00
	1930s	Vase	8"	No Mark	Matte Colors	$85.00 – 110.00

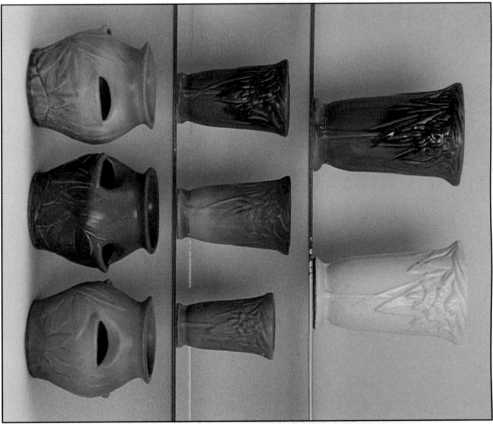

	Year	Description	Size	Mark	Available Glazes	Value
Row 1	1930s	Vase	8"	No Mark	Matte Colors	$50.00 – 80.00

Both vases on this row are the same with different glazes pictured. Wide range in values due to glazes.

	Year	Description	Size	Mark	Available Glazes	Value
Row 2	1930s	Vase	6"	No Mark	Matte Colors	$50.00 – 70.00
Row 2	1930s	Vase – Same as left same row.				
Row 3	1930s	Vase	5"	No Mark	Matte Colors	$45.00 – 60.00
Row 3	1930s	Vase	6¼"	No Mark	Matte Colors	$45.00 – 85.00

All vases on this row are the same with different glazes pictured. Wide range in values due to glazes.

PAGE 29

Top

	Year	Description	Size	Mark	Available Glazes	Value
Row 1	1930s	Vase	8"	No Mark	Matte Colors	$50.00 – 80.00

All three vases on this row are the same with different glazes pictured. Wide range in values due to glazes. Blue is not very common.

	Year	Description	Size	Mark	Available Glazes	Value
Row 2	1930s	Vase	6"	No Mark	Matte Colors	$40.00 – 70.00
Row 2	1930s	Jardiniere w/saucer	4"	No Mark	Matte Colors	$25.00 – 35.00
	1930s	Vase – Same as left same row. Also sold in 5" size; same value.				

Bottom

	Year	Description	Size	Mark	Available Glazes	Value
Row 1	1930s	Jardiniere w/saucer	6"	No Mark	Matte Colors	$40.00 – 55.00
	1930s	Jardiniere w/saucer – Same as Row 2 middle above, different glaze.				
Row 2	1930s	Jardiniere w/saucer – Same as left same row.				
	1930s	Jardiniere – 9" Same pattern as above.		No Mark	Matte Colors	$125.00 – 150.00
	1930s	Vase	10"	No Mark	Matte Colors	$85.00 – 100.00

Low sand Butterfly design porch jars. Available in matte glazes. No marks. 11" size – shown in white. *$125.00 – 175.00.* 14" size – shown in aqua. *$175.00 – 225.00.*

Vase – 14". Offered in several glazes. See pages 41 & 59. *$200.00 – 250.00.* Sand Butterfly pattern, 20" sand jar, matte glazes – see page 54. *$450.00 – 600.00.*

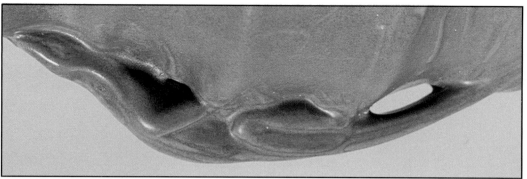

Close-up of lizard handle.

Lizard handle vase. One of the most artistic vases of this era. Matte glazes. Offered in two sizes, 9" & 10", as shown, with equal value. $300.00 – 400.00.

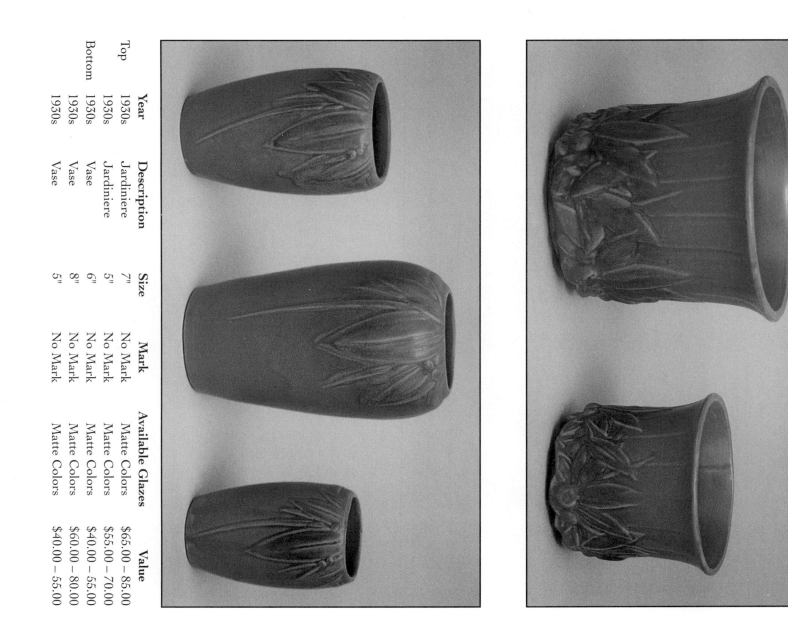

	Year	Description	Size	Mark	Available Glazes	Value
Top	1930s	Jardiniere	7"	No Mark	Matte Colors	$65.00 – 85.00
	1930s	Jardiniere	5"	No Mark	Matte Colors	$55.00 – 70.00
Bottom	1930s	Vase	6"	No Mark	Matte Colors	$40.00 – 55.00
	1930s	Vase	8"	No Mark	Matte Colors	$60.00 – 80.00
	1930s	Vase	5"	No Mark	Matte Colors	$40.00 – 55.00

| 1930s | Jardiniere | 6½" | No Mark | Matte Colors | $85.00 – 110.00 |
| 1930s | Jardiniere | 7½" | NM | Matte Colors | $85.00 – 110.00 |

One of few pieces with glazes from this era that is marked "NM."

Sand jar, 18". Matte colors. *$400.00 – 500.00.*

Pedestal & jardiniere sets: Taller same as set pictured on left on page 22. Jardiniere 8½"; Pedestal 12½". $250.00 – 350.00. Smaller set shown for size comparison, detail below.

Page 35

	Year	Description	Size	Mark	Available Glazes	Value
Top						
Row 1	1930s	Sand Butterfly Jardiniere	7"	No Mark	Matte Colors	$60.00 – 85.00
	1930s	Sand Butterfly Jardiniere	5"	No Mark	Matte Colors	$35.00 – 45.00
Row 2	1930s	Sand Butterfly Jardiniere – Same as middle, same row.				
	1930s	Flower Pot	3"	No Mark	Matte Colors	$30.00 – 40.00
	1930s	Flower Pot	3"	No Mark	Matte Colors	$30.00 – 40.00
	1930s	Centerpiece – Same as page 27, bottom, row 1.			Matte Colors	$45.00 – 65.00
Bottom						
Row 1	1930s	Jardiniere	8"	No Mark	Matte Colors	$65.00 – 85.00
	1930s	Jardiniere 5" – Same as page 32, top.			Matte Colors	$55.00 – 70.00
	1930s	Jardiniere	4"	No Mark	Matte Colors	$45.00 – 60.00
Row 2	1930s	Vase	12"	No Mark	Matte Colors	$200.00 – 300.00
	1930s	Urn – Same as page 22.			Matte Colors	$25.00 – 40.00
	1930s	7" Jardiniere / 6½" Pedestal		No Mark	Matte Colors	$200.00 – 250.00

All 1930s planters in matte glazes.

			Value
Row 1	4"	No Mark	$40.00 – 50.00
	5½"	No Mark	$55.00 – 70.00
Row 2	6"	No Mark	$60.00 – 80.00
	5"	No Mark	$55.00 – 70.00

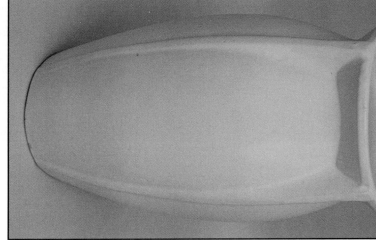

Vase, 14", matte glazes. Also found in burgundy glaze with black drip. $200.00 – 250.00.

PAGE 37						
		Year	Description	Size	Mark	Available Glazes	Value
Top		1930s	Vase	8"	No Mark	Matte Colors	$65.00 – 75.00
		1930s	Vase	6"	No Mark	Matte Colors	$40.00 – 50.00
		1930s	Vase	5"	No Mark	Matte Colors	$40.00 – 50.00
Bottom		1930s	Vase	14"	No Mark	Matte Colors	$150.00 – 200.00
		1930s	Vase	12"	No Mark	Matte Colors	$125.00 – 175.00
		1930s	Vase	10"	No Mark	Matte Colors	$80.00 – 100.00

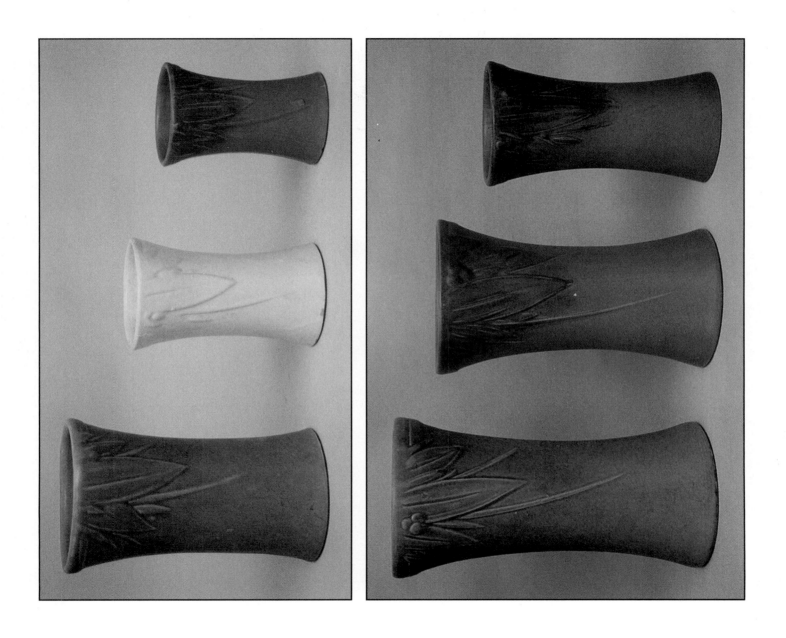

Jardiniere, 6½", 1930s in matte glaze. Small handles on either side at top. $65.00 - 85.00.

PAGE 39

	Year	Description	Size	Mark	Available Glazes	Value
Top Left	1930s	Jardiniere	10½"	No Mark	Matte Colors	$150.00 – 175.00
Top Right	1930s	7" Jardiniere / 6½" Pedestal		No Mark	Matte Colors	$200.00 – 250.00
		Same as page 35 bottom, row 2.				
		Both sets are identical – different glazes.				
Middle	1930s	Flower Pot w/ saucer	4"	No Mark	Matte Colors	$35.00 – 45.00
	1930s	Flower Pot w/ saucer	6"	No Mark	Matte Colors	$50.00 – 70.00
	1930s	Flower Pot w/ saucer	5½"	No Mark	Matte Colors	$30.00 – 40.00
Bottom	1930s	Centerpiece Bowl		No Mark	Matte Colors	$50.00 – 70.00
	1930s	Candleholder		No Mark	Matte Colors	$35.00 – 45.00

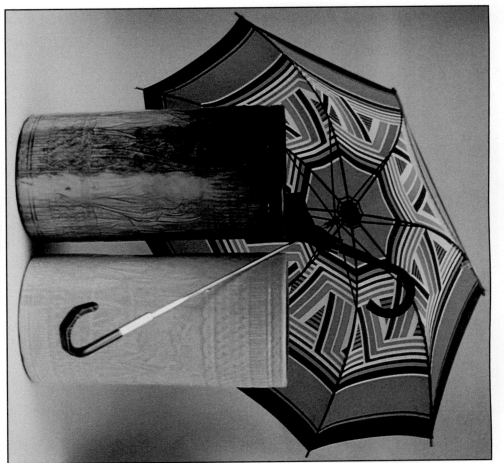

21" umbrella stands, $300.00 – 400.00. Same as shown on page 16.

Umbrella stand, 19", 1940s. Natural and matte glazes. $250.00 – 350.00.

Same sphinx jar in different glaze.

Close-up of sphinx head.

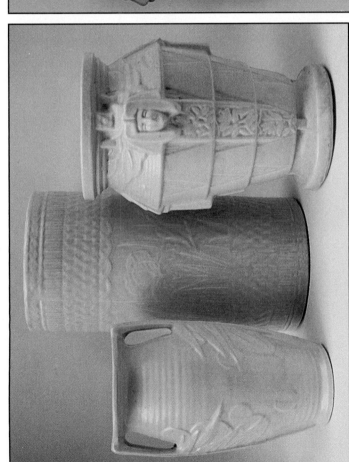

14" vase. $150.00 – 200.00. Other glazes shown on pages 30 & 59. Umbrella stand, same as pictured on previous page and below left. Sphinx sand jar, 16", 1930s. Matte glazes. $500.00 – 650.00.

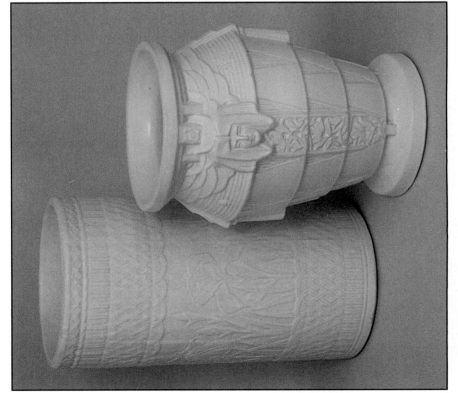

Same umbrella stand and sphinx jar as noted above.

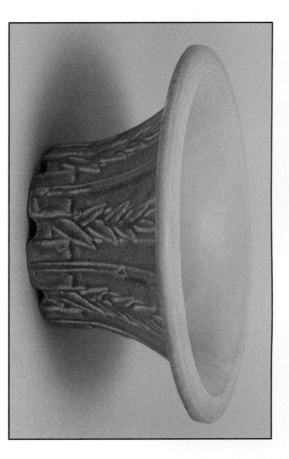

Decorative bowl, same as middle row below. $45.00 – 60.00.

Page 45

	Year	Description	Size	Mark	Available Glazes	Value
Top	1930s	Hanging Basket	5"	No Mark	Matte Colors	$40.00 – 55.00
	1930s	Hanging Basket	6"	No Mark	Matte Colors	$35.00 – 50.00
	1930s	Hanging Basket – Same as left – same row.				
Middle	1930s	Bowl	5"	No Mark	Matte Colors	$45.00 – 60.00
	1930s	Console Bowl	8"	No Mark	Variety Colors	$50.00 – 70.00
	1930s	Bowl – Same as left – same row.				
Bottom	1930s	Vase	7"	No Mark	Matte Colors	$100.00 – 125.00
	1930s	Vase – Same as left - same row.				

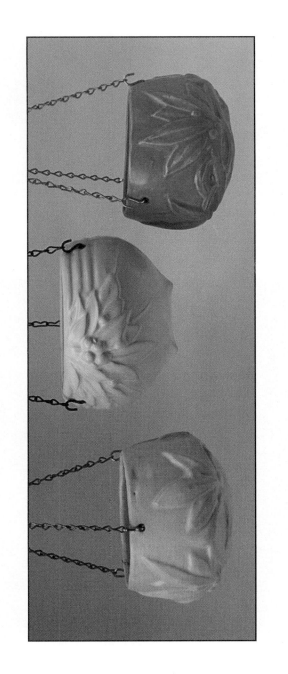

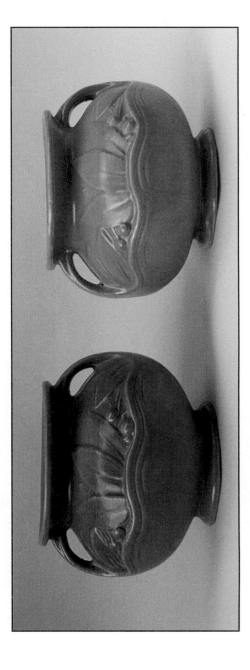

Jardiniere, 5", $55.00 - 70.00.

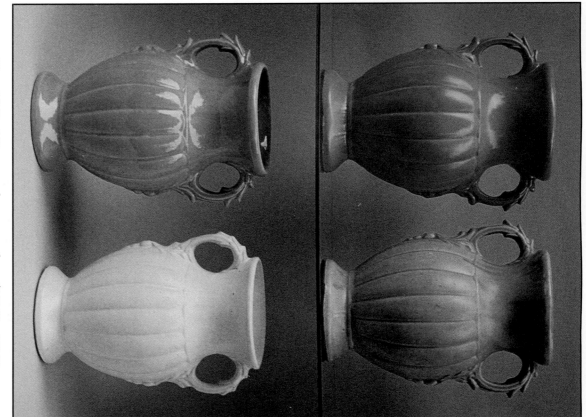

Vase, 1940s, 12", no mark, matte colors. $100.00 – 150.00.

PAGE 45

	Year	Description	Size	Mark	Available Glazes	Value
Top						
Row 1	1930s	Hanging Basket	5"	No Mark	Matte Colors	$40.00 – 55.00
	1950s	Jardiniere	6"	No Mark	Matte Colors	$55.00 – 75.00
Row 2	1930s	Holly Jardiniere	4"	No Mark	Matte Colors	$30.00 – 45.00
	1950s	Holly Jardiniere	4½"	No Mark	Matte Colors	$35.00 – 50.00
	1930s	Holly Jardiniere – Same as middle, same row.				
Bottom						
Row 1	1920s	Vase	7"	No Mark	Matte Colors	$75.00 – 100.00
	1950s	Hanging Basket	6"	No Mark	Matte Colors	$40.00 – 55.00
	1930s	Vase – Same as left – same row.				
Row 2	1940s	Vase	12"	No Mark	Matte Colors	$100.00 – 150.00
	1950s	Holly Jardiniere	10½"	No Mark	Onyx	$90.00 – 110.00

Many of the pieces included in the previous section were also sold in an onyx finish. This was the same glaze sold on pieces by the Brush-McCoy Co. at approximately the same time, making it difficult to determine which compa-

ny produced a given piece. If the bottom has a number mark, it is a Brush-McCoy product. Other than that, the shape of the pottery is about the only clue.

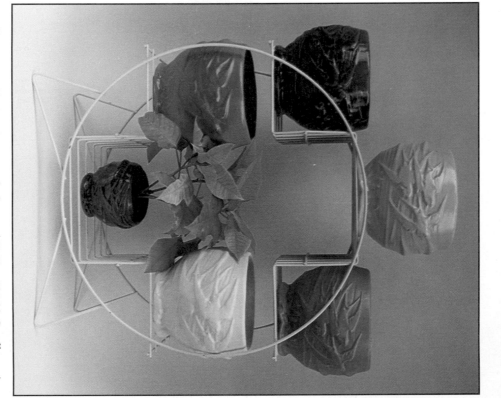

Swallows 7" jardiniere in several glazes. $85.00 – 125.00. Swallows jardiniere, 4". $45.00 – 65.00.

6" vase also pictured in several glazes. $55.00 – 80.00.

The 8" vases on this page show the wide range of glazes produced during this era. $45.00 – 85.00.

Hand decorating.

Left: Inscription etched on vase: "To Mama, From Evelyn, San Diego – 1935."

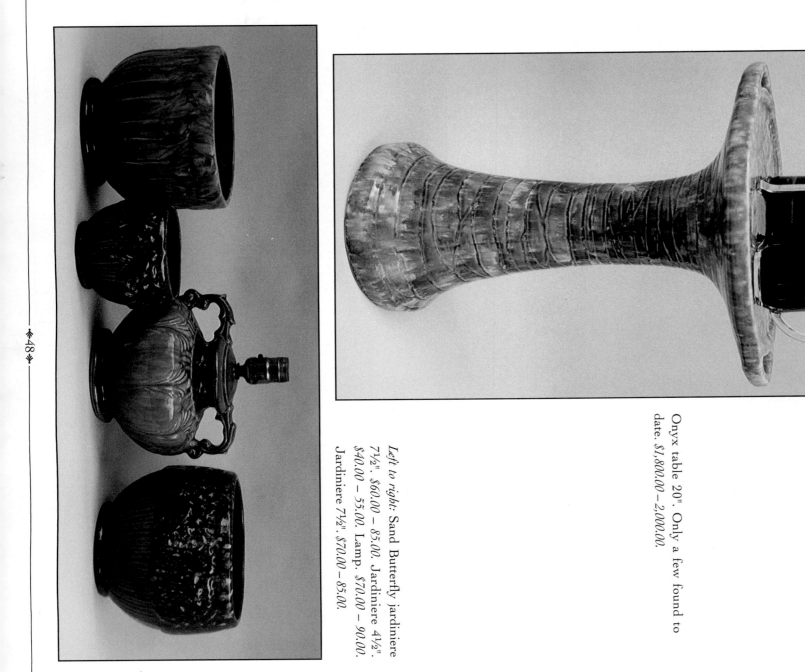

Left to right: Sand Butterfly jardiniere 7½". $60.00 – 85.00. Jardiniere 4½". $40.00 – 55.00. Lamp. $70.00 – 90.00. Jardiniere 7½". $70.00 – 85.00.

Onyx table 20". Only a few found to date. $1,800.00 – 2,000.00.

Smaller sizes: 8½" Holly jardinieres with 12½" pedestals. $250.00 – 500.00. *Larger size:* 10½" Holly jardiniere with 18½" pedestal. $450.00 – 500.00.

Pedestal and jardiniere sets. *Smaller size:* 7" jardiniere with 6½" pedestal. $200.00 – 250.00. *Larger size:* 8½" Jardiniere with 12½" pedestal. $250.00 – 550.00.

Pitcher with duck neck handle. 1930s. Several colors. $75.00 – 90.00. Pitcher marching ducks, various colors. $85.00 – 100.00.

Vase, 8", 1930s, several glazes. $55.00 – 70.00. Jardiniere 4½", 1930s, several glazes. $50.00 – 65.00. Glazes pictured not common.

Jardinieres 10½", $150.00 – 175.00, 8½", $50.00 – 75.00, and 7", $35.00 – 50.00.

Dog: "Pansy" the Pug owned by Louie & Eleanore Geissel of Seattle, Washington.

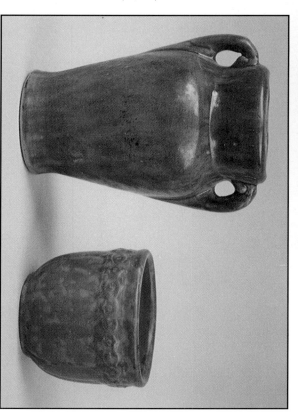

NM MARK

In the latter part of the '30s, McCoy started to mark pieces "NM." The vast majority of pieces in the NM era were made in pastel glazes.

Oil jars pictured in several glazes. The top jar is 15" with no mark. The balance of the jars on the stand are 12" and marked "NM." The jar with handles on the floor is 15" with no mark. 15", $250.00 – 300.00. 12", $125.00 – 200.00.

4" Oil jars on stand, various glazes, marked NM. $35.00 – 55.00.
Other oil jar, 12", marked NM. $125.00 – 200.00.

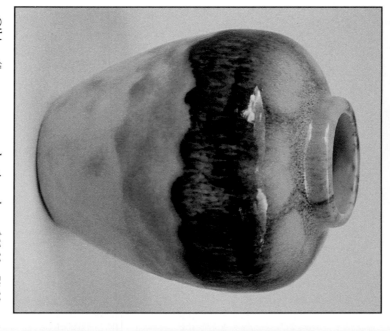

Oil jar, 4", rare, non-production glaze. $60.00 – 75.00.

	Year	Description	Size	Mark	Available Glazes	Value
Row 1	1940s	Vase	8"	No Mark	Gloss Colors	$40.00 – 50.00
	1940s	Jardiniere	6"	No Mark	Gloss Colors	$35.00 – 45.00
	1940s	Vase – Same as vase to the left, different glaze.				
Row 2	1940s	Vase	10"	No Mark	Gloss Colors	$55.00 – 70.00
	1940s	Vase	6"	No Mark	Gloss Colors	$35.00 – 45.00
	1940s	Vase – Same as vase to the left, different glaze.				
Row 3	1940s	Vase	12"	No Mark	Pastel Colors	$90.00 – 125.00
	1940s	Vase – Same as vase to the left, different glaze.				

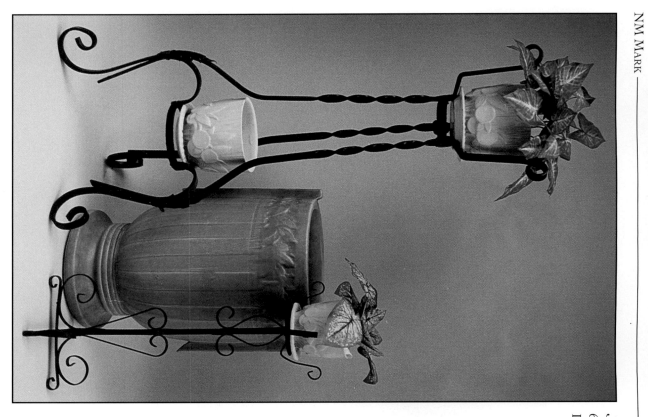

Jardiniere 5", 1940s, gloss glazes, no mark, $35.00 – 45.00. 6" jardiniere, $40.00 – 55.00. 4" jardiniere, $30.00 – 40.00. Large 20" Sand Butterfly sand jar, $450.00 – 600.00.

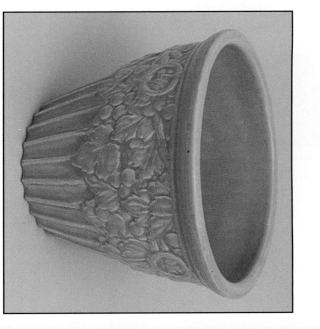

Porch jar, 1940s, white or green glaze, marked NM, 11" x 9½", $150.00 – 200.00.

Page 55

	Year	Description	Size	Mark	Available Glazes	Value
Top	1940s	Planter	3½"	NM	Variety	$30.00 – 40.00
Left middle and middle	1940s	Planter	3½"	NM	Variety	$90.00 – 110.00
	Unusual glaze and glaze formula.					
Lower left	1940s	Planter	3½"	NM	Variety	$80.00 – 100.00
	Glaze formula on Planter.					
	1940s	Planter	3½"	NM	Variety	$90.00 – 110.00
	Unusual glaze and glaze formula.					
Lower right	1940s	Planter	7"	McCoy	Variety	$40.00 – 60.00

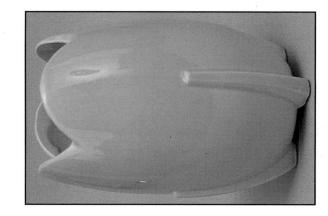

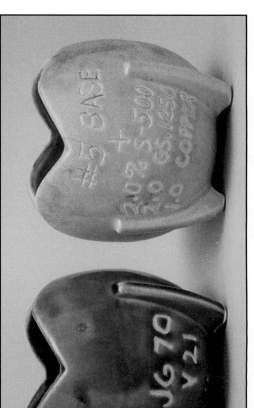

All pieces on pages 56 – 57 are the Basketweave pattern. (See also page 25). The yellow glaze below was not a standard catalog glaze although a few jardinieres have been found. The pedestals will have an NM mark on the top platform. The 7½" size jardiniere has no mark but the medium and large jardinieres have been found with and without the NM mark. The pink or coral glaze pieces were actually cataloged as "peach." This color is a little harder to find and commands a higher price.

Jardiniere, 7½", yellow. $75.00 – 100.00.

Page 57

Description	Size	Green or White	Peach
Jardiniere	7½"	$60.00 – 75.00	$65.00 – 80.00
Jardiniere/Pedestal	8½"/12½"	$250.00 – 300.00	$275.00 – 325.00
Jardiniere/Pedestal	10½" / 18½"	$450.00 – 500.00	$475.00 – 550.00

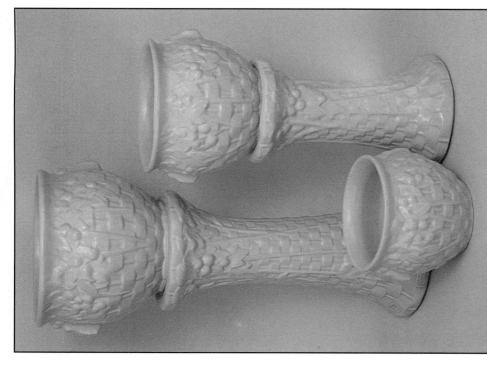

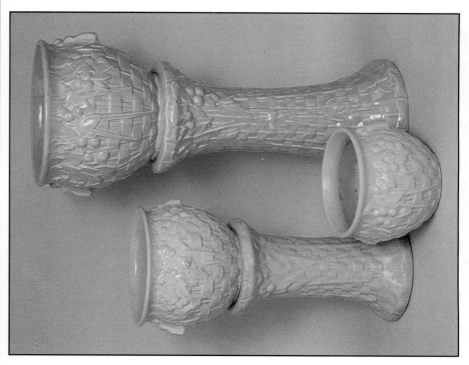

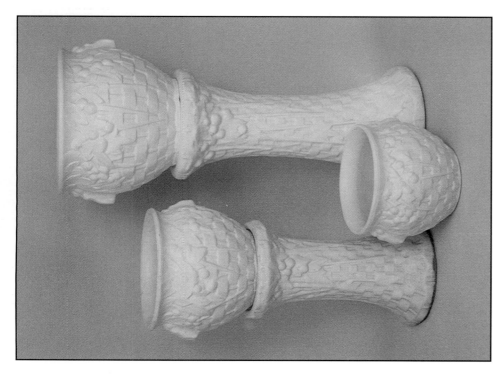

	Year	Description	Size	Mark	Available Glazes	Value
Left	1940s	Vase	10"	USA	Matte Colors	$75.00 – 100.00
Right	1940s	Vase	12"	USA	Matte Colors	$90.00 – 110.00
Below	1940s	Vase	10"	USA	Matte Colors	$75.00 – 100.00

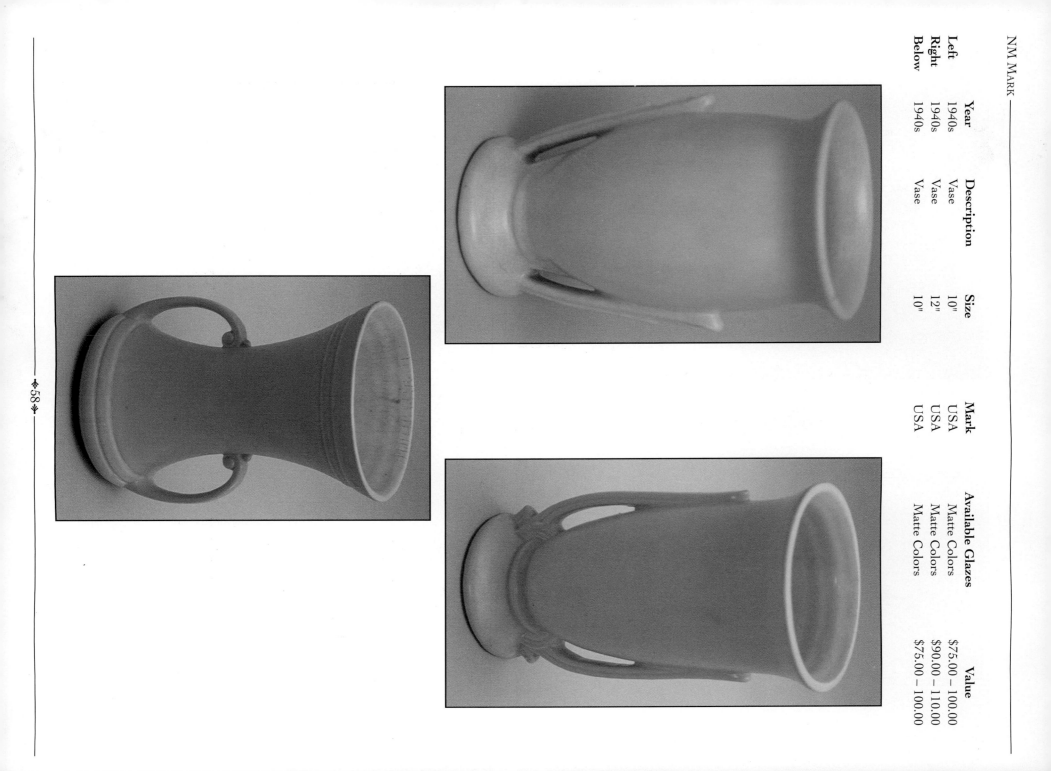

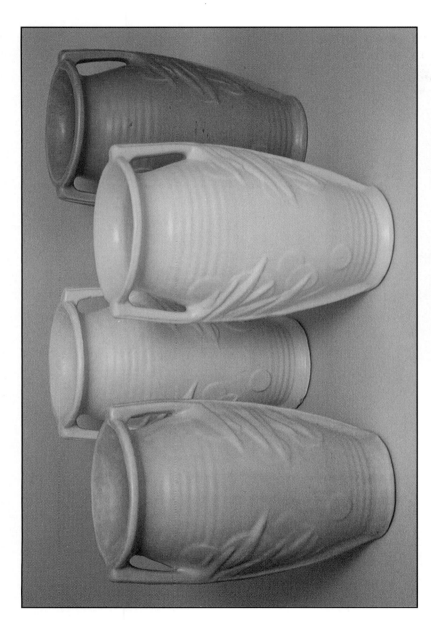

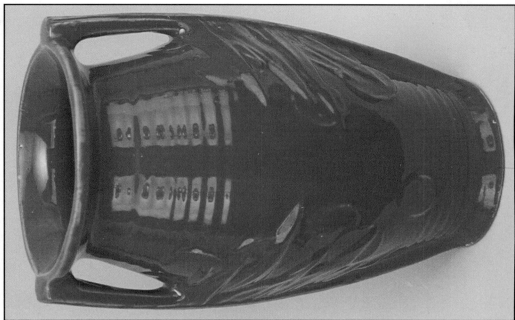

All vases pictured are the same with different color glazes. Vase 1930s – 40s, 14", no mark, variety of colors. $250.00 – 350.00.

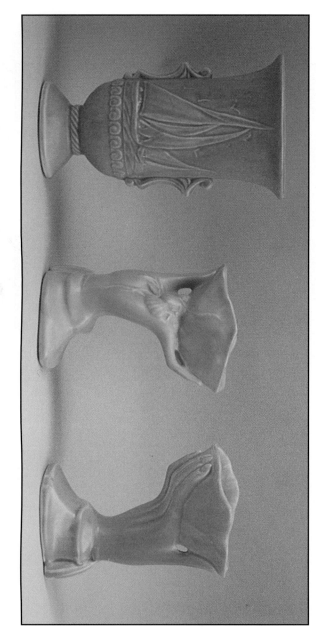

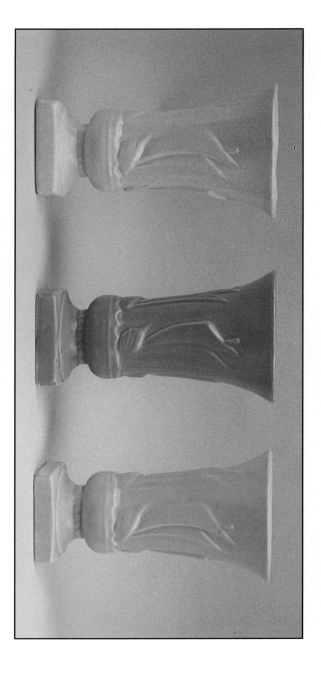

PAGE 60	Year	Description	Size	Mark	Available Glazes	Value
Top	1940s	Vase	8"	McCoy	Variety Colors	$50.00 – 65.00
	All four vases on this row are the same – different glazes.					
Middle	1942	Sailboat Vase	9"	NM	Matte Colors	$50.00 – 65.00
	All three vases on this row are the same – different glazes.					
Bottom	1940s	Sailboat Vase	9"	NM and No Mark	Matte Colors	$60.00 – 75.00
	1943	Hand Vase	7"	NM	Matte Colors	$75.00 – 90.00
	Vase – Opposite side of same vase to left.					

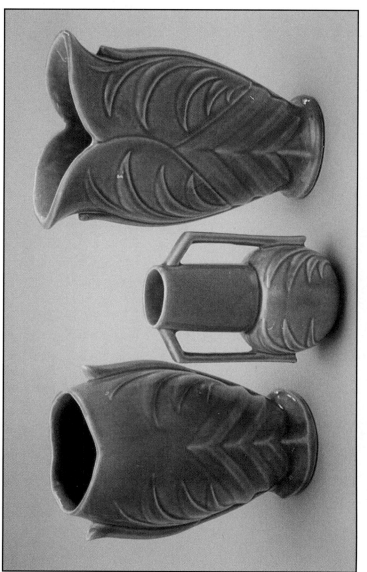

All 1940s vases in a variety of colors. 7", marked USA, $50.00 – 75.00. 5", no mark, $45.00 – 60.00. 8", marked NM or no mark, $45.00 – 65.00.

Heart vase pictured with old cupid print, 6", variety colors, no mark. $50.00 – 70.00.

PAGE 63

	Year	Description	Size	Mark	Available Glazes	Value
Top						
Row 1	1940s	Vase	6"	NM	Variety Colors	$60.00 – 75.00
	1940s	Vase	7½"	No Mark	Yellow or White	$75.00 – 100.00
Row 2		Vase – Opposite side of same vase to left.				
	1940s	Heart Vase	6"	No Mark	Variety Colors	$50.00 – 70.00
	1940s	Garden Dish	8½" x 5"	NM	Green	$65.00 – 85.00
	1940s	Vase	8"	NM	Variety Colors	$50.00 – 70.00
Bottom						
Row 1	1940s	Vase	8"	NM/No Mark	Variety Colors	$45.00 – 65.00
	1940s	Cornucopia Planter	4"	McCoy	Variety Colors	$25.00 – 35.00
Row 2	1940s	Vase	7"	USA	Variety Colors	$50.00 – 70.00
	1940s	Vase	9"	USA	Matte Colors	$40.00 – 50.00
	1940s	Vase	8"	NM	Matte Colors	$45.00 – 60.00
	1940s	Vase	8"	NM	Matte Colors	$65.00 – 85.00

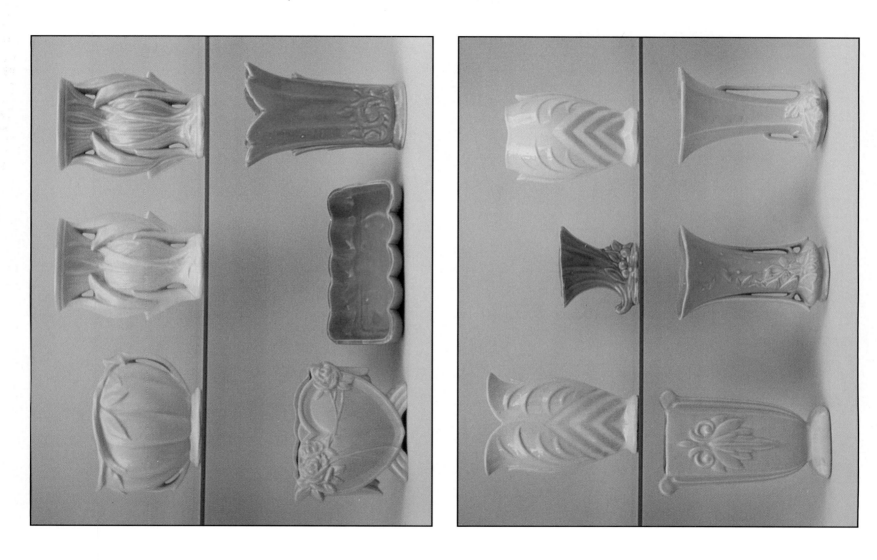

PAGE 65	Year	Description	Size	Mark	Available Glazes	Value
Top						
Row 1	1940s	Jardiniere	4½" Tall	NM	Pastel Colors	$45.00 – 60.00
	1940s	Jardiniere	3½" Tall	NM	Pastel Colors	$35.00 – 45.00
	The above jardinieres were also sold in a 6" tall size.					
	1940s	Vase	6"	NM	White	$50.00 – 70.00
Row 2	1940s	Fernery	4" x 7"	No Mark	Variety Colors	$45.00 – 60.00
	1940s	Fernery	9½"	NM	Pastel Colors	$40.00 – 50.00
	Deer fernery also sold with no mark; if no mark, top edge of piece will not have the braided decoration.					
Bottom						
Row 1	1940s	Jardiniere	3½"	NM	Pastel Colors	$40.00 – 50.00
	1940s	Jardiniere	6"	NM	Pastel Colors	$50.00 – 65.00
Row 2	1940s	Flower Bowl	9½"	McCoy	White	$35.00 – 45.00
	1940s	Swan Vase	6"	No Mark	Pastel Colors	$35.00 – 45.00

Bird bookends, 6". 1940s, marked NM, pastel color glazes. *$175.00 – 225.00.*

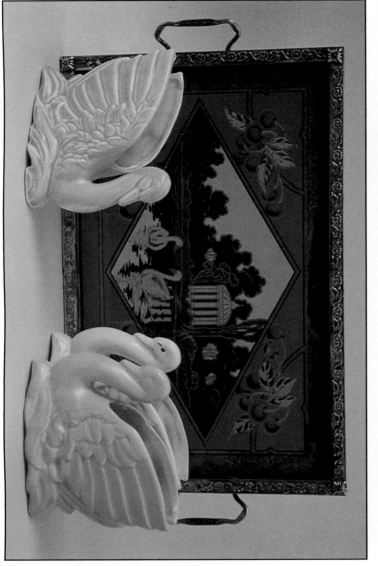

Swan vases, 6", no mark, pastel colors. Same as on next page. Pictured with beautiful swan accent tray. *$35.00 – 45.00.*

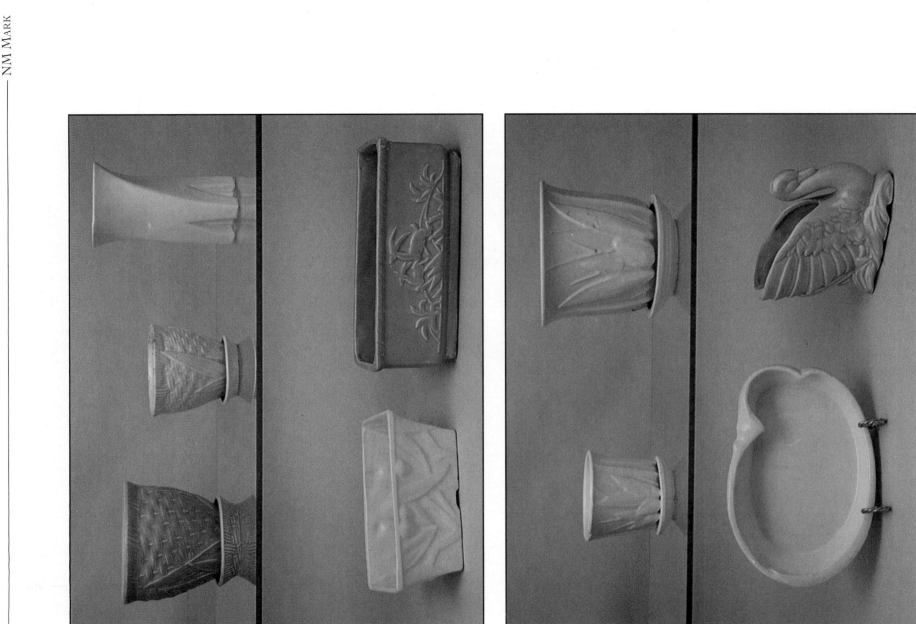

	Year	Description	Size	Mark	Available Glazes	Value
Top						
Row 1	1940s	Planter	5"	NM	Variety Colors	$35.00 – 50.00
	1940s	Planter	3" x 6"	NM	Variety Colors	$35.00 – 50.00
	1940s	Bulb Bowl	6"	NM	Variety Colors	$40.00 – 50.00
Row 2	1940s	Garden Dish	9½" x 7½"	NM	Pastel Colors	$85.00 – 110.00
	1940s	Vase	8"	McCoy	Pastel Colors	$40.00 – 60.00
	1940s	Hands Novelty Tray	8½"	NM	Variety Colors	$100.00 – 125.00
Bottom						
Row 1	1940s	Flower Pot	3½"	NM	Pastel Colors	$25.00 – 35.00
	Same as left, this row, different glaze.					
	1940s	Hands Novelty Tray	5¾"	NM	Variety Colors	$35.00 – 50.00
	All three hand trays on this row are the same – different glazes.					
Row 2	1940s	Vase	9"	NM	Pastel Colors	$40.00 – 60.00
	1940s	Vase	9"	McCoy	Pastel Colors	$40.00 – 60.00
	1940s	Vase	9"	USA	Pastel Colors	$40.00 – 60.00

Vase, 1940s, 7", no mark, gloss colors. $55.00 – 70.00.

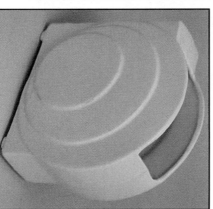

Vase, 1940s, 6¾" tall, USA mark, variety colors. $75.00 – 90.00.

Parrot vase, 1940s, 7½", NM, variety colors. $45.00 – 60.00. Donkey, 1940s, 7", no mark, variety colors. $60.00 – 70.00. These two pieces are pictured in a non-production glaze.

Vase, 1940s, McCoy mark, variety glazes. $75.00 – 100.00. Parrot vase, same as above left photo. $45.00 – 60.00. Hands novelty tray, 8½" long, NM, variety colors. $100.00 – 125.00.

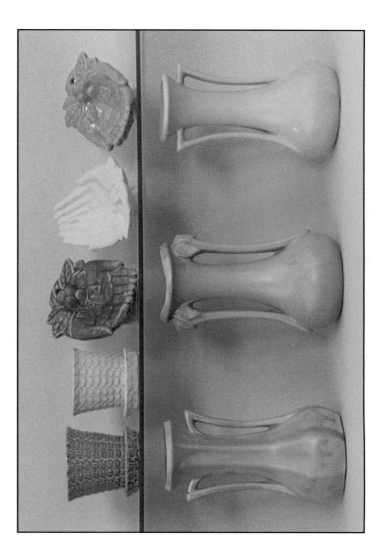

	Year	Description	Size	Mark	Available Glazes	Value
Top	1940s	Mary Ann Shoe Planters	5" Long	NM	Pastel Colors	$25.00 – 40.00
		All shoes on both rows are the same except for glaze color.				
Bottom						
Row 1	1940s	Baa Baa Black Sheep	4½"	NM	Variety Colors	$45.00 – 60.00
		All planters on this row are the same – different glazes.				
Row 2	1940s	Parrot Planter – Same as pictured at far left, page 66.				$45.00 – 60.00
	1940s	Donkey – Same as pictured at far left, page 66.				$60.00 – 70.00
	1940s	Kitten Planter	6"	NM	Variety Colors	$45.00 – 60.00

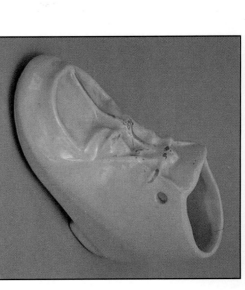

Right: Mary Ann shoe same as described above except for factory holes meant for a ribbon. *$35.00 – 45.00.*

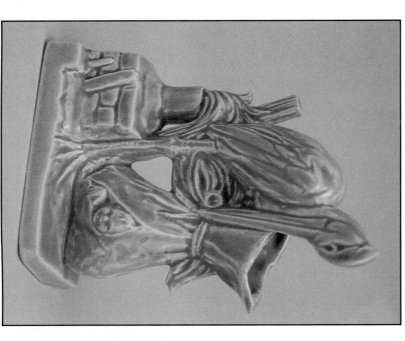

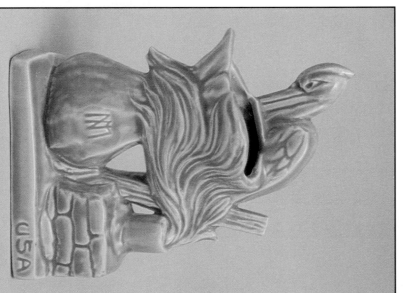

Stork planter, 1940s, 7" tall, marked NM, green glaze. Very rare piece. *$300.00 – 400.00*. Views shown of both sides. Dry bottom on piece. Written in pencil on the bottom: "Bob made this for me when he worked at McCoy. 1946." Signed "Mildred."

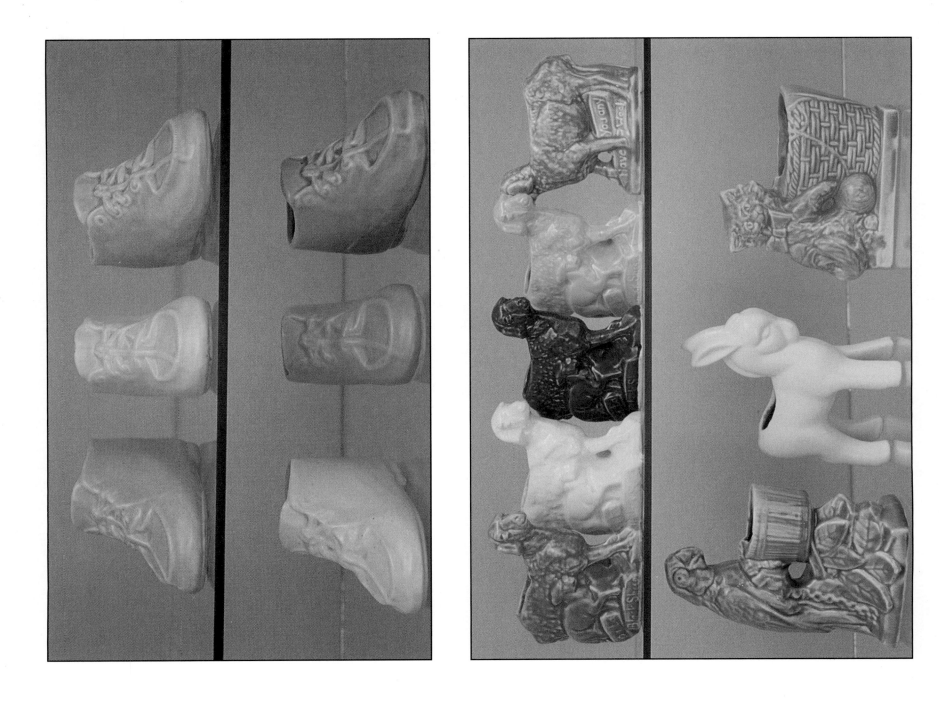

PAGE 71

	Year	Description	Size	Mark	Available Glazes	Value
Top						
Row 1	1940s	Horse Bookends	8"	USA	Variety Colors	$100.00 – 125.00
Row 2	1940s	Sand Butterfly Trough	8½" Long	No Mark	Variety Colors	$35.00 – 45.00
	All three troughs on this row are the same — different glazes.					
Bottom						
Row 1	1940s	Dog Dish	6"	McCoy	Green, Maroon	$60.00 – 75.00
	1950s	Cuspidor	7½"	McCoy	Green, Maroon	$40.00 – 50.00
	McCoy Reproduction – Marked "Authentic McCoy Reproductions, Circa 1917 by McCoy."					
	1940s	Dog Dish	7½"	McCoy	Brown, Green, Yellow	$60.00 – 75.00
	Lettering: "To Man's Best Friend, His Dog."					
Row 2	1940s	Flower Bowl	8¼"	NM	Pastel Colors	$40.00 – 50.00
	Same bowl, different colors.					

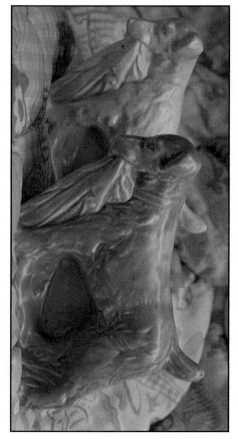

Dogs with holder, 1940s, 7" x 5", NM mark, pastel matte colors. $60.00 – 75.00.

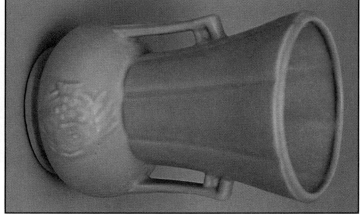

Vase with fish, 1940s, 10" tall, USA mark, pastel colors. $55.00 – 70.00.

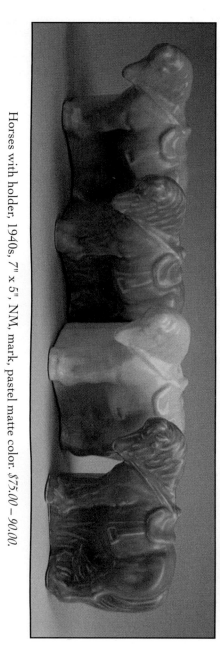

Horses with holder, 1940s, 7" x 5", NM, mark, pastel matte color. $75.00 – 90.00.

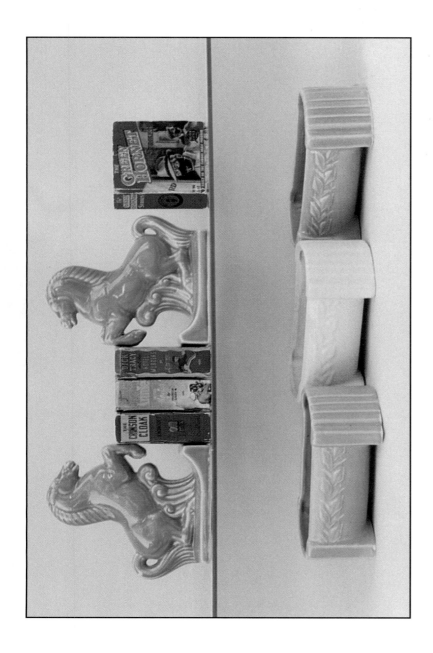

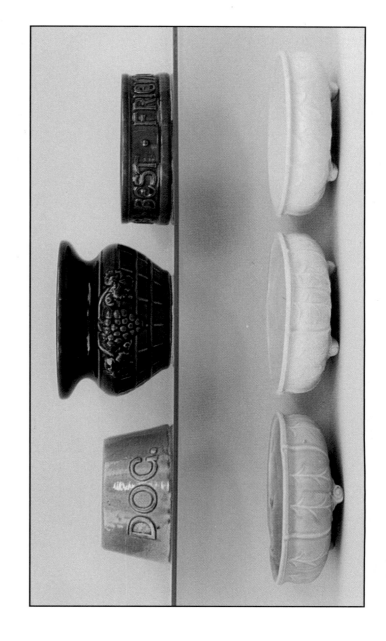

Elephant pitcher, 1940s, 7" x 5", NM mark, variety colors. $250.00 – 300.00. Donkey pitcher, 1940s, 7" x 5", NM mark, variety colors. $200.00 – 250.00.

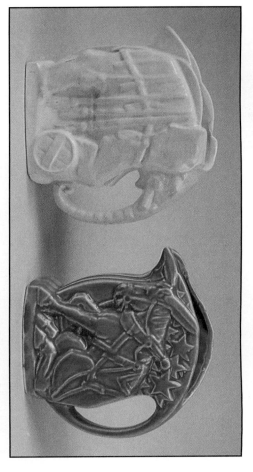

Backwards birds, 1940s, 4" tall, NM mark. Colors shown. $50.00 – 60.00.

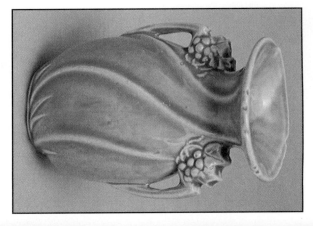

Vase, 1940s, 5½", no mark, variety colors. $75.00 – 100.00.

PAGE 73	Year	Description	Size	Mark	Available Glazes	Value
Top						
Row 1	1940s	Hanging Basket	7½"	No Mark	Bright Colors	$40.00 – 50.00
	1940s	Hanging Basket	7½"	No Mark	Green, Yellow	$50.00 – 60.00
	1940s	Hanging Basket – Same as this row left.				
Row 2	1940s	Dragonfly Planter	3½"	No Mark	Pastel Matte	$30.00 – 40.00
	1940s	Flower Pot	3½"	No Mark	Bright Colors	$30.00 – 40.00
	1940s	Flower Pot	3½"	No Mark	Bright Colors	$35.00 – 45.00
Bottom						
Row 1	1940s	Dragonfly Planter	5½"	No Mark	Pastel Matte	$50.00 – 65.00
	1940s	Vase	5½"	No Mark	Bright Colors	$25.00 – 35.00
	1940s	Vase	8"	No Mark	Bright Colors	$45.00 – 60.00
Row 2	1940s	Dragonfly Planter	4½"	No Mark	Pastel Matte	$50.00 – 60.00
	1940s	Vase – Same as blue vase above.				
	1950s	Jardiniere	6"	McCoy	Chartreuse, Yellow	$40.00 – 50.00

Fawn planter, 1940s, 4½" x 5", NM mark, pastel colors. Pictured with plastic pins. $45.00 – 60.00. Lavender color only $85.00 – 100.00.

Candleholder bookends, 1940s, 6" tall, NM mark, pastel colors & mustard/rust glaze. $125.00 – 150.00.

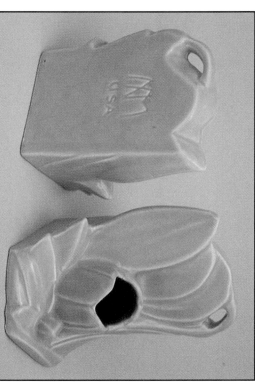

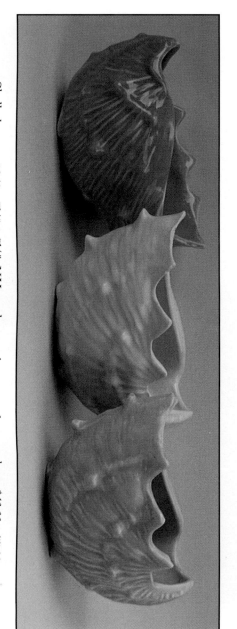

Shell planters, 1940s, 7½" x 5½", NM mark, pastel matte and rose colors. $40.00 – 55.00.

Dutch shoes, 1940s, 5" & 2" sizes, no mark, variety colors. 5", $20.00 – 30.00. 2", $50.00 – 65.00.

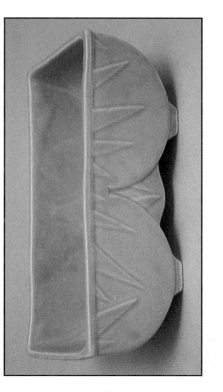

Fernery, 1940s, 4½" x 10", NM mark, pastel matte colors. $75.00 – 90.00.

HOBNAIL LINE

In the early 1940s, Nelson McCoy produced two different lines of pastel glaze pieces usually with matte finish, the Hobnail and the Butterfly, and both have become highly sought after by collectors. The Hobnail was produced in the shapes pictured on the next few pages. Several of the shapes are shared by the Butterfly line. Hobnail pieces, with the addition of leaves in their pattern at top are also frequently found with a gloss glaze in white, green, or yellow.

Hobnail ferneries showing all of the standard glazes produced in the matte pastel colors.

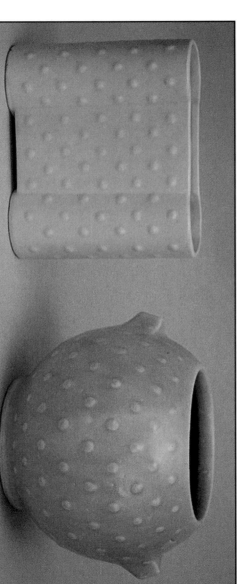
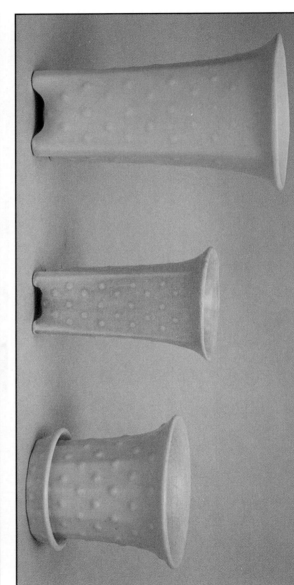
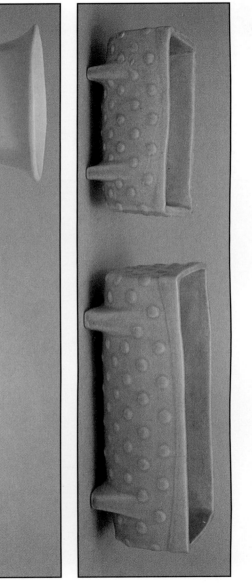

	Year	Description	Size	Mark	Available Glazes	Value
Row 1	1940s	Fernery	5½"	NM	Pastel Matte Colors	$25.00 – 35.00
	1940s	Fernery	8¼"	NM	Pastel Matte Colors	$30.00 – 40.00
Row 2	1940s	Vase	8"	NM	Pastel Matte Colors	$60.00 – 75.00
	1940s	Vase	6"	NM	Pastel Matte Colors	$50.00 – 65.00
	1940s	Flower Pot	5"	NM	Pastel Matte Colors	$35.00 – 45.00
Row 3	1940s	Castlegate Vase	6"	No Mark	Pastel Matte Colors	$150.00 – 200.00
	1940s	Jardiniere	6"	No Mark	Pastel Matte Colors	$75.00 – 100.00

Jardinière is very similar to the Hobnail cookie jars.

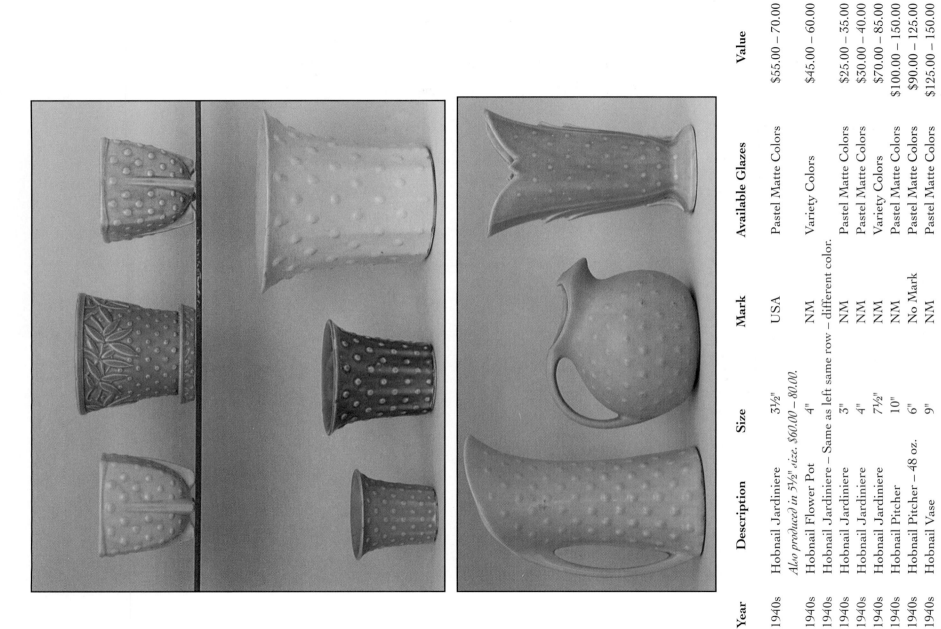

	Year	Description	Size	Mark	Available Glazes	Value
Top						
Row 1	1940s	Hobnail Jardiniere	3½"	USA	Pastel Matte Colors	$55.00 – 70.00
		Also produced in 5½" size. $60.00 – 80.00.				
	1940s	Hobnail Flower Pot	4"	NM	Variety Colors	$45.00 – 60.00
	1940s	Hobnail Jardiniere – Same as left same row – different color.				
Row 2	1940s	Hobnail Jardiniere	3"	NM	Pastel Matte Colors	$25.00 – 35.00
	1940s	Hobnail Jardiniere	4"	NM	Pastel Matte Colors	$30.00 – 40.00
	1940s	Hobnail Jardiniere	7½"	NM	Variety Colors	$70.00 – 85.00
Bottom	1940s	Hobnail Pitcher	10"	NM	Pastel Matte Colors	$100.00 – 150.00
	1940s	Hobnail Pitcher – 48 oz.	6"	No Mark	Pastel Matte Colors	$90.00 – 125.00
	1940s	Hobnail Vase	9"	NM	Pastel Matte Colors	$125.00 – 150.00

Console bowls, 1940s, NM mark, 11" and 5" shown, also made 8" size, pastel color glazes. 11", $60.00 – 75.00; 8", $35.00 – 50.00; 5", $45.00 – 60.00.

Hand vase, 1940s, no mark, 6½" tall, white color glaze. $100.00 – 150.00.

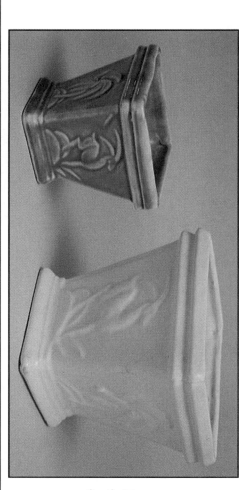

Deer planters, 1940s, 4" and 5½" tall, no mark, variety colors. 4", $30.00 – 40.00; 5½", $35.00 – 45.00.

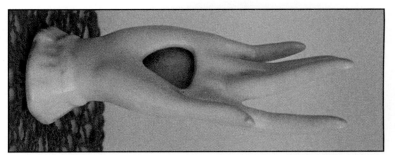

PAGE 79	Year	Description	Size	Mark	Available Glazes	Value
Top						
Row 1	1940s	Hand Vase	8¼"	NM	Variety Colors	$30.00 – 50.00
		All vases on this row are the same. Many will be found with no mark.				
Row 2	1940s	Vase	5¾"	McCoy	Variety Colors	$20.00 – 30.00
	1940s	Pelican with Cart	8" Long	No Mark	Yellow, White, Green	$35.00 – 45.00
	1940s	Vase	6"	No Mark	Variety Gloss Colors	$30.00 – 35.00
Bottom						
Row 1	1940s	Hand Planter	7¾"	NM	Pastel Colors	$35.00 – 45.00
	1940s	Cornucopia Vase	7"	McCoy	Matte Pastels	$50.00 – 65.00
	1940s	Hands Planter – Same as first piece this row – different color.				
Row 2	1940s	Cornucopia Vase	7½"	McCoy	Variety Gloss Colors	$30.00 – 40.00
	1940s	Cornucopia Vase – Same as first piece this row – different color.				
	1940s	Uncle Sam Vase	7½"	McCoy	Variety Gloss Colors	$50.00 – 60.00

Although it was not a specific catalog line, the Lily Bud pieces as they are called by collectors are a very desirable early 1940s line. All of the shapes that are a part of this unofficial line are pictured. They have been found in all the pastel matte glazes but the lavender seems to be the most elusive and should probably command at least a 20% premium on the values listed.

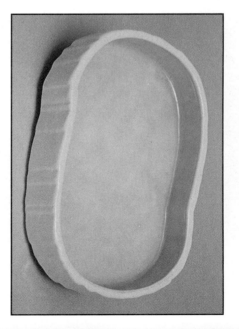

Fernery, 1940s, 4½" x 10", NM mark, variety of colors, shown in mustard/rust glaze. $60.00 – 75.00. Only three shapes of McCoy have been found with this glaze. Other two pieces: Butterfly wall pocket, page 106, and candleholder bookends, shown in different glaze on page 74.

Flower bowl, 1940s, 6½" x 9½", NM mark, white with yellow or turquoise internal color. $30.00 – 40.00.

Bookends, 5¾" pastel matte colors, see also on page 83, top row. $150.00 – 200.00. "Banana" planter, 8½", pastel matte colors, see also on next page, middle row. $40.00 – 50.00.

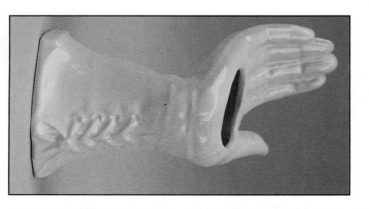

Hand with glove vase, 1940s, 8¼" tall, NM mark, harder to find than similar vase on page 79, top row. $150.00 – 200.00.

	Description	Size	Mark	Available Glazes	Value
Top	Planter	6½"	NM	Pastel Matte Colors	$45.00 – 60.00
	"Cross" Planter	7½"	NM	Pastel Matte Colors	$50.00 – 65.00
Middle	"Banana" Planter	8½"	NM	Pastel Matte Colors	$40.00 – 50.00
	Candleholder	5"	NM	Pastel Matte Colors	$30.00 – 40.00
	Planter	6½"	NM	Pastel Matte Colors	$45.00 – 60.00
Bottom	Garden Dish	7¾" x 6"	NM	Pastel Matte Colors	$60.00 – 75.00
	Garden Dish	5½" x 4½"	NM	Pastel Matte Colors	$45.00 – 60.00

	Year
Top	1940s
	1940s
Middle	1940s
	1940s
	1940s
Bottom	1940s
	1940s

Doe and fawn planter, 1940s, 7" tall, NM mark, pastel matte colors. $50.00 – 60.00. Lion planter, 1940s, 8¾" x 4", NM mark, pastel matte colors. $80.00 – 110.00.

Below: The three styles of Lily Bud wall pocket. All 1940s. They were all made in the pastel matte glazes.

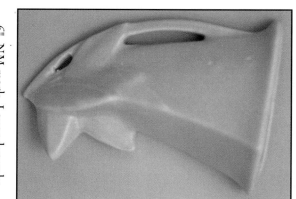

6", NM mark. Lavender only. $75.00 – 100.00.

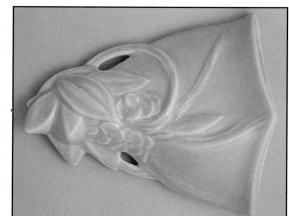

8", McCoy mark. $250.00 – 500.00.

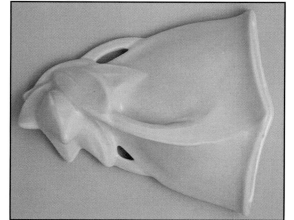

8", NM mark. $200.00 – 250.00.

Page 83

	Year	Description	Size	Mark	Available Glazes	Value
Top	1940s	Vase	5"	NM	Pastel Matte Colors	$60.00 – 75.00
	1940s	Bookends	5¾"	NM	Pastel Matte Colors	$150.00 – 200.00
Middle	1940s	Vase	10"	NM	Pastel Matte Colors	$80.00 – 100.00
	1940s	Vase	8"	NM	Pastel Matte Colors	$50.00 – 65.00
Bottom	1940s	Planter	11½" Long	NM	Pastel Matte Colors	$60.00 – 75.00

Stretch Animals are another collection of Nelson McCoy that has become very popular. They were all cataloged from the late '30s to the very early '40s. The terminology of "stretch" animal is a description used in the Huxford's book on McCoy. These pieces were actually part of a larger general product group called "Novelty Flower Holders and Planters." However, their design has certainly been captured

by the "stretch" designation. In the 1942 catalog, the Pony sold for $.75 a dozen!!

None of these pieces are marked and are all dry bottom. The catalog colors are pastel shades: blue, white, yellow, and green. However a few pieces, particularly the small lion, have been found in other gloss glaze colors.

Ramming and standing goats, variety of glazes shown.

PAGE 85

	Year	Description	Size	Mark	Available Glazes	Value
Top	1940s	Lion	7½" x 5½"	No Mark	Pastel Matte	$200.00 – 250.00
	1940s	Lion	5¼" x 4"	No Mark	Pastel Matte	$125.00 – 150.00
Middle	1940s	Pony (Horse)	5⅜" x 3½"	No Mark	Pastel Matte	$75.00 – 90.00
	1940s	Ramming (Butting) Goat	5½" x 3¼"	No Mark	Pastel Matte	$200.00 – 250.00
	1940s	Goat	5¼" x 4¾"	No Mark	Pastel Matte	$80.00 – 100.00
Bottom	1940s	Dog	7¼" x 5¾"	No Mark	Pastel Matte	$200.00 – 250.00
	1940s	Hound (Dachshund)	8¼" x 5"	No Mark	Pastel Matte	$175.00 – 225.00

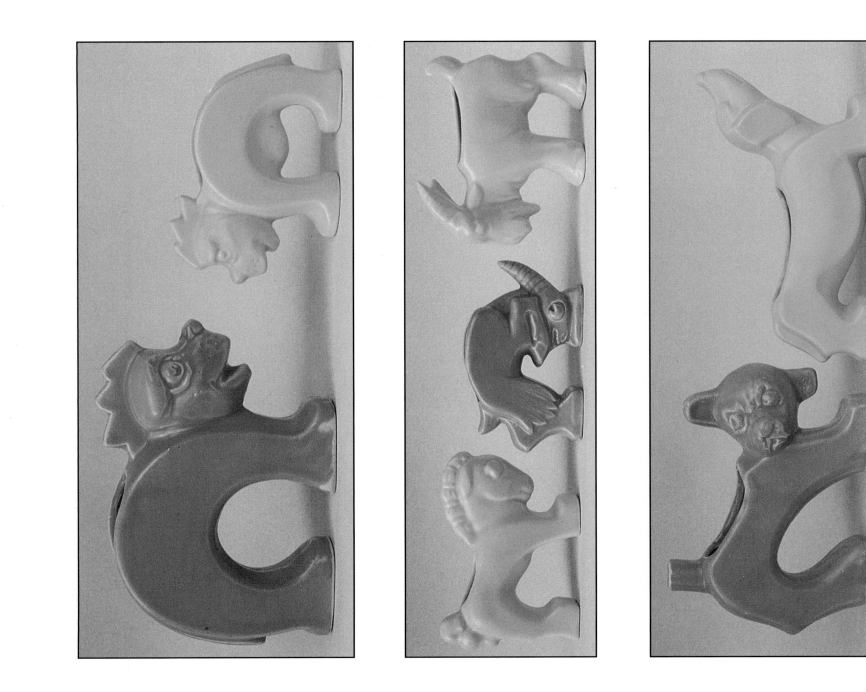

There were eight different pieces offered as part of a flower holder line in the late '30s to early '40s. They were offered in the matte pastel colors, white, yellow, aqua, and blue, and also sold in a pink/rose glaze, usually gloss but some have been found in matte finish. As pictured in some of the shapes, a few non-production glazes can also be found. The gold samples pictured are from the Sunburst Line of the '50s but are the same size and considered part of the same

line by collectors even though they were sold much later.

If the piece has good detail (early out of mold life), you can usually find an "NM" mark along the bottom edge with the exception of the pigeon which is not marked. Many seem not to be marked but they are "the Real McCoy." All pieces are dry bottom. The yellow and rose/pink glazes are more difficult to find and are valued separately. The non-production glaze samples also carry higher values.

Left and below: Fish, 4¼" x 3¼", NM mark. $75.00 – 150.00. Yellow and rose. $100.00 – 175.00.

Vase, 3½" x 3¼", NM mark. $30.00 – 40.00. Yellow and rose. $50.00 – 60.00.

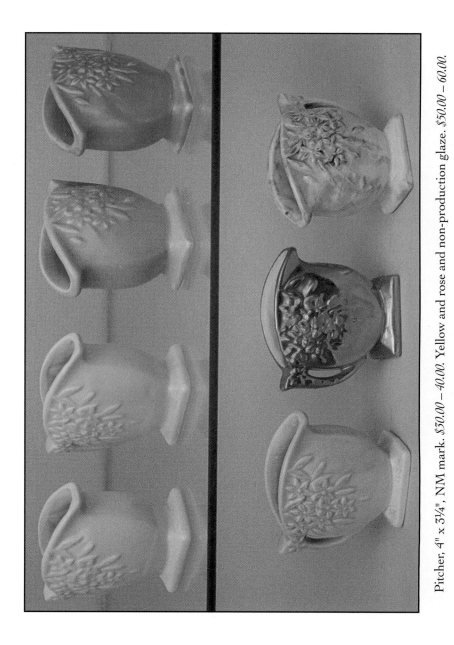

Pitcher, 4" x 3¼", NM mark. $30.00 – 40.00. Yellow and rose and non-production glaze. $50.00 – 60.00.

Left & below: "Hands of friendship" (catalog description) commonly called "Praying Hands," 4" x 3", NM mark. $50.00 – 60.00. Yellow and rose. $80.00 – 100.00.

Pigeon, 4" x 3½", NM mark. $40.00 – 50.00. Yellow and rose. $80.00 – 100.00.

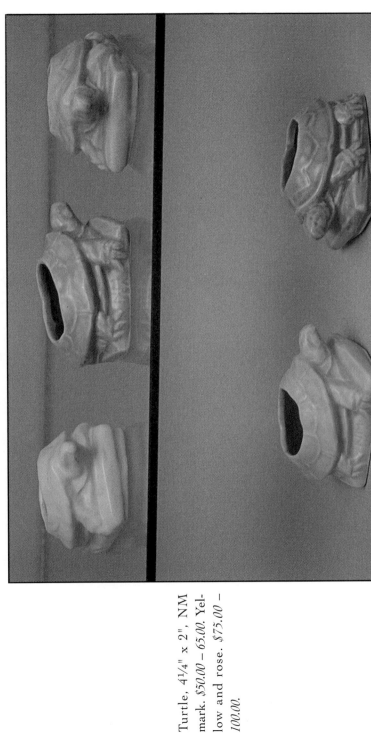

Turtle, 4¼" x 2", NM mark. $50.00 – 65.00. Yellow and rose. $75.00 – 100.00.

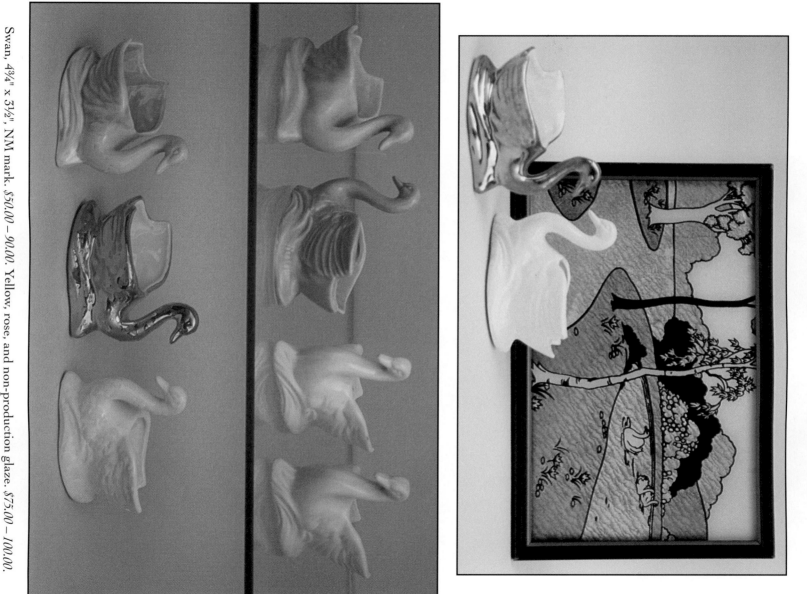

Swan, 4¾" x 3½", NM mark. $50.00 – 90.00. Yellow, rose, and non-production glaze. $75.00 – 100.00.

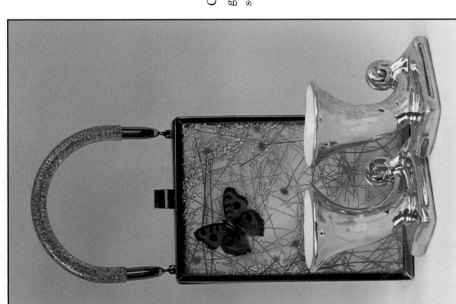

Cornucopia, 4" x 3¼", Sunburst Gold glaze. $30.00 – 40.00. Also pictured below, second row.

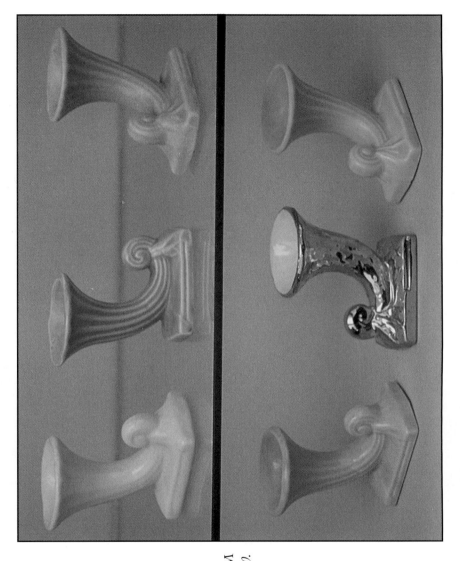

Cornucopia, 4" x 3¼", NM mark. Top row, $30.00 – 40.00. Yellow and rose. $60.00 – 80.00.

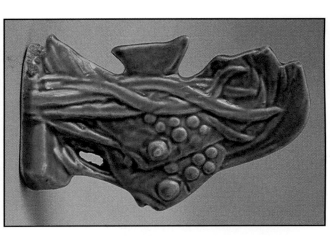

Left: Angelfish, 1940s, white or green, no mark, 6" tall. $150.00 – 200.00.

Right: Seahorse, 1940s, white or green, no mark, 6" tall. $250.00 – 500.00.

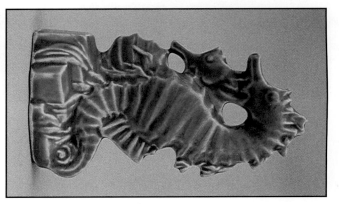

Elephant, 1940s, 7½" x 5½", no mark, variety glaze colors. $25.00 – 35.00.

PAGE 93

	Year	Description	Size	Mark	Available Glazes	Value
Top						
Row 1	1940s	Witch	3"	USA	Brown, Green	$200.00 – 250.00
	1940s	Gnome (Hillbilly)	3"	USA	Brown, Green	$200.00 – 250.00
	1940s	Gnome, back view.				
Row 2	1940s	Cat	3"	USA	Gloss Variety	$200.00 – 250.00
	1940s	Turtle – Same as pg. 89, shown here for size comparison.				$40.00 – 50.00
Left middle	1940s	Turtle	3¼"	NM	Brown	$150.00 – 200.00
	1940s	Pelican	3"	No Mark	White, Yellow	$150.00 – 200.00
	1940s	Rabbit	1½"	USA	Gloss Variety	$200.00 – 250.00
Right middle	1940s	Frog	3⅛"	NM	Green	$200.00 – 250.00
	1940s	Frog	3½"	NM	Green	$200.00 – 250.00
Bottom	1940s	Fish	3"	No Mark	Variety Colors	$100.00 – 150.00

Hairline on the left would significantly lower the value.

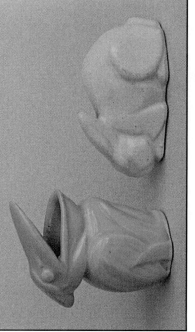

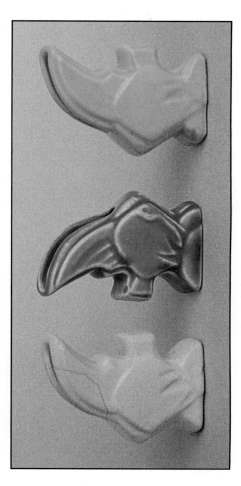

FLOWER BOWL ORNAMENTS

These very popular pieces were sold as a series of flower bowl ornaments. They are commonly known as some of the "ladder pieces" as displayed in the Huxford McCoy book. They were all made only in matte white and were part of the late 1930s product offering. In the bottom right photo on the next page, we show you that all these pieces are from "cored" molds. When looking for these pieces, this coring fact should help in eliminating some of those purchases that end up in that "other" collection.

Duck ornament pictured with North Dakota Prairie picture.

Bird (commonly called wren) ornament pictured with North Dakota Prairie picture.

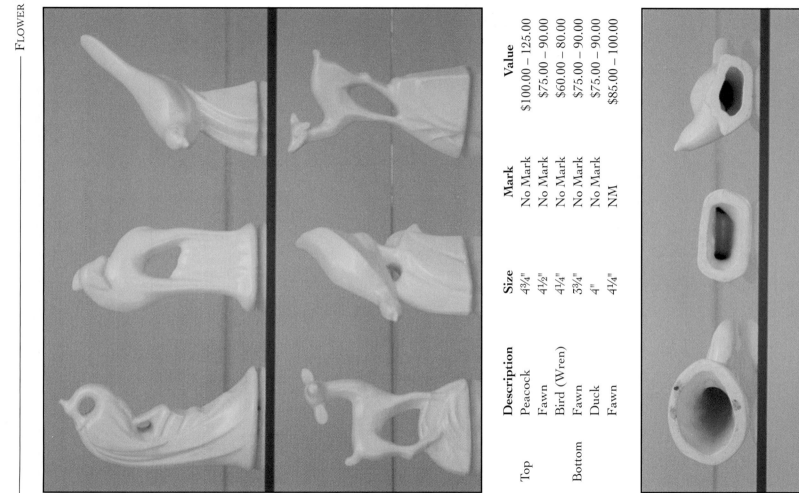

	Description	Size	Mark	Value
Top	Peacock	4¾"	No Mark	$100.00 – 125.00
	Fawn	4½"	No Mark	$75.00 – 90.00
	Bird (Wren)	4¼"	No Mark	$60.00 – 80.00
Bottom	Fawn	5¾"	No Mark	$75.00 – 90.00
	Duck	4"	No Mark	$75.00 – 90.00
	Fawn	4¼"	NM	$85.00 – 100.00

BUTTERFLY LINE

As noted earlier, the Butterfly pattern pieces were sold in the early 1940s. They have consistently been one of the most popular lines to collect. There were twenty-six different shapes made. The "divided planter" alone was made in white only; All other pieces were made in six pastel glazes,

blue, yellow, aqua, lavender, pink (coral), and white. A few pieces have been found in other glazes but these are rare and were not standard production. All pieces have either an NM mark or USA mark. The only exception is one of the ferneries. The USA marks are subtle and frequently not readable.

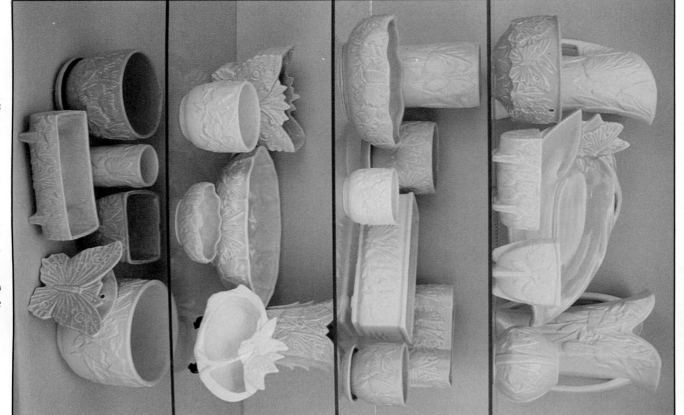

All twenty-six shapes of the butterfly line.

The hanging basket has been found with and without holes. At this time, this fact has not seemed to make a difference in value. We have listed the rarer pink (coral) glaze separately for pricing since it demands some degree of premium price, depending on the shape. As you will note in the photos, the pink (coral) glaze was produced in a very wide range of shades sometimes looking like a different glaze when comparing one piece to another. The butterfly line and floral vases started Pat and Craig Nissen collecting McCoy pottery.

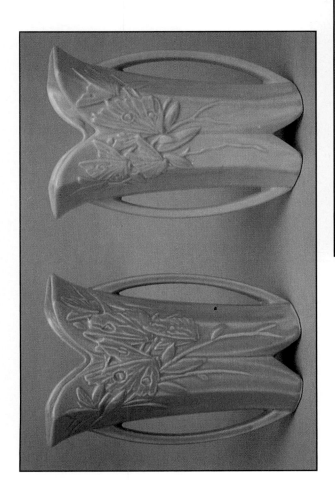

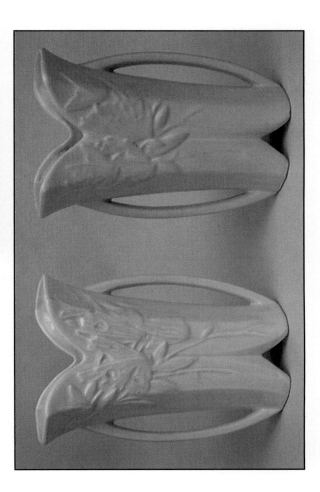

Double handle vases, 10", USA mark, pictured are the six standard glaze colors. *$150.00 – 200.00. Coral, $175.00 – 225.00.*

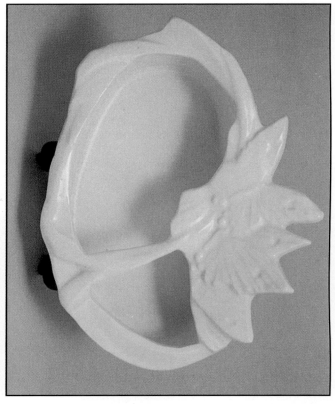

Divided planter, 7½" x 5½", NM mark. Piece made in white only. $125.00 – 150.00.

Wall pocket, 7" x 6", NM mark. Green, white, yellow, $200.00 – 250.00; blue, $250.00 – 500.00; lavender and coral (none known found), $500.00 – 400.00.

PAGE 99

	Description	Size	Mark		Value
Top	Platter	14" x 8½"	NM	Coral:	$250.00 – 300.00
Middle	Jardiniere	5¼" x 5¼"	USA	Coral:	$300.00 – 400.00
	Jardiniere	3¾" x 3¾"	USA	Coral:	$125.00 – 175.00
Bottom	Flower Pot	6½"	NM	Coral:	$150.00 – 200.00
	Flower Pot	5"	NM	Coral:	$75.00 – 95.00
	Flower Pot	3¾"	NM	Coral:	$100.00 – 125.00
				Coral:	$85.00 – 110.00
				Coral:	$100.00 – 150.00
				Coral:	$50.00 – 75.00
				Coral:	$80.00 – 100.00
				Coral:	$40.00 – 50.00
				Coral:	$60.00 – 75.00

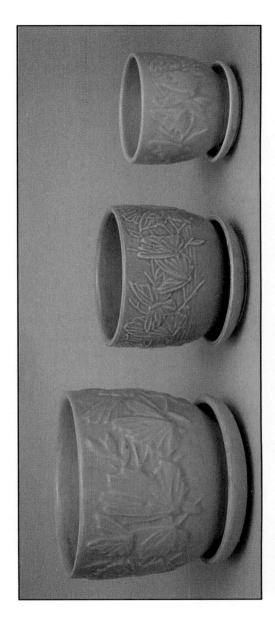

Jardiniere, 7½", NM marked, non-production color. $150.00 – 200.00. Ivy vase, 4½", same as page 105, bottom row, non-production color. $75.00 – 100.00.

Console bowl with floral bouquet, 8½" x 6". $60.00 – 80.00. Also shown on page 103, first item, top row.

PAGE 101

	Description	Size	Mark	Value
Top	Pitcher	10"	NM	Coral: $150.00 – 200.00
	Vase	9"	NM	Coral: $175.00 – 225.00
Middle	Fernery	8¼" x 4"	NM	Coral: $100.00 – 125.00
	Fernery	5½" x 3¼"	NM	Coral: $75.00 – 95.00
Bottom	Jardiniere	7½"	NM	Coral: $150.00 – 200.00
	Jardiniere	4½"	NM	Coral: $50.00 – 60.00
	Jardiniere	3½"	NM	Coral: $40.00 – 50.00

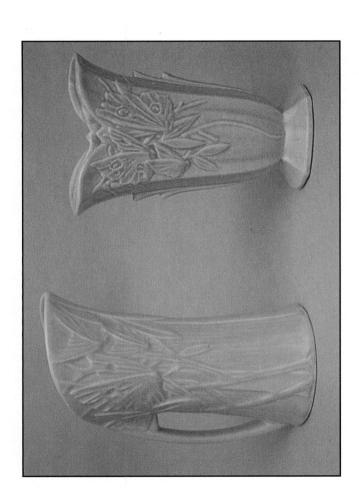

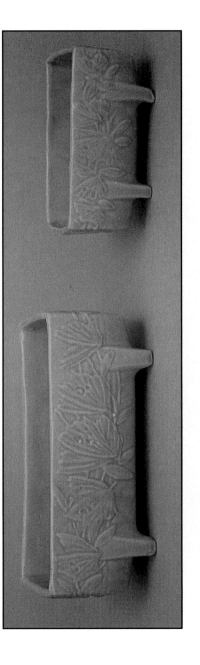

	Description	Size	Mark		Value
Top	Console Bowl	8½" x 6"	NM	Coral:	$60.00 – 80.00
					$80.00 – 100.00
	Console Bowl	5" x 3¾"	NM	Coral:	$50.00 – 60.00
					$75.00 – 85.00
Middle	Console Bowl	11" x 7½"	NM	Coral:	$75.00 – 90.00
					$100.00 – 125.00
Bottom	Castle Gate Vase	7" x 6"	USA	Coral:	$100.00 – 125.00
					$150.00 – 200.00
	Butterfly Vase	7½" x 5½"	USA	Coral:	$75.00 – 100.00
					$100.00 – 125.00

Butterfly vase, 7½" x 5½", marked USA. $75.00 – 100.00.

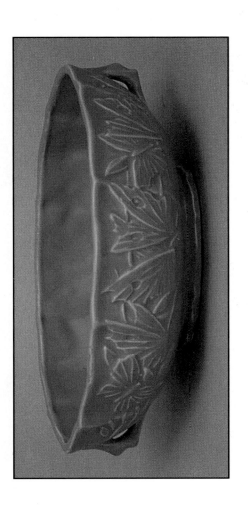

Butterfly vase, 7½" x 5½", USA. $75.00 – 100.00. Vase, 8¼", NM. $50.00 – 60.00.

PAGE 105

	Description	Size	Mark		Value
Top	Fernery	9" x 3½"	No Mark	Coral:	$75.00 – 95.00
	Also made with braided rim, NM mark. Similar to Deer Fernery, page 65.				$100.00 – 125.00
Middle	Hanging Basket	6½"	NM	Coral:	$175.00 – 225.00
	Hanging Basket Planter	6½"	NM	Coral:	$250.00 – 300.00
					$175.00 – 225.00
Bottom	Vase	8¼"	NM	Coral:	$250.00 – 300.00
					$50.00 – 60.00
	Vase	6¼"	NM	Coral:	$60.00 – 70.00
					$30.00 – 45.00
	Ivy Vase	4½"	USA	Coral:	$45.00 – 60.00
					$40.00 – 50.00
					$75.00 – 90.00

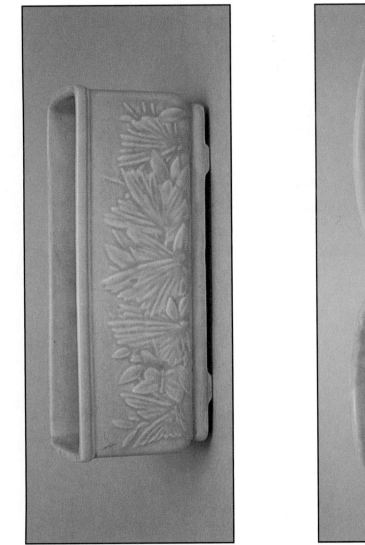

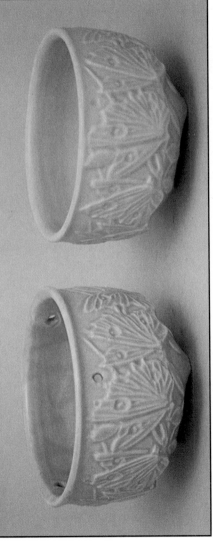

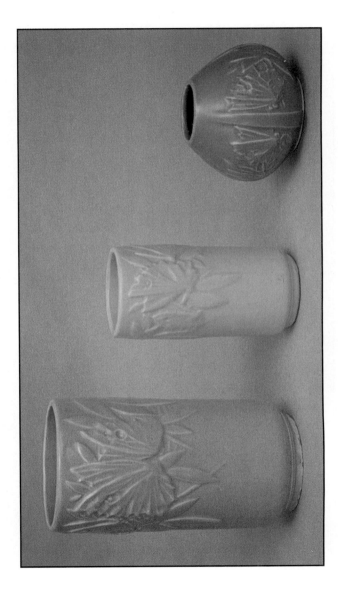

McCoy wall pockets are another very popular area of Nelson McCoy pottery. So many of these wonderful pieces are getting hard to find because not only are the numbers of McCoy collectors increasing, but also there are many wall pocket collectors after these same pieces. In the last year, there were at least two books released just on the topic of wall pockets.

The vast majority of McCoy wall pockets was produced in two eras. Several are from the 1940s and found mainly in pastel matte glazes. The largest selection and quantity were produced from the late 1940s through most of the 1950s. These were made in a wide range of shapes with many brilliant colored glazes.

Brilliant 1940s vase pictured with vintage hankerchief & necklace. 7½", USA. $55.00 – 70.00.

Leaves and Berries pattern wall pocket, 1940s, no mark, 7" long, variety gloss colors. $150.00 – 250.00.

Butterfly wall pocket, rare glaze, 1940s, NM mark, 7" long. $500.00 – 400.00.

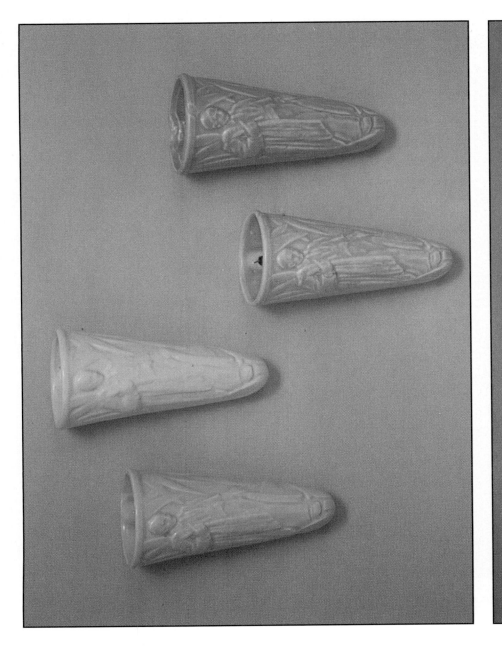

Top: Wall pocket, Mexican, 7½" long, no mark, pastel colors as shown. Sample has been found with cold paint. $50.00 – 60.00. *Bottom:* Butterfly wall pocket, 7" x 6", NM mark, pastel colors. Green, white, yellow, $200.00 – 250.00; blue, $250.00 – 350.00; lavender and coral (none known to be found), $300.00 – 400.00.

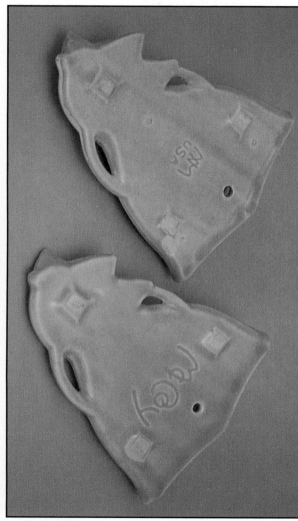

Markings on backs of wall pockets on next page.

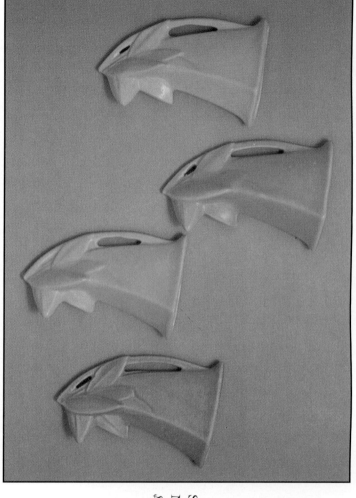

Smallest Lily Bud wall pocket, 1940s, NM mark, 6" long, pastel matte colors. $50.00 – 75.00. Lavender, $75.00 – 100.00.

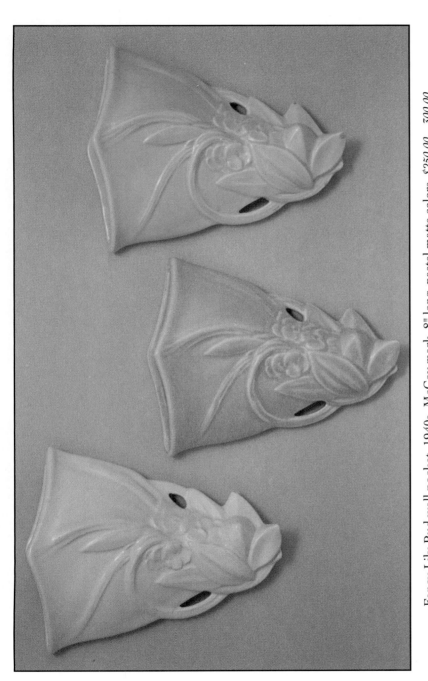

Fancy Lily Bud wall pocket, 1940s, McCoy mark, 8" long, pastel matte colors. $250.00 – 300.00.

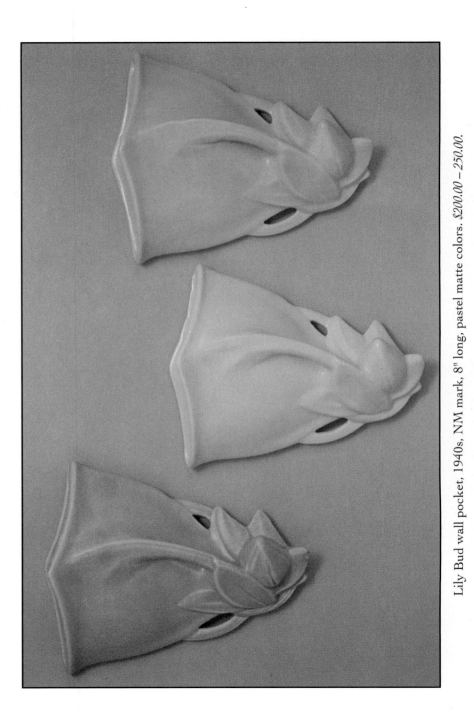

Lily Bud wall pocket, 1940s, NM mark, 8" long, pastel matte colors. $200.00 – 250.00.

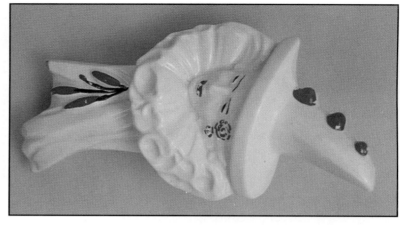

Clown wall pocket, 1940s, 8" long, McCoy mark. $100.00 – 150.00.

Lady with bonnet wall pocket, 1940s, 8" long, McCoy mark. Wall pocket pictured with polka dot pattern was production decoration. Other pieces shown were not standard decoration. $50.00 – 90.00.

PAGE 111

Top

Lily wall pockets, late 1940s, McCoy mark, 6½" long, yellow or white. Decorated as shown, $85.00 – 100.00. Blossomtime wall pockets, late 1940s, McCoy mark, 7¾" long, yellow or white. Decorated as shown, $95.00 – 150.00.

Bottom

Dutch shoe wall pockets, late 1940s, McCoy mark, 7½" long. Gloss colors as shown, $40.00 – 50.00. Look for glaze in mounting hole to be sure the piece is a production wall pocket and not a planter that has been altered.

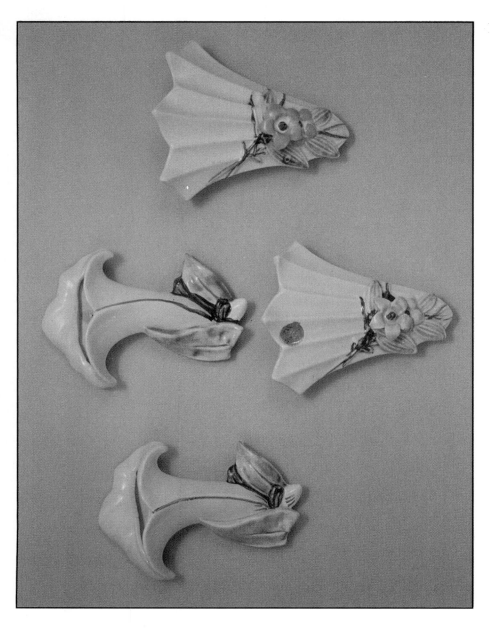

Bellows wall pocket, mid 1950s, McCoy mark, 9½" x 4½". Yellow with brown bisque glaze and ivory with green spray glaze are production glazes. Bellows wall pocket in center in black with blue spray glaze was not a production glaze. Standard glazes, $80.00 – 100.00. Black/blue glaze, $200.00 – 250.00.

PAGE 113

Top

Lovebirds wall pocket, early 1950s, McCoy mark, 8½" x 6", metallic trivet decorated as pictured left and right. Left wall pocket bird decoration more difficult to find. $75.00 – 90.00. Owls wall pocket, early 1950s, McCoy mark, 8½" x 6", yellow trivet brown decorated. $65.00 – 80.00.

Bottom

Iron wall pocket, early 1950s, McCoy mark, 8½" x 6", metallic trivet with gray iron, gray trivet with yellow iron, metallic trivet with yellow iron, and chartreuse trivet with metallic iron. $50.00 – 75.00.

The clock wall pocket, made in the mid-1950s, is definitely one of the most desirable pieces in the wall pocket collection but hard to find without damage. Check closely for a repaired wing or tail on the bird. Also, the weights will frequently be chipped. The catalog glazes were listed as green

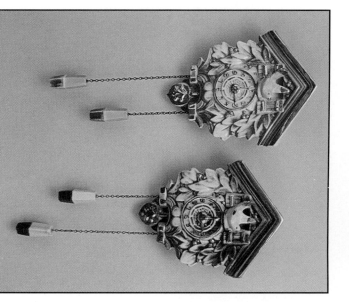

gray or brown decorated, but they have been found in a number of glaze colors as well as gold trimmed. The body of all pieces is 8" long without consideration for the weight chain where length can vary greatly. All are marked McCoy.

Burgundy/blue and green/brown combinations with gold trim accent. $150.00 – 200.00

Glazes pictured are, clockwise, green, brown, green/brown, and gray/brown. $125.00 – 150.00

Glazes pictured are burgundy/blue combination, gray, and yellow. $125.00 - 150.00.

All of the clock wall pockets were made with two different style faces, a roman numeral face and numeric face. Value is the same.

Cornucopia wall pocket, mid 1950s, McCoy mark, 8" x 6½", yellow with brown bisque glaze and ivory with green bisque glaze. $75.00 – 90.00. Mailbox wall pocket, mid 1950s, McCoy mark, 7" x 5½", green glaze. $90.00 – 100.00.

Page 117

Top

Flower with bird wall pocket, late 1940s, McCoy mark, 6½" x 5", glazes were blue, yellow, or pink decorated. Check closely for bird damage. $40.00 – 55.00.

Bottom

Bird bath wall pocket, late 1940s, McCoy mark, 6½" x 5", glazes were blue, yellow, or green decorated. Check closely for bird damage. $85.00 – 100.00.

Fan wall pocket, mid 1950s, McCoy mark, 8½" x 8", glazes green, pink, or blue, on facing page, were produced first, followed a few years later by the Sunburst gold and white, both with a drip style texture. $75.00 – 90.00.

Violin wall pocket, mid 1950s, McCoy mark, 10¼". Glazes brown or aqua with contrasting strings were produced first, followed a few years later by white and tan. Also pictured is an aqua violin wall pocket with gold trim. Brown or aqua, $100.00 – 150.00; white or tan, $150.00 – 200.00; gold trim, $200.00 – 250.00.

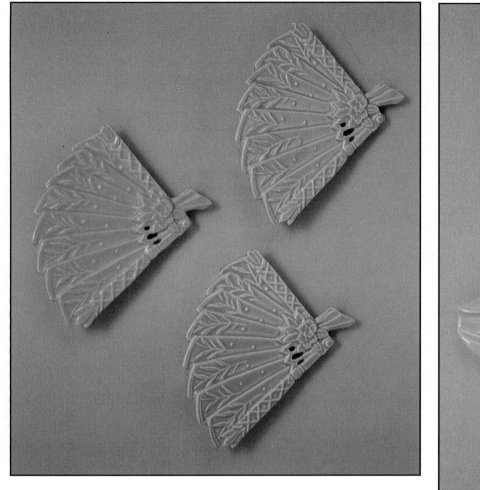

Fan wall pockets, mid 1950s,
McCoy mark. $75.00 – 90.00.

Leaf wall pocket, mid 1950s, McCoy mark, 7" x 5½", glazes pink, yellow, or ivory with sprayed decoration.
$35.00 – 50.00. Urn wall pocket, mid 1950s, McCoy mark, 6½" x 4½", chartreuse with brown flecks or pink
with black flecks glazes. $30.00 – 45.00.

The fruit wall pockets were initially produced in the early 1950s. None of them are marked and all are about 7" x 6". The standard green leaves with the catalog color of the fruit was called the "natural color" glaze. If you find one with a letter on the back, this is the initial of the production worker; workers initialed the pieces they made since they were paid by the piece.

Pear wall pocket. Shown in natural glaze and with brown leaves. Natural, $65.00 – 80.00. Brown leaves, $150.00 – 200.00. Bananas wall pocket, can also be found with brown leaves. Natural, $125.00 – 150.00. Brown leaves, $175.00 – 225.00.

PAGE 121

Top

Grapes wall pocket. Bottom wall pocket is the natural color glaze and the least difficult to find. The dark example on the left is called concord and the light green color on the top is actually called "white." The far right wall pocket color is red. $80.00 – 100.00. Concord, $200.00 – 225.00. White (grapes actually pale green color), $125.00 – 150.00. Red, $200.00 – 225.00.

Bottom

Apple wall pocket. Left is the natural color glaze. The center wall pocket has very rare olive leaves. The far right shows brown leaves. Natural, $50.00 – 60.00. Olive leaves, $200.00 – 225.00. Brown leaves $150.00 – 200.00.

Pictured are two experimental glaze wall pockets. Lower picture shows some degree of formula indication on their backs. If you look at the formula markings, it appears the left is ½ yellow and ½ orange in comparison to the right one that indicates one orange and two yellow. Note: At the very top of the right piece in the lower picture, the "gate" (the entrance to the mold for the material when made) has never been finished off. $200.00 – 250.00.

PAGE 123

Top

Orange wall pocket. Left is the natural color glaze and the least difficult to find. The natural glaze is actually orange cold paint over a yellow glazed orange. The yellow wall pocket pictured is what the orange looks like before the cold paint. It is difficult to find a piece with the cold paint in perfect condition. The orange with the black writing says "Souvenir of Miami, 1953." The far right orange has the orange color under glaze, no cold paint. Natural, $65.00 – 80.00. Dated 1953, $150.00 – 200.00. Yellow, $40.00 – 50.00. Glazed orange, $80.00 – 95.00.

Bottom

Umbrella wall pocket, mid 1950s, McCoy mark, 8¾" x 6". Production gloss glazes: yellow, black, or green. The gold wall pockets were part of the Sunburst line made a couple years later. Note both white and pink interiors. The black color has also been found in a matte finish. Gloss glazes, $60.00 – 75.00. Gold, $70.00 – 85.00. Matte black, $150.00 – 200.00.

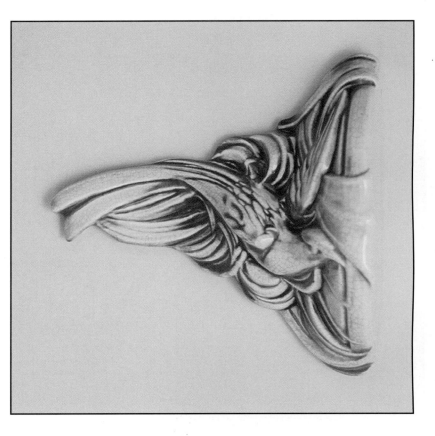

Wall bracket (bird shelf), 1948, 9" x 8", sprayed green and brown, or white, no mark. Very few have been found. $600.00 – 700.00.

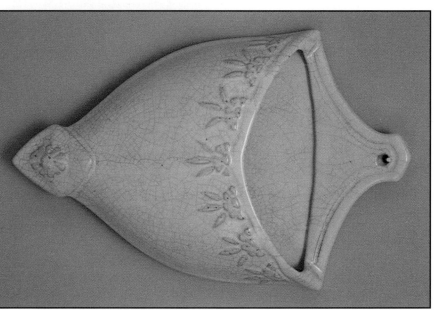

Early American wall pocket, 1966, McCoy mark, antique crackle finish, part of Early American line that year, 9" long. Very few have been found. $250.00 – 350.00.

Above and Below: Flower wall pocket vase, late 1940s, no mark, 6" square. Sold in a variety of colors. Dark blue and darker brown with green accent are very difficult to find. The piece with the typical rustic glaze was from the Rustic line of the late 1940s and is without question, the easiest McCoy wall pocket to find; they must have sold "a ton" of them. Rustic, $50.00 – 55.00; Turquoise, coral, yellow, or white, $35.00 – 50.00; dark blue or brown/green, $90.00 – 110.00.

Matchbox holder shown with original box, same speckled finish as above. McCoy mark, 5¾" x 3¼", late 1970s. $50.00 – 40.00.

Frame for mirror, early 1980s, 13" x 7½", blue/white speckled, no mark. $50.00 – 60.00. Wall pocket in same finish, no mark, early 1980s, 9½" long. $40.00 – 75.00.

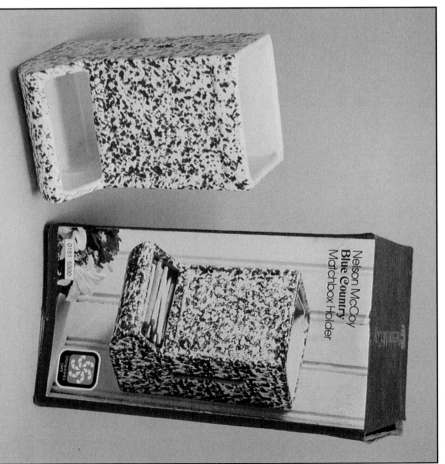

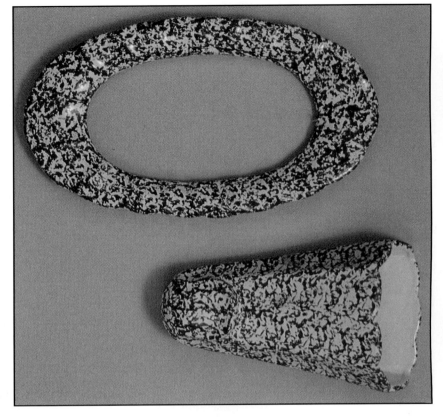

PAGE 127

Top and Middle
Wall pocket (tongue), early 1980s, no mark, 9½" long. Sold in a variety of colors and patterns. Many of these were part of a line of pieces with the similar pattern/glaze. $40.00 – 75.00.

Bottom
Matchbox holders, same as previous page, McCoy mark, 5¾" x 3¼", late 1970s. $50.00 – 40.00. Wall candleholder, no mark, 11" x 5½", late 1970s-early 80s. $25.00 – 35.00.

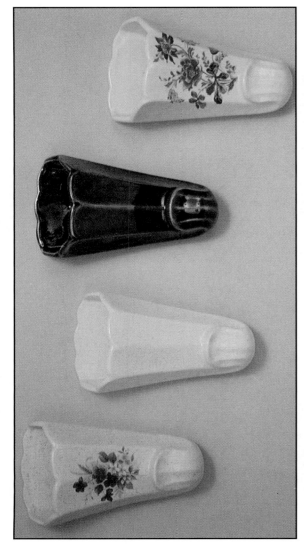

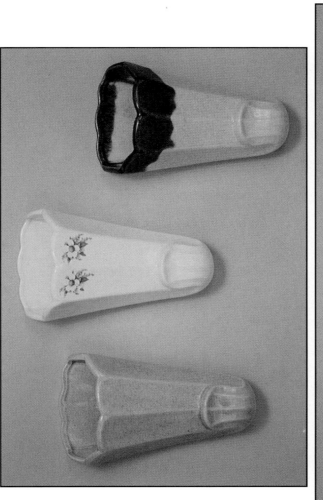

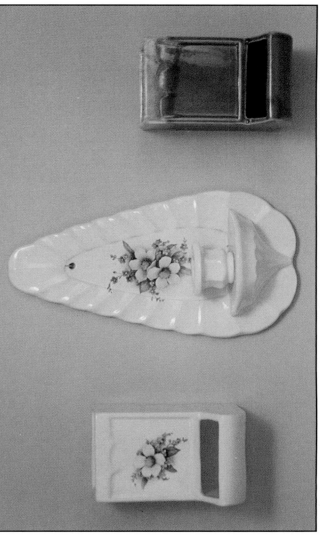

In 1953, McCoy released the fruit planter line. As you can obviously see, they closely resemble the fruit wall pockets. The lemon and pomegranate were never produced as wall pockets. Planters were 6½" x 5" in size with natural color finish. As with the wall pockets, the orange was the only one with cold paint as the top finish. You can see on the

orange on the bottom row of facing page how much of the cold paint has been lost. The difficulty in finding each individual fruit is directly related to the value as indicated. All of the planters are marked McCoy. A few pieces have been found with brown leaves, similar to the wall pockets, which adds 50% to values.

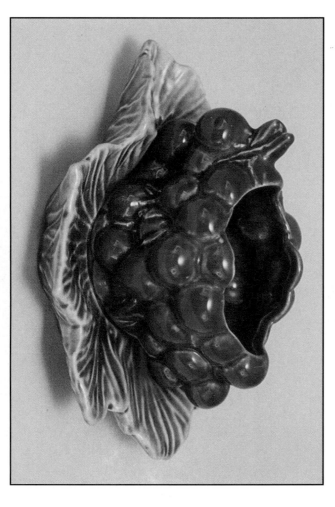

Grapes planter. $125.00 – 150.00.

Bananas. $100.00 – 125.00. Lemon. $75.00 – 100.00.

Pear. $35.00 – 50.00. Apple. $35.00 – 50.00.

Pomegranate. $100.00 – 125.00. Orange. $40.00 – 60.00.

Dog feeder, late 1930s, 7½". Around the outside of the feeder: "Man's Best Friend, His Dog." Both pieces the same. Brown, yellow or green glaze. $60.00 – 75.00.

Left: Spaniel feeder, late 1930s, 6½", green, yellow, red, or blue glaze. $85.00 – 100.00. *Right:* Cat feeder, late 1950s, 6", green, yellow, red, or blue glaze. $60.00 – 75.00.

Left and right: details on previous page. *Center:* Hunting dog feeder, late 1930s, 5"; also sold in a 6" size. No mark. *$45.00 – 60.00.* "Muffy" (4-year-old Bichon Frise – wouldn't let us give out her weight!), is part of the Nissen family.

Flower pots, early 1950s. Shown on decorative plant stand, 3", 3½", 4". All marked McCoy, variety of gloss colors. Later hobnail with leaves pattern. Original hobnail pieces were early 1940s. $25.00 – 40.00.

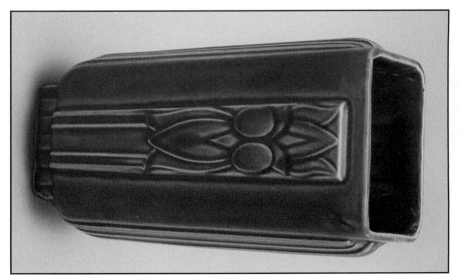

Vase, 1940s, 9", McCoy mark, dark green, white. $50.00 – 60.00.

PAGE 133

	Year	Description	Size	Mark	Available Glazes	Value
Row 1	1940s	Vase	8"	McCoy	Variety Gloss Colors	$40.00 – 55.00
	1940s	Vase — Same as vase before.				
	1940s	Vase	7½"	USA	White, Yellow	$40.00 – 60.00
Row 2	1940s	Vase	6"	McCoy	Variety Gloss Colors	$30.00 – 35.00
	1940s	Vase — Same as vase before.				
	1940s	Vase	6"	McCoy	Variety Gloss Colors	$25.00 – 30.00
	1940s	Vase	5"	McCoy, No Mark	Variety Colors	$35.00 – 50.00
Row 3	1940s	Vase	6"	McCoy	Variety Gloss Colors	$35.00 – 40.00
	1940s	Vase	8"	McCoy	Variety Gloss Colors	$45.00 – 60.00
	1940s	Vase	7"	McCoy	Variety Gloss Colors	$35.00 – 40.00
Row 4	1940s	Vase	8"	USA	Wide Variety Colors	$40.00 – 60.00
	Some of these vases are marked McCoy.					
	1940s	Vase	9"	McCoy	Green, White, Yellow	$50.00 – 70.00
	1940s	Vase — Same as this row left but with McCoy mark.				

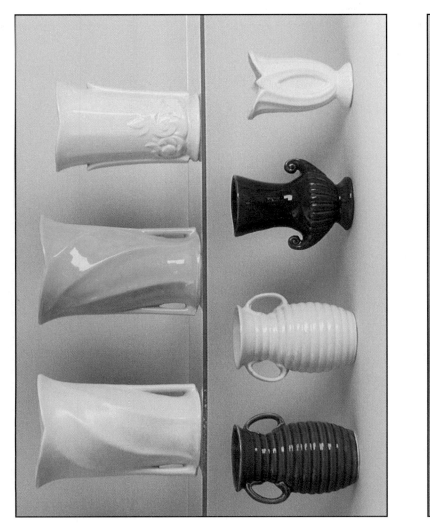

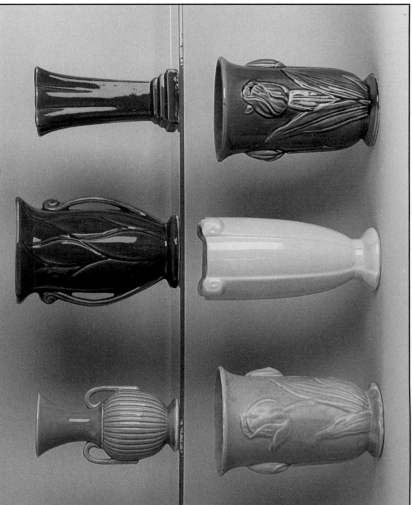

Page 155

Year	Description	Size	Mark	Available Glazes	Value
Top					
Row 1					
1940s	Duck w/egg Planter	7" x 3¼"	McCoy	White, Yell. Decorated	$25.00 – 30.00
1940s	Twin Shoes	4½" x 5½"	McCoy	Pink , Blue	$25.00 – 30.00
1940s	Snowman Planter	6" x 4"	McCoy	White Decorated	$50.00 – 60.00
Row 2					
1940s	Jardiniere	7¾"	McCoy	White, Green, Coral	$35.00 – 50.00
1940s	Flower Pot	3"	No Mark	Variety Colors	$15.00 – 20.00
1940s	Flower Pot	3¾"	No Mark	White, Green, Yellow	$20.00 – 25.00
1940s	Flower Pot	5", 6"	No Mark	White, Green, Yellow	$35.00 – 45.00
Bottom					
Row 1					
1940s	Double Ducks with eggs planter	6" x 3"	McCoy	White, Yellow, Coral	$30.00 – 35.00
1940s	Pelican			Lavender	
1940s	Pelican	7¾" x 5¾"	NM	Gloss & Matte Colors	$35.00 – 50.00
1940s	Pelican — Same as middle this row.				
Row 2					
1940s	Pitcher	7"	McCoy or No Mark	Wide Variety Colors	$25.00 – 40.00
	Pitcher has been found with inscription, "Treasure Island, San Francisco, 1939."				
1940s	Jardiniere	7½"	NM or No Mark	Pastel Colors	$50.00 – 60.00
1940s	Donkey	7"	No Mark	Variety Gloss Colors	$25.00 – 30.00

Snowman planter pictured with vintage penguin pins, 6" x 4", McCoy mark, white decorated. $50.00 – 60.00.

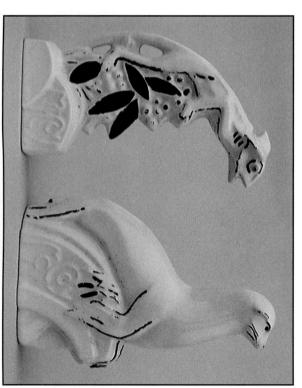

Great iguana and seal figural pieces, 1940s, McCoy mark, both are 6½" tall. Only a couple of each found. $250.00 – 500.00 each.

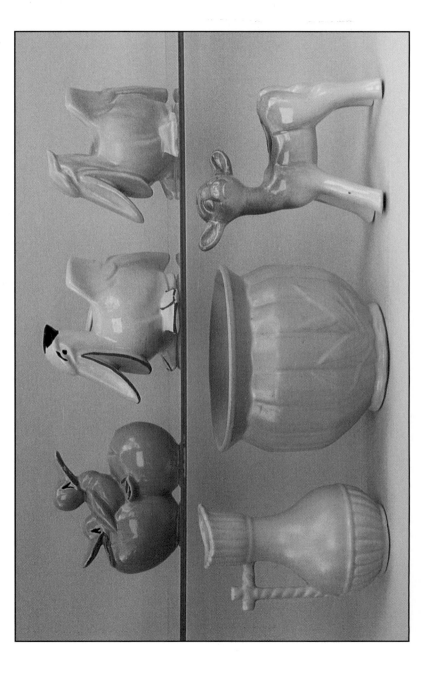

	Year	Description	Size	Mark	Available Glazes	Value
Top						
Row 1	Late 1940s	Vase	8¼"	McCoy	Variety Matte & Gloss	$30.00 – 40.00
	Late 1940s	Vase	8¼"	McCoy	Variety Gloss Colors	$30.00 – 40.00
	Late 1950s	Vase	5", 8", 10"	McCoy	White, Green, Yellow	$25.00 – 30.00
Row 2	1950	Jardiniere	7½"	McCoy	Chartreuse, Pink, Yellow	$35.00 – 45.00
	1950	Jardiniere	6" x 7"	McCoy	Green, Yellow	$35.00 – 45.00
	1950	Jardiniere	7½"	McCoy	Blended Glaze	$40.00 – 50.00
Bottom						
Row 1	1940s	Urn Vase	6½"	McCoy	Green, Yellow, White	$40.00 – 50.00
	Late 1940s	Flower Pot	3¾"	McCoy	Green, Yellow, Pink	$25.00 – 30.00
	Late 1940s	Jardiniere	5"	McCoy	White, Green, Peach	$25.00 – 30.00
	Late 1940s	Cornucopia Vase	8" x 7½"	McCoy	Pastel Matte Colors	$75.00 – 90.00
Row 2	Late 1940s	Vase	9"	McCoy	Pastel Matte Colors	$45.00 – 60.00
	Late 1940s	Vase	9"	McCoy	Variety Matte & Gloss	$45.00 – 60.00
	Early 1940s	Vase	9"	USA	Pastel Matte Colors	$45.00 – 60.00

Left: 10" vase, 1940s, McCoy mark, variety of pastel matte glazes. $75.00 – 100.00. *Right:* 9" vase, 1940s, McCoy mark, pastel matte colors. $45.00 – 60.00.

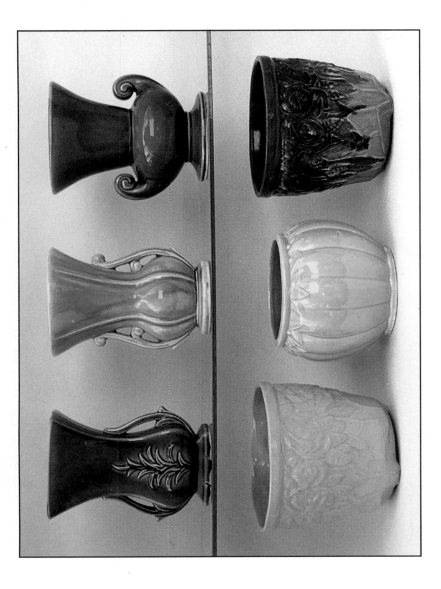

Jardinieres, 1950, 3½", marked McCoy, both offered in turquoise, yellow, and green. $45.00 – 60.00 each.

Pitcher, 9½", 1953, McCoy mark, variety gloss colors. $50.00 – 60.00. Reamer, 1949, 8" long, yellow or white. $60.00 – 75.00.

PAGE 159

	Year	Description	Size	Mark	Available Glazes	Value
Top						
Row 1	1953	Penguin Spoonrest	7" x 5"	McCoy	Green, Yell. Decorated	$100.00 – 150.00
	1953	Butterfly Spoonrest	7½" x 4"	McCoy	Green, Yellow Gloss	$100.00 – 150.00
	1953	Butterfly Spoonrest — same as middle this row.				
	These butterfly pieces were not part of the early '40s Butterfly line although the style of the butterfly is similar.					
Row 2	1940s	Pitcher – 32 oz.	6½"	McCoy	White, Green, Yellow	$30.00 – 40.00
	1940s	Teapot	12 & 30 oz.	McCoy	Brown Gloss	$30.00 – 40.00
	1940s	Pitcher – Same as left this row.				
Bottom						
Row 1	1964	Pitcher	5½"	McCoy	Variety Gloss Colors	$30.00 – 35.00
	1940s	Bean Pot – 2 qt.	6½"	McCoy	Brown Gloss	$30.00 – 40.00
	1964	Pitcher — Same as left this row.				
Row 2	1949	Pitcher – 55 oz.	8"	McCoy	Variety Gloss Colors	$40.00 – 50.00
	1953	Pitcher	7½"	McCoy	Variety Gloss Colors	$40.00 – 50.00
	1950s	Pitcher	7½"	No Mark	Variety Gloss Colors	$50.00 – 60.00
	This pitcher was made in 22, 32, 48, and 64 oz. sizes. Value range accounts for sizes.					

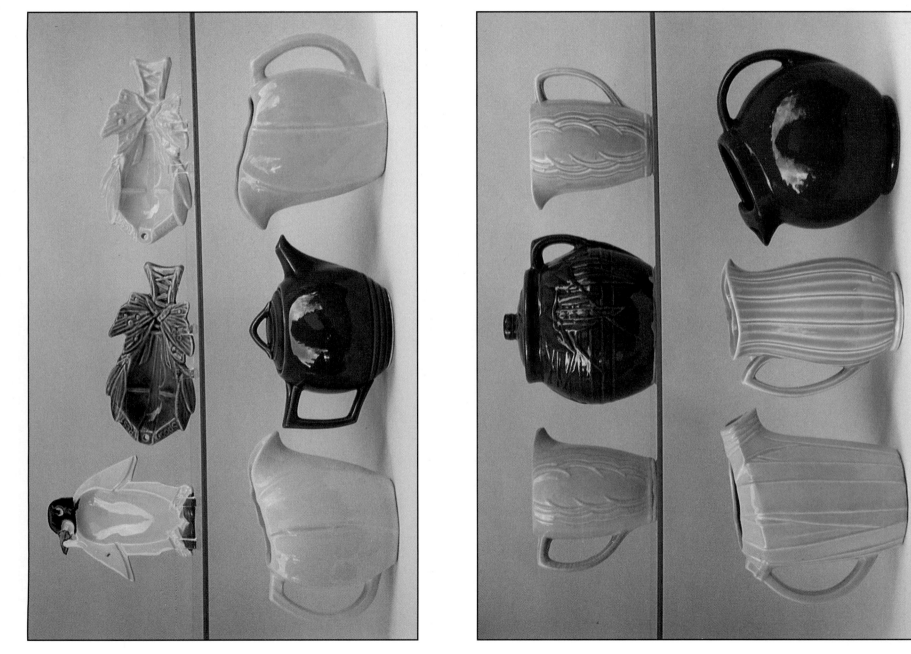

Madonna planter, 1950s, 6" tall, marked McCoy, white, very few have been found. $250.00 – 500.00.

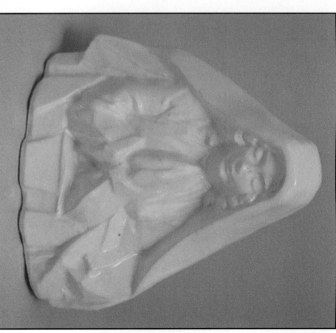

Bird planters pictured with lovely vintage tray. Details listed below.

PAGE 141

	Year	Description	Size	Mark	Available Glazes	Value
Top	1955	Wheelbarrow w/ Rooster Planters	10½" x 7"	McCoy	White, Green or Yellow	$100.00 – 125.00
Middle	1940s	Goose w/ Cart	8" x 4¾"	NM or McCoy	White, Green, Yellow	$35.00 – 45.00
	1940s	Pelican w/ Cart	8¼" x 4"	No Mark	White, Green, Yellow	$35.00 – 45.00
Bottom	1940s	Bird Planter	7" x 6¾"	USA	White, Green, Yellow	$25.00 – 35.00
	1940s	Bird Planter	4½" x 4½"	USA	White, Green, Yellow	$20.00 – 25.00

Both pieces this row are dry bottom. USA mark is on side near bottom edge.

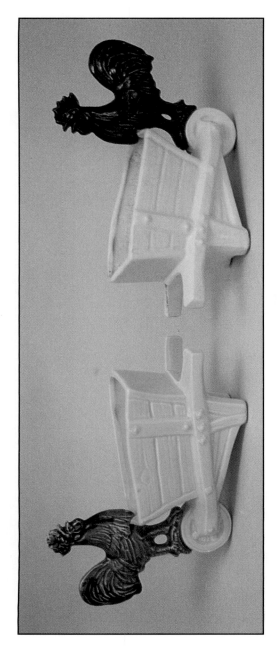

Page 143	Year	Description	Size	Mark	Available Glazes	Value
Top						
Row 1	1940s	Pitcher	7"	No Mark	Variety Colors	$35.00 – 50.00
	1940s	Ice Jug – 48 oz.	7"	No Mark	Variety Colors	$35.00 – 50.00
Row 2	1940s	Bird Pitcher – 32 oz.	6"	McCoy, No Mark	White, Green, Yellow	$35.00 – 50.00
	1940s	Bird Pitcher — Same as other pitcher this row.				
Bottom						
Row 1	1940s	Daisy Teapot		McCoy	Decorated as shown*	$40.00 – 50.00
	1940s	Creamer – 8 oz.		McCoy	Decorated as shown	$20.00 – 25.00
	1940s	Sugar – 8 oz.		McCoy	Decorated as shown*	$20.00 – 25.00
Row 2	1950	Vase	12"	McCoy	White, Green, Yellow	$50.00 – 60.00
	1950	Vase — Same as other vase this row.				

*Also in white and a variety of pastels.

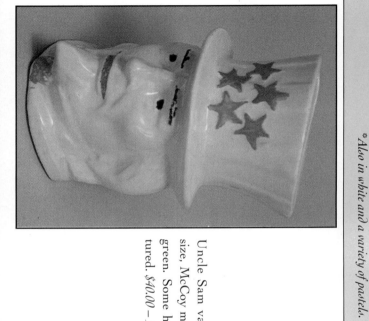

Uncle Sam vase, early 1940s, 7½" size, McCoy mark, white, yellow, and green. Some hand decorated as pictured. $40.00 – 50.00.

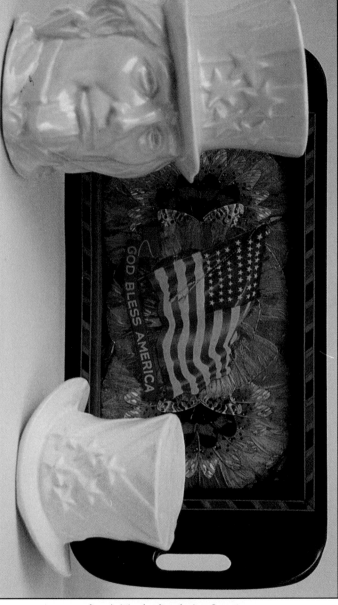

Uncle Sam vase, early 1940s, 7½", McCoy mark, white, yellow, and green. $40.00 – 50.00. Hat planter, 1941, 4", variety colors. $20.00 – 50.00.

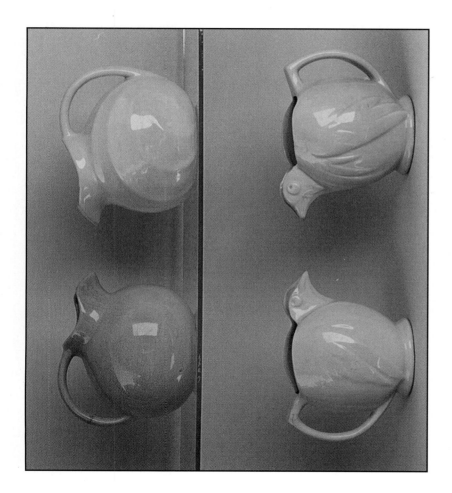

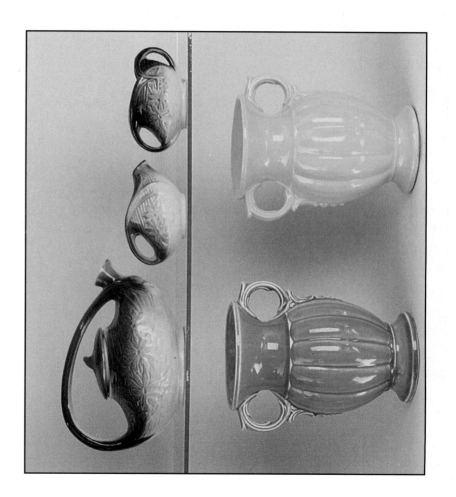

Vase with contrasting leaf, shown in both glazes sold, chartreuse and shrimp overdrip, 1955, McCoy mark. $100.00 – 125.00.

Vase, early 1940s, marked McCoy, 6", variety of colors. Pattern similar to early wall pocket. $40.00 – 50.00.

PAGE 145

	Year	Description	Size	Mark	Available Glazes	Value
Top	1955	Vase with Contrasting Leaf	9"	McCoy	Chartreuse or Shrimp Overdrip	$100.00 – 125.00
	1953	Ivy Vase	9"	McCoy	Hand Decorated	$90.00 – 110.00
		Matches tea set below.				
Middle	1950s	Ivy Teapot – 6 Cup		McCoy	Hand Decorated	$50.00 – 60.00
	1950s	Creamer – 8 oz.		McCoy	Hand Decorated	$20.00 – 25.00
	1950s	Sugar – 8 oz.		McCoy	Hand Decorated	$20.00 – 25.00
Bottom	1950s	Vase	12"	McCoy	White, Green, Black	$80.00 – 100.00
	1950s	Vase	10"	McCoy	White, Green, Black	$65.00 – 80.00
		Same vase was also sold in 14" size. $60.00 – 75.00.				

PAGE 147

	Year	Description	Size	Mark	Available Colors	Value
Top						
Row 1:	1964	Low Centerpiece	8½"	McCoy	White, Black, Pink, Orange	$15.00 – $20.00

This 8½" x 4½" low rectangular center piece was part of the Artisan line that contained an additional 15 shapes.

	Year	Description	Size	Mark	Available Colors	Value
	1950	Hanging Basket	3½"	No Mark	Green, & Yellow	$40.00 – $50.00
	1951	Jardiniere Bowl	3¾"	No Mark	Green, Pink & Yellow	$30.00 – $40.00
Row 2:	1951	Pitcher Vase	8"	McCoy	Green, Pink & Yellow	$25.00 – $30.00
	1951	Triple Planting Dish	10"	No Mark	Green, Pink & Yellow	$25.00 – $35.00
Bottom						
Row 1:	1950	Jardiniere	7"	McCoy	White, Green & Peach	$30.00 – $40.00
	1951	Bird Ashtray	5¼"	No Mark	Green, Blue, Pink & Yellow	$35.00 – $45.00
	1956	Fan Vase	10½"	McCoy	White, Green, Yellow	$40.00 – $60.00
Row 2:	1948	Embossed Vase	7"	McCoy	Green, Coral, Yellow	$35.00 – $45.00
	1950	Pot & Saucer	6"	McCoy	Green, Yellow, and Turquoise	$25.00 – $30.00

This pot & saucer also available in 4" and 5" sizes.

	Year	Description	Size	Mark	Available Colors	Value
	1948	Vase			Same as the green vase shown on this shelf.	$35.00 – $45.00

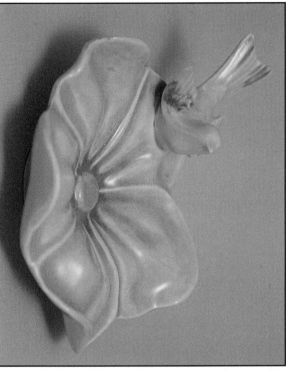

Bird ashtray, green color, white birds were also produced. $35.00 – 45.00.

Rare Cope monkey planter with good cold paint, 5½", no mark. $100.00 – 200.00.

Piano planters, 1959, 5" x 6", white, yellow fleck, and matte black. Pictured with musical theme silhouettes. $100.00 – $150.00.

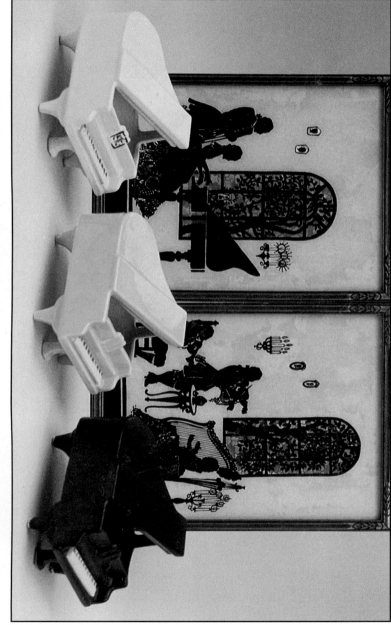

PAGE 149

Top

	Year	Description	size	Mark	Available colors	Value
Row 1:	1951	Clown & Pig Planter	8½"	McCoy	White/Hand Decorated	$80.00 – $100.00
	1956	Cornucopia Vase	7"	McCoy	Yellow, Green, Aqua & Pink	$25.00 – $35.00
	1947	Pig Planter	6"	No Mark	White/Hand Decorated	$20.00 – $25.00
Row 2:	1947	Planting dish	8"	McCoy	Matte White & Gloss Green	$20.00 – $25.00
	1945	Swallows Planting Dish	4"	McCoy	White/Hand Decorated	$20.00 – $30.00
	1947	Planting Dish	9"	McCoy/No Mark	Matte White & Gloss Green	$20.00 – $30.00

Bottom

	Year	Description	size	Mark	Available colors	Value
Row 1:	1947	Planting Dish	9"	McCoy	Matt White & Gloss Green	$20.00 – $25.00
	1947	Bulb Bowl	7"	McCoy	White Green & Yellow	$15.00 – $20.00
	1947	Swan Planter	7½"	McCoy	White/Hand Decorated	$30.00 – $45.00
Row 2:	1956	Vase	7"	McCoy	White, Green, & Turquoise & Pink	$25.00 – $30.00
	1948	Centerpiece Bowl	11"	McCoy	Green, Yellow, Turquoise & Coral	$30.00 – $40.00
	1941	Shell Planting Vase	6"	McCoy	Matte White & Pink	$20.00 – $30.00

Swan, planting dish, 1955, 10½". Produced in two color combinations with either a white or yellow swan. This must have been produced for only a short time, hard to find. $200.00 – 250.00.

Vases, 9", McCoy mark. Vase without handle, 1943, pictured in blue, also available in white and green. Vases with handles, 1947, green, white, and peach. $50.00 – 60.00.

PAGE 151

	Year	Description	Size	Mark	Available colors	Values
Top						
Row 1:	1956	Basketweave Planter	7½"	McCoy	Yellow, Pink, Lime	$15.00 – 20.00
		This 7½" x 3½" planter was spray decorated at the factory for effect.				
	1947	Panel Vase	7"	McCoy	Green, Coral & Yellow	$30.00 – 45.00
Row 2:	1949	Double Cache Pot	10½"	McCoy	Green, Yellow Decorated	$35.00 – 45.00
	Both colors produced are shown, but also found with a yellow/green bird.					
Bottom						
Row 1:	1948	Peacock Vase	8"	McCoy	White, Green & Yellow	$35.00 – 45.00
	1948	Double Handled Vase	8"	McCoy	Green, Coral & Yellow	$35.00 – 45.00
	1950	Flower Vase	8"	No Mark	Green, Yellow & White	$25.00 – 35.00
Row 2:	1948	Vase	9"	McCoy	Green, Coral & Yellow	$35.00 – 45.00
	1948	Vase	8"	McCoy	Green, Coral & Yellow	$25.00 – 35.00
	1948	Same 9" Vase as shown in yellow on this shelf			Green, Pink & Yellow	$25.00 – 45.00

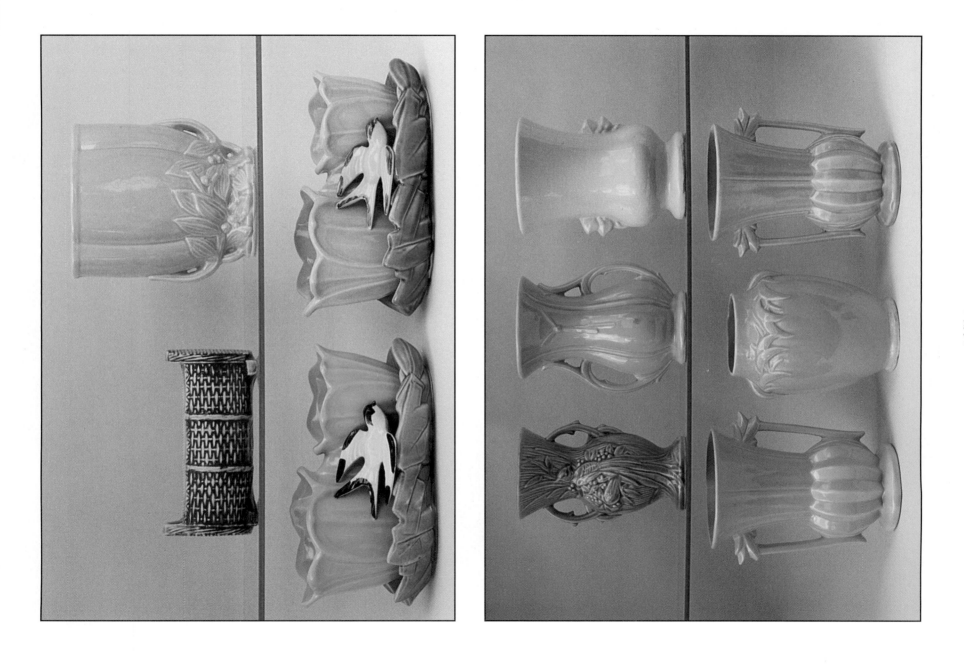

Sand jar, 10" x 14", McCoy mark, pastel green, matte white, gloss brown. $200.00 – $250.00.

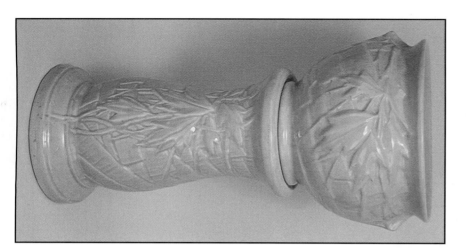

1955, 9½"/14½", jar has McCoy mark, green, matte white, brown/green blend. $500.00 – $550.00 set.

Pedestal, 1955, 14½", no mark, brown/green blend. Shown being used as table with glass 14" top. Great Idea! The other pieces (coffee pot, candleholder & dish) are shown elsewhere in the book. Pedestal only: $125.00 – $150.00.

Green porch jar, 1955, 10" x 11", McCoy mark. This was one of the few pieces McCoy offered with or without a drainage hole. $125.00 – $175.00. Sand jar, 14" x 10", McCoy mark, gloss brown. $200.00 – $250.00.

Rabbit & stump planter, 1951, 5½", McCoy mark, shown in the most common color, ivory with brown spray decorated. Pictured in front of a North Dakota prairie picture. $60.00 – 75.00.

Left & Right: Rabbit & stump planter shown in rare color combinations of yellow/purple and blue/yellow. It was also produced in pink/blue. $100.00 – 125.00.

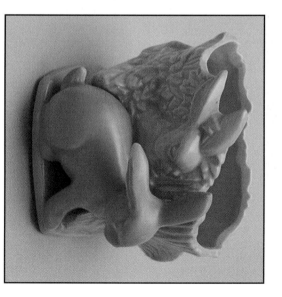

Bear, 5½" x 7", 1940s–50s, McCoy mark, yellow with red cold painted ball also with brown bear. Pictured here with a Goldilocks & The Three Bears jigsaw puzzle. $100.00 – 125.00.

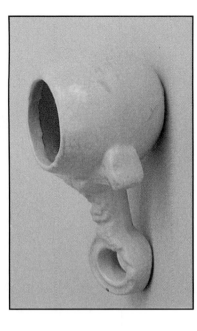

Baby rattle planter, 5½" x 3", 1954, cold painted, produced in pink and blue. $75.00 – 100.00.

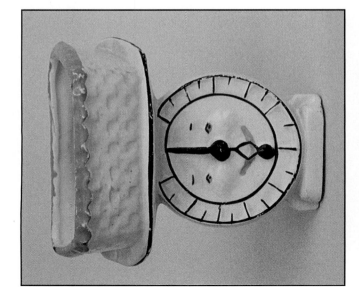

Baby scale planter, 5" x 5½", 1954, no mark, decorated in pink and blue. $60.00 – 75.00.

Raggedy Ann block planter, 5¼" x 4½", 1954, no mark, cold painted. $75.00 – 100.00.

Lamb planter, 5" x 4½", 1954, no mark, also produced with pink and blue cold paint. $60.00 – 75.00.

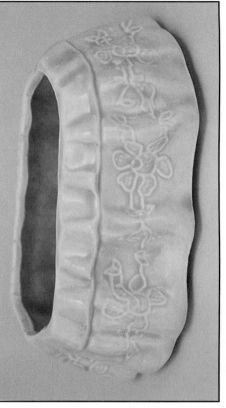

Baby crib planter, 6½" x 4", 1954, no mark, produced in pink and blue. $60.00 – 75.00.

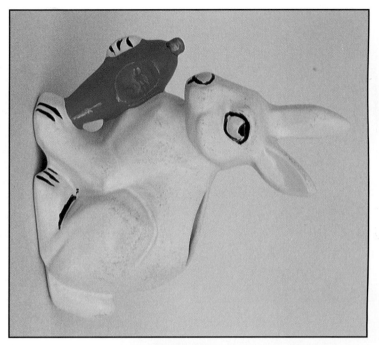

White rabbit planter with great cold paint, McCoy mark, 7¼" tall, hard to find. $100.00 – 125.00 depending on paint.

Yellow rabbit planter all ready for Easter, 7¼", McCoy mark, 1950s. $100.00 – 125.00.

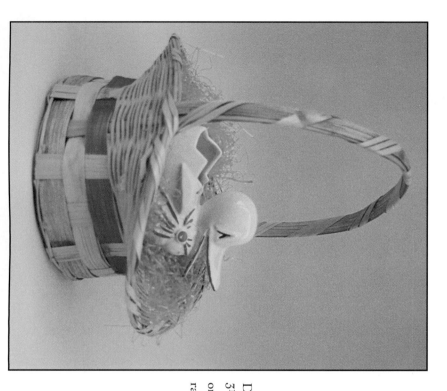

Duck with egg planter, 7" x 3¼", 1950, McCoy mark, white or yellow with cold paint decoration. $25.00 – 50.00.

	Year	Description	Size	Mark	Available colors	Value
Top	1959	Puppy Planter	6¼" x 6"	McCoy	White/ Black & Brown Decoration	$60.00 – 75.00
	1953	Cat Planter	7" x 4"	McCoy	White/Pink or Coral/Gray	$40.00 – 50.00
Middle	1950s	Rabbit Carrot Planter	7¼"	McCoy	White or Yellow with Cold Paint	$100.00 – 125.00
	1950s	Panda & Crib Planter	6"	McCoy	White with Cold Paint Decorated	$75.00 – 100.00
Bottom	1953	Lamb Planter	8½" x 7¼"	McCoy	White w/Pink & Gray w/ blue	$50.00 – 60.00
	1954	Lamb Planter	8½ x 7¼"	McCoy	White with Pink or Blue Cold Paint	$60.00 – 70.00

1955 Lamb Planter also pictured on page 165 with pink cold paint. 1954 Lamb on the right is hardest to find.

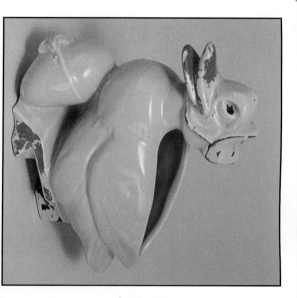

Duck with egg planter, some cold paint still intact, rare. *$100.00 – $125.00.*

Lamb planters. *Left,* 1953. $50.00 – 60.00. *Right,* 1954. $60.00 – 70.00. Lambs are pictured with a vintage child's play case.

PAGE 159

	Year	Description	Size	Mark	Available colors	Value
Top						
Row 1	1955	Squirrel Planters	5" x 4½"	McCoy	Brown or Gray Decorated	$25.00 – 30.00
		Squirrel #1 is matte gray and a rare color. The second two pieces are the catalog colors.				$20.00 – 25.00
Row 2	1957	Birds in Nest Planter	5" x 4"	McCoy	Yellow or Green Decorated	$35.00 – 45.00
	1953	Lamb Planter	8½" x 7¼"	McCoy	White with Pink or Blue paint	$50.00 – 60.00
	1957	Birds in Nest Planter (Shown here)		McCoy	Yellow with Green Decoration	$35.00 – 45.00
Bottom						
Row 1	1957	Small Fawn Planter	5" x 3½"	McCoy	Brown/Green or Tan Decoration	$20.00 – 25.00
	1957	Driftwood Planter	8½" x 3½"	McCoy	White/Gray Bisque, Birchwood	$20.00 – 30.00
	1957	Driftwood Planter, *Pictured to show side view*		McCoy	Chartreuse/Green Bisque	$20.00 – 30.00
Row 2	1950	Windproof Ashtray 5½" x 7"		McCoy	Yellow, Pink, or Ivory with Spray	$30.00 – 35.00
		This piece was also made as a wall pocket.				
	1957	Basket Planter	9" x 5¼"	McCoy	Ivory/Green or Yellow/Brown	$40.00 – 50.00

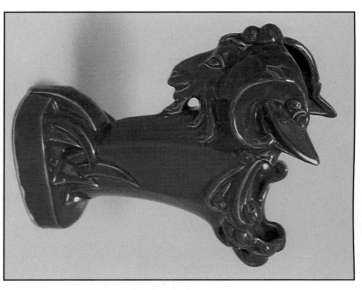

Ram's head vase shown in burgundy. This may be the hardest color to find. Very Art Deco. *$125.00 – $175.00.*

1956 Stork Planters attending a birthday party for a newborn. We're sure they were sent with flowers. *$60.00 – $75.00.*

PAGE 161

	Year	Description	Size	Mark	Available colors	Value
Top						
Row 1:	1956	Poodle Planter	7½" x 7½"	McCoy	Pink, Lime, Black & Burgundy	$60.00 – 75.00
		(Pictured is the lime color with reverse side showing. Black & burgundy glazes are harder to find.)				$50.00 – 60.00
Row 2:	1956	Stork Planter	7½" x 7"	McCoy	Pink & Lime Decorated	$60.00 – 75.00
		(Pictured is the pink glaze with great cold paint, also shows reverse side.)				$40.00 – 50.00
Bottom						
Row 1:	1949	Scottie Planting Dish	8"	McCoy	Green & Ivory with Brown Spray	$40.00 – 50.00
	1952	Dog with Cart Planter	8½"	McCoy	Green & Ivory with Brown Spray	$30.00 – 35.00
Row 2:	50s	Ram's Head Vase	9½"	McCoy	Black, Burgundy & Chartreuse	$100.00 – 150.00
	1956	Poodle Planter	7½"	McCoy	Black with Red Cold Paint	$75.00 – 100.00
		(Ram's head vase shown in chartreuse & the reverse side from other pictured.)				$125.00 – 175.00

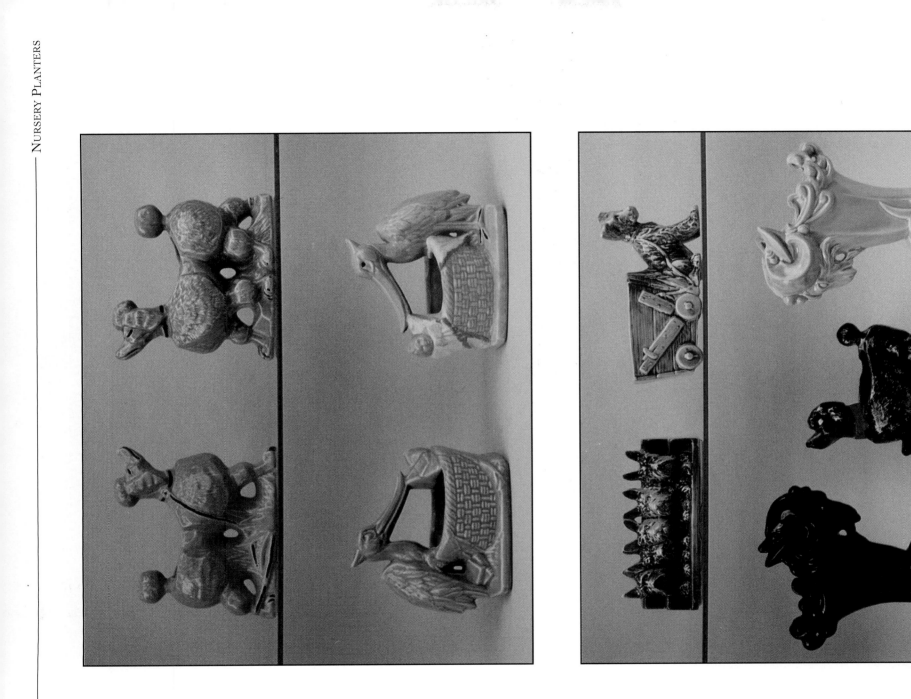

Like many of the pieces pictured in this book, these large fan vases are getting hard to find. Worth looking for...They are beautiful!

Large fan vase, McCoy mark, white and green agate. $250.00 – 350.00. Pictured with an aluminum tray.

Large fan vase, 13½" x 10", McCoy mark, black. $250.00 – 350.00.

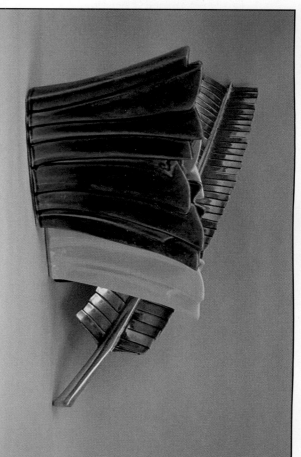

Grape vase, 9", 1951, McCoy mark, rare blue and yellow. $125.00 – 175.00.

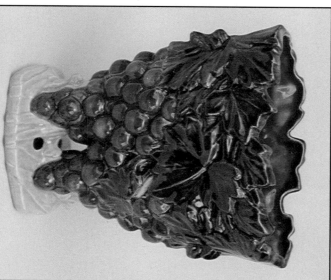

Grape vase, 1951, 9", McCoy mark, two-tone decorated. $45.00 – 60.00. Grape Pitcher vase, 1951, 9", two-tone, McCoy mark. $35.00 – 45.00.

Grape pitcher vase, McCoy mark, brown and yellow. $35.00 – 45.00. Grape vase, McCoy mark, brown and yellow. $45.00 – 60.00.

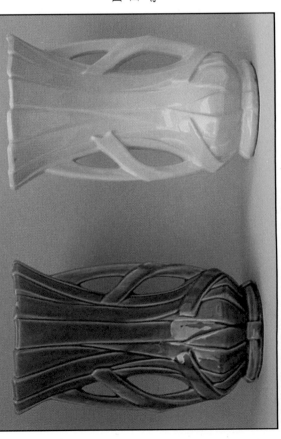

Large double handled vase, 12", 1947, McCoy mark, gloss white and green. $75.00 – 100.00.

The flower form vases have become very popular among McCoy collectors. Many collectors only collect the flower form vases in their various colors and decorations. Margaret Hanson began collecting McCoy with these beautiful pottery pieces.

The 1955 Pink Poppy vase shown above is both the front and back of this beautiful example. This is one of only a few McCoy produced pieces to be as attractive on the back as it was on the front. The front is on the left.

PAGE 165

	Year	Description	Size	Mark	Available colors	Value
Top	1955	Poppy Vase	8½"	McCoy	Pink Decorated	$600.00 – 700.00
		(Pink color can vary greatly.)				
	1955	Poppy Vase	8½"	McCoy	Yellow Decorated	$700.00 – 800.00
		(Yellow is rare and more valuable.)				
Middle	1956	Wide Lily Vase	8½"	McCoy	White or Yellow Decorated	$350.00 – 400.00
	1956	Wide Lily vase	8½"	McCoy	White or Yellow Decorated	$350.00 – 400.00
		(Note: available in matte or gloss glaze. The yellow color was cataloged, but is very rare.)				
Bottom	1950	Chrysanthemum Vase	8"	McCoy	Pink or Yellow	$100.00 – 125.00
	1950	Chrysanthemum Vase	8"	McCoy	Pink or Yellow	$100.00 – 125.00

The two vases displayed with the lovely basket of silk flowers below are fine examples of the McCoy flower form vases. The Hyacinth and Double Tulip vases are highly sought after by collectors.

PAGE 167

	Year	Description	Size	Mark	Available colors	Value
Top	1950	Triple Lily Vase	8½"	McCoy	White or Yellow	$40.00 – 60.00
	1950	Triple Lily Vase	8½"	Mccoy	White or Yellow	$40.00 – 60.00

These were available in matte or gloss, pictured here with the original McCoy paper labels.

	Year	Description	Size	Mark	Available colors	Value
Middle	1950	Hyacinth Vase	8"	McCoy	Pink or Blue/Green Leaves	$100.00 – 125.00
	1950	Hyacinth Vase	8"	McCoy	Pink or Blue/Green Leaves	$100.00 – 125.00
	1950	Hyacinth Vase	8"	McCoy	Pink or Blue/Green Leaves	$100.00 – 125.00

Shown here are the three main colors produced, blue, pink, & lavender. Some non-standard colors have been found.

	Year	Description	Size	Mark	Available colors	Value
Bottom	1948	Double Tulip Vase	8"	McCoy	White, Rose Decorated	$75.00 – 90.00
	1948	Double Tulip Vase	8"	McCoy	White, Yellow Decorated	$75.00 – 90.00
	1948	Double Tulip Vase	8"	McCoy	White, Pink Decorated	$75.00 – 90.00

As with many McCoy pieces produced, we have three colors of a vase that was only supposed to be done in two. Again, it's just more for you to find.

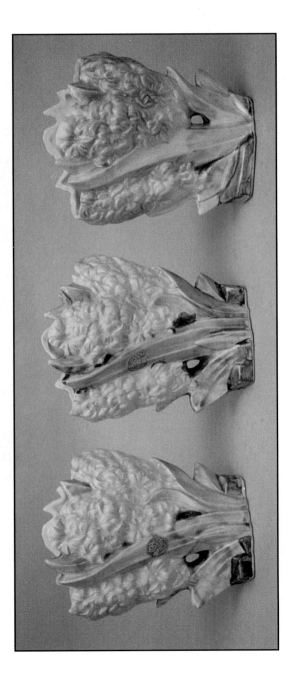

Planter bookends, 6¼" x 5½" each, rare color, green with ivory and tan spray. Shown here with a colorful Smith Frederick foil picture. They make perfect book ends for the nightstand because they were sold with felt bottoms. $90.00 – 125.00 pair.

PAGE 169

	Year	Description	Size	Mark	Available colors	Value
Top						
Row 1:	1953	Magnolia Vase	8¼"	McCoy	Pink Tint w/Green Leaves	$150.00 – 175.00
	1953	Lower Tulip Vase	6½"	McCoy	White w/Hand Decoration	$85.00 – 110.00
Bottom						
Row 1:	1956	Triple Pot Planter	12½" x 4½"	McCoy	Pink, Yellow, Orange Decorated	$90.00 – 120.00
		12½" x 4½" Triple Pot in pink w/green trim. The orange color had tan trim w/green leaves.				
Row 2:	1953	Planter Bookends	6¼" x 5½"	McCoy	Green/Yellow, Gray/Maroon	$90.00 – 125.00
						$90.00 – 125.00
		Shown here are the other two colors available at time of introduction; these were sold with felt bottoms.				

PAGE 171

	Year	Description	Size	Mark	Available colors	Value
Top						
Row 1:	1955	Planting Dish with Bud	11"	McCoy	Yellow or Chartreuse	$50.00 – 60.00
		The bud was applied and decorated after the piece was removed from the mold.				
Row 2:	1955	Single Cache Planter	9"	McCoy	Yellow/Green, Pink/Black	$65.00 – 75.00
Row 2:	1955	Hummingbird Planter	11"	McCoy	Pink w/Green Base	$75.00 – 100.00
					Blue w/Black Base	
Bottom						
Row 1:	1955	Large Centerpiece	12" x 6"	McCoy	Brown or Ruby w/Green	$50.00 – 60.00
Row 1:	1955	Small Centerpiece	8" x 4"	McCoy	Brown or Yellow w/Green	$40.00 – 50.00
Row 2:	Large Centerpiece pictured to show the back side of the planter and the brown blended glaze.			McCoy	Brown or Yellow w/Green	$50.00 – 60.00
	Small Centerpiece in brown blended glaze comparing the different sizes.					$40.00 – 50.00

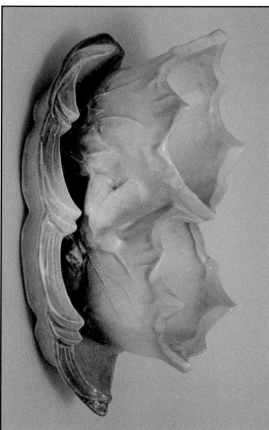

Hummingbird double cache planter, 1955, 11" x 5". Hard to find. *$75.00 – 100.00.*

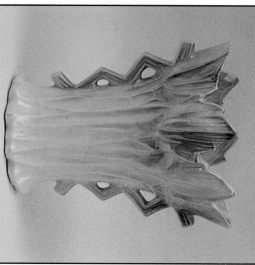

Left: 1955 – 9" petal vase. Ivory or chartreuse with green petals. This is a very desirable vase and is highly sought after by the flower form collectors. *$150.00 – 175.00.*

Floral vase, 9" high, McCoy mark. This example was found by an avid McCoy collector and purchased for under $10.00. The current value is much higher! *$150.00 – 200.00.*

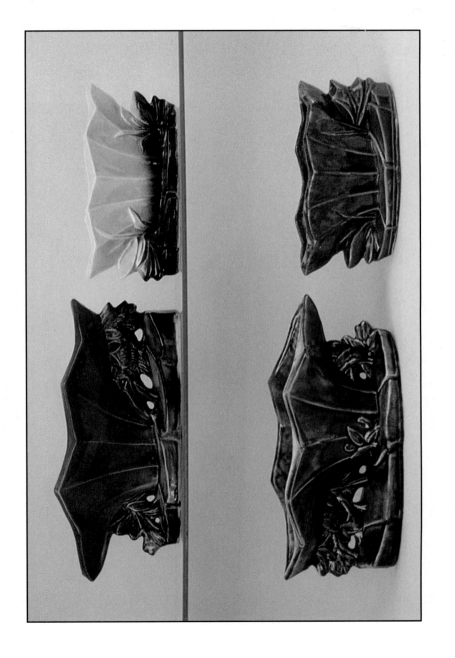

Lily bookends, 1948, 5½" x 5", green with decorated lily. These are as beautiful as they look. $125.00 – 150.00. Lily bud vases, 1947, 8", white or yellow, hand decorated. $60.00 – 75.00. Note: The white vase has an original paper label.

PAGE 173

	Year	Description	Size	Mark	Available colors	Value
Top						
Row 1:	1953	Two-tone Vase	9"	McCoy	Gray/Green	$40.00 – 50.00
	1953	Two-tone Vase shown in the gray/green combination.			Gray/Green, Yellow/Green, Chartreuse/Green	$40.00 – 50.00
Row 2:	1954	Small Fan Vase	10"	McCoy	Chartreuse/Green, Yellow/Brown	$45.00 – 55.00
		Pictured is the second color of the small fan vase. This vase looks good on either side.			Chartreuse/Green, Yellow/Brown	$45.00 – 55.00
Bottom						
	1954	Tall Fan Vase	14½"	McCoy	Green or Yellow/Decorated Foot	$150.00 – 200.00
		Tall fan vase shown for color and reverse side comparison. These are very impressive vases.				$150.00 – 200.00

BLOSSOMTIME LINE

This is the complete Blossomtime line from McCoy. First produced in 1946, this line had to be a popular choice of the consumer as seen by its availability in many antique stores and malls. As usual, you will find some pieces had been produced in flower colors other than shown in the catalogs. The blue flower shown on the bottom row is a good example.

Blossomtime wall pocket, 1946, 8" with original paper label, yellow with applied pink flower. $95.00 – 150.00.

Here are three examples, 8" vase, 6" square jardiniere, and 5" square jardiniere, of the white white glaze with the rare non-cataloged flower colors. Add 20% for the rare flower colors.

Page 175

	Year	Description	Size	Mark	Available colors	Value
Top	1946	Square Jardiniere	6"	McCoy	White or Yellow with Pink Flowers	$40.00 – 50.00
	1946	Square Jardiniere	5"	McCoy	White or Yellow with Pink Flowers	$30.00 – 40.00
	1946	Planting Dish	8"	McCoy	White or Yellow with Pink Flowers	$40.00 – 50.00
Middle	1946	Divided Handled Vase	7"	McCoy	White or Yellow with Pink Flowers	$50.00 – 60.00
	1946	Handled Vase	6¼"	McCoy	White or Yellow with Pink Flowers	$40.00 – 50.00
	1946	Urn Vase	6½"	McCoy	White or Yellow with Pink Flowers	$40.00 – 50.00
Bottom	1946	Tall Vase	8"	McCoy	White or Yellow with Pink Flowers	$50.00 – 60.00
	1946	Small Vase	6"	McCoy	White or Yellow with Pink Flowers	$30.00 – 40.00
	1946	Tall Rectangular Vase	8"	McCoy	White or Yellow with Pink Flowers	$50.00 – 60.00

The blue flower decoration is rare.

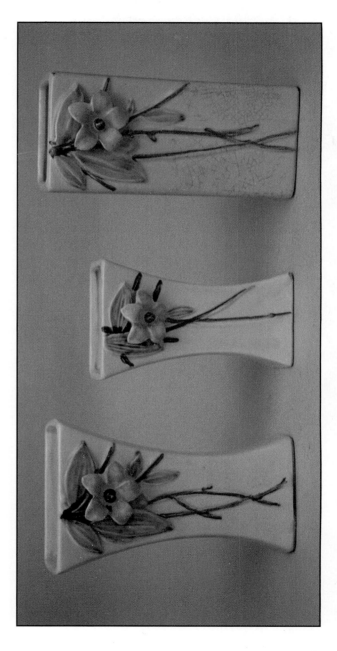

WILD ROSE LINE

This beautiful pastel glazed line of vases and planters was produced in 1952. It contained six shapes that are all pictured on page 177. The available colors were lavender, yellow, blue, and pink. The rose was hand painted in pink; the pink version had a yellow painted rose. This is a highly sought-after line.

Fine examples of the four pastel glazes. Planters, 8" x 3½", McCoy mark. $50.00 – 60.00 ea.

A beautiful example of the 4½" vase shown in light pink with a yellow rose, McCoy mark. $65.00 – 80.00. Non-production color combination.

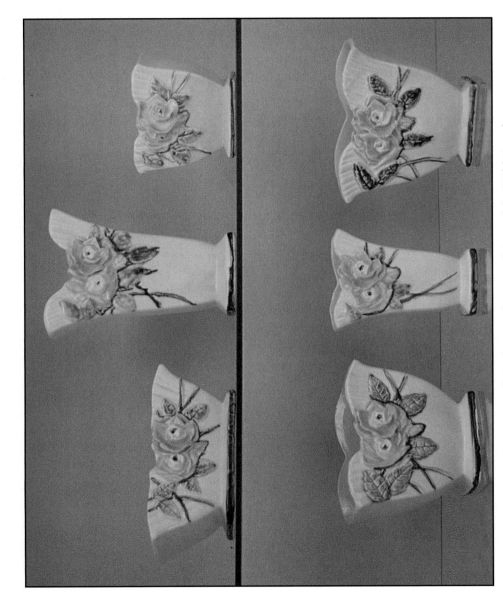

Pictured above are all the known shapes and sizes of the Wild Rose line.

	Year	Description	Size	Mark	Available colors	Value
Row 1:	1952	Planter	8" x 3½"	McCoy	Lavender, Yellow, Blue & Pink	$50.00 – 60.00
	1952	Tall Vase	8" x 5½"	McCoy	Lavender, Yellow, Blue & Pink	$75.00 – 90.00
	1952	Small Jardiniere	4" x 4"	McCoy	Lavender, Yellow, Blue & Pink	$40.00 – 50.00
Row 2:	1952	Square Jardiniere	6" x 6" x 6"	McCoy	Lavender, Yellow, Blue & Pink	$75.00 – 90.00
	1952	Small Vase	6½" x 4½"	McCoy	Lavender, Yellow, Blue & Pink	$40.00 – 50.00
	1952	Large Jardiniere	6" x 2½" x 6"	McCoy	Lavender, Yellow, Blue & Pink	$75.00 – 90.00

These sports planters have bisque glaze on the outside with gloss finished interiors, with the exception of the boxing gloves, which may also be gloss finished outside and inside. They are very collectible for both McCoy collectors and sports and auto collectors. Because of their popularity, they are seldom found for sale and many collectors have traded for these collectibles.

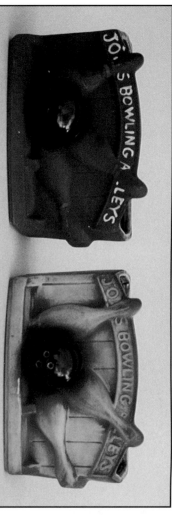

Two different colors of the bowling planter. Both have green interiors. The tan color is not cataloged. $125.00 – 175.00.

Football planter shown in antique finish with a vintage trophy. $75.00 – 100.00.

Page 179					
Year	**Description**	**Size**	**Mark**	**Available colors**	**Value**
Top					
1957	Baseball Glove Planter	6" x 6"	No Mark	Brown Spray/Yellow or Green Int.	$150.00 – 200.00
1957	Boxing Gloves Planter	6½" x 5½"	No Mark	Brown Spray/Blue or Pink Int.	$100.00 – 125.00
1957	Football Shoe Planter	7" x 4½"	McCoy	Brown Spray/Yellow or Green Int.	$75.00 – 100.00
Middle					
1957	Convertible Planter	9½" x 4½"	No Mark	Brown Spray/Yellow or Green Int.	$60.00 – 80.00
	This auto planter is also available in the hard-top version.				
Bottom					
1957	Fisherman Planter	6" x 4½"	McCoy	Brown Spray/Yellow or Green Int.	$150.00 – 200.00
1957	Bowling Planter	6½" x 4"	McCoy	Brown Spray/Yellow or Green Int.	$125.00 – 175.00
1957	Golf Planter	6" x 4"	McCoy	Brown Spray/Yellow or Green Int.	$150.00 – 200.00

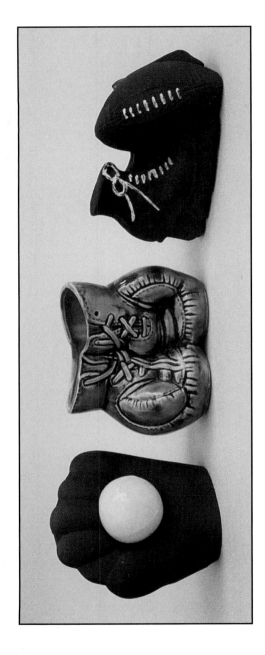

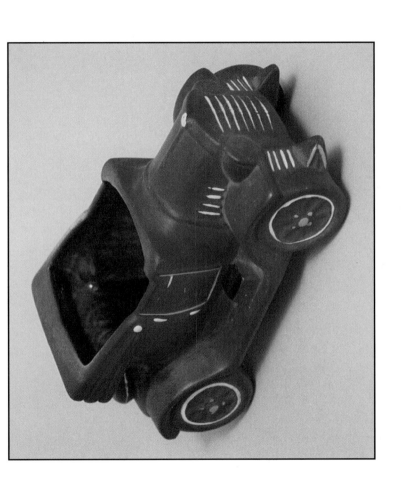

Most of the gold decorated pieces found were not decorated by McCoy. They sold many of their pieces to the Shafer Company of Zanesville, Ohio. Shafer added the 23K gold trim enhancement and then sold the pieces themselves. Of course, some pieces were still marked McCoy and Shafer frequently put a stamp on the bottom. They did not decorate

all pieces the same. The fawn vase has been found without the gold trim on the deer and we are showing two examples of the spinning wheel planter. The following section contains many outstanding examples of Shafer's work and the different look it gave to the McCoy Pottery.

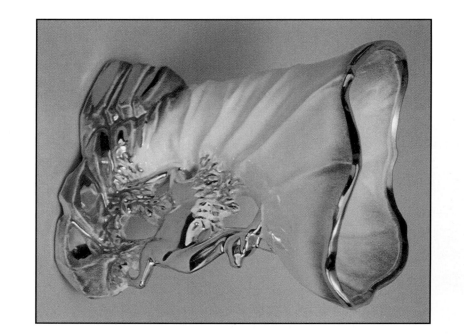

Shafer
23 K. Gold
Guaranteed

PAGE 181

	Year	Description	Size	Mark	Glaze	Value
Top	1956	Shell Planter	5" x 4"	McCoy	Yellow	$30.00 – 40.00
	1956	Wagon Wheel Planter	12" x 4"	McCoy	Green	$100.00 – 125.00
Middle	1941	Tulip Vase	8" high	No Mark	Yellow	$60.00 – 80.00
	1946	Pitcher Vase	9" high	McCoy	Yellow/Green	$60.00 – 80.00
Bottom	1947	Flower Vase	9" high	McCoy	Yellow	$80.00 – 100.00
	1954	Sunflower Vase	9" high	McCoy	Yellow	$70.00 – 90.00

This vase has the following inscription:"1949 Iowa State Glad Show, Waterloo."

Like the pieces pictured on page 183, here is another one of those great finds! This 1953 spinning wheel planter decorated in gold and sold by Shafer has the following verse, under the glaze, and hand written on the wheel: "A Mile to a friend's house is never too far." $90.00 – 110.00.

PAGE 183	Year	Description	Size	Mark	Glaze	Value
Top	1953	Puppy Planter	7½" x 4½"	McCoy	Gray & Green Decorated	$50.00 – 60.00
	1943	Frog & Lotus	5" x 4"	No Mark	Green & Yellow Decorated	$35.00 – 40.00
Middle	1953	Spinning Wheel Planter	7¼" x 7¼"	McCoy	Gray Blend Decorated	$70.00 – 90.00
	1953	Kitten Planter	7" x 4½"	McCoy	Gray & Green Decorated	$50.00 – 60.00
Bottom	1954	Village Smithy Planter	7½" x 6½"	McCoy	Gray Blend Decorated	$50.00 – 65.00
	1953	Old Mill Planter	7½" x 6½"	McCoy	Gray & Green Decorated	$50.00 – 65.00

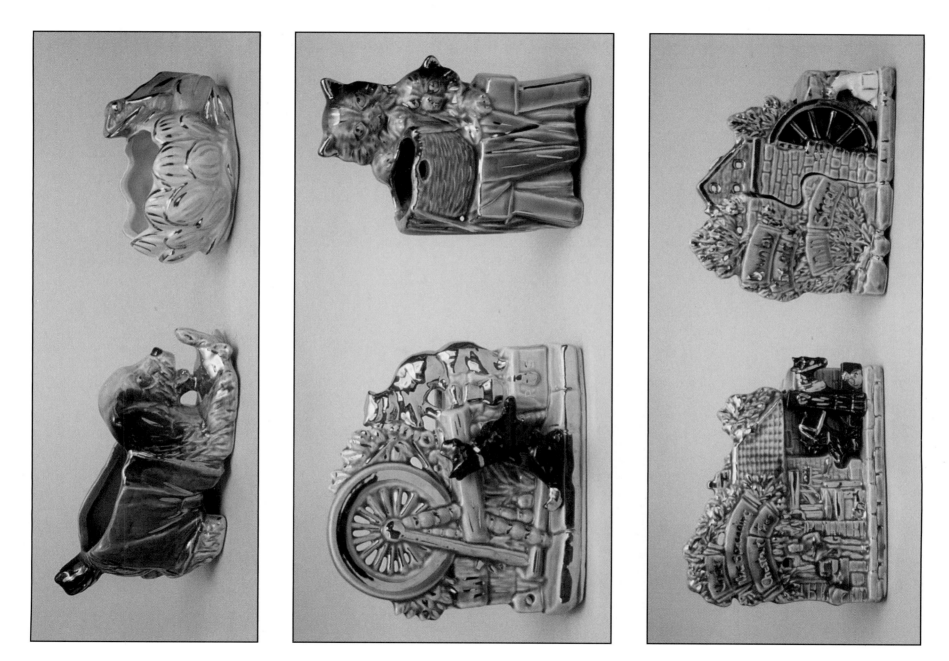

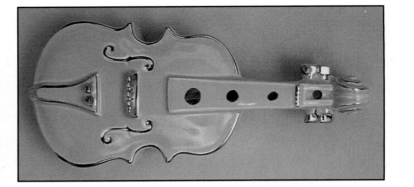

Top: Bird of Paradise, 12½" x4½", 1946 , McCoy mark. $60.00 – 75.00.
Middle: Bud vase 7¼", 1956, McCoy mark. $30.00 – 40.00.
             Planting dish, 7¼", 1956, McCoy mark. $30.00 – 40.00.
Bottom: Stork planter, 7½"x 7, 1956, McCoy mark. $60.00 – 75.00.
             Baby carriage planter, 7¾" x 6", 1955, McCoy mark. $60.00 – 75.00.

Violin wall pocket, 1957, 10¼". This wonderful example of the McCoy violin wall pocket is a real prize. $200.00 – 250.00.

Pictured is the bird of paradise planter with a reverse painted serving tray. $60.00 – 75.00.

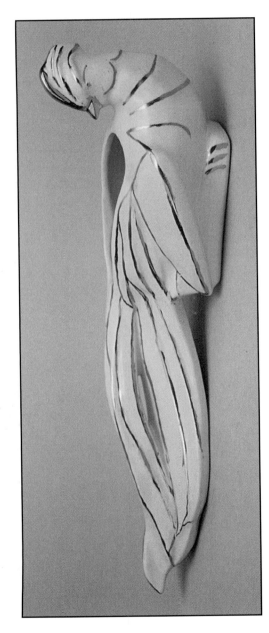

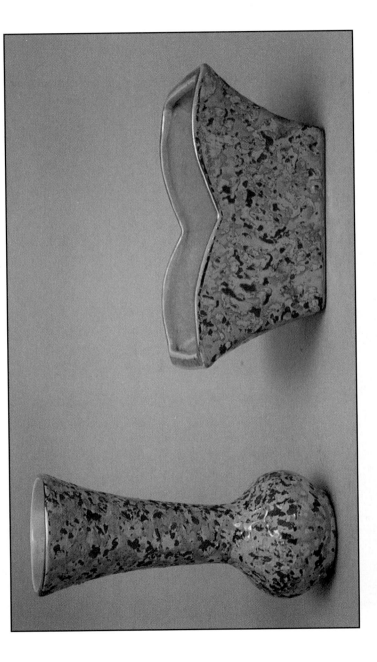

	Year	Description	Size	Mark	Glaze	Value
Top	1950	Fancy Lotus Leaf Pot	4½"	McCoy	Yellow	$40.00 – 45.00
	1953	Water Lily Planter	7½" x 4½"	McCoy	Yellow & Green	$45.00 – 50.00
Middle	1953	Magnolia Vase	8¼" x 7"	McCoy	White & Pink	$200.00 – 250.00
	1953	Double Tulip	6½" x 8"	McCoy	White & Pink	$150.00 – 200.00
Bottom	1951	Grape Vase	9"	McCoy	Yellow/Gold	$75.00 – 90.00
	1951	Grape Vase	9"	McCoy	Green & Ivory	$75.00 – 90.00

Gold decorated clock with standard numerals. First produced in 1952, this is a popular choice among wall pocket collectors. $150.00 – 200.00.

Burgundy/gold-trim lion, 15" x 5½", 1950. Hard to find in this color and trim. $75.00 – 100.00.

Hand-decorated Liberty Bell planter with rare gold bell and the wrong date, 8th. July 1776, 10½" x 8¼", 1954. These planters are a prize for gold-trim collectors. $300.00 – 400.00.

PAGE 189

	Year	Description	Size	Mark	Glaze	Value
Top	1956	Triple Pot	12½" x 4½"	McCoy	Green & Pink	$125.00 – 175.00
Middle	1943	Hands Ashtray	5¾"	McCoy	Yellow	$65.00 – 75.00
	1950	Novelty Dish with Bird	10"	McCoy	Yellow & Green	$45.00 – 55.00
Bottom	1942	Horse Bookends	8"	No Mark	White	$125.00 – 150.00

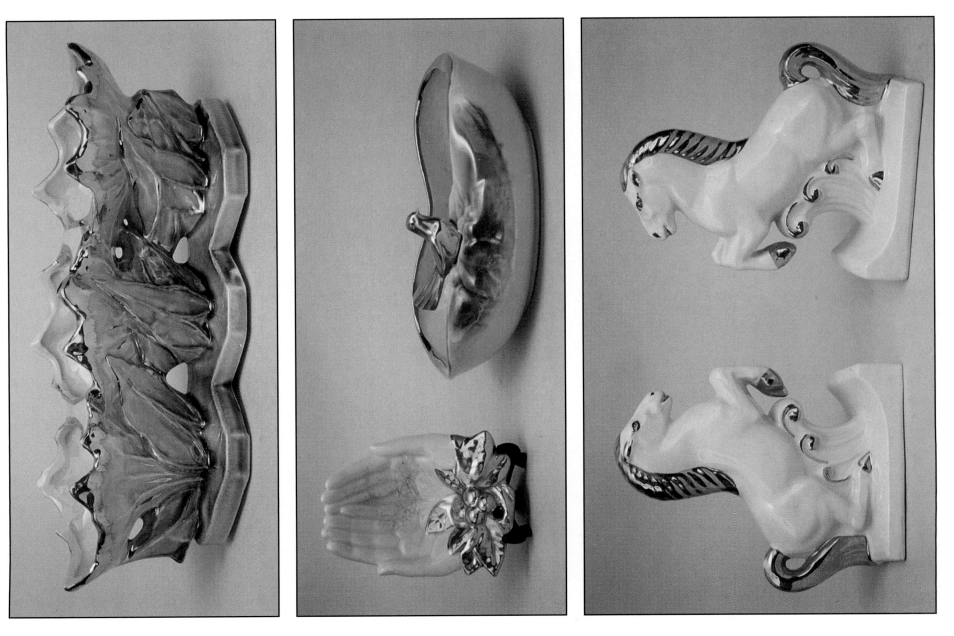

	Year	Description	Size	Mark	Glaze	Value
Top	1955	Gondola Candy Boat	11½" x 3½"	McCoy	Black Gloss	$75.00 – 95.00
Middle	1948	Lily Bookends	5½"	No Mark	Green with Decorated Lily	$150.00 – 200.00
Bottom	1954	Log Planter	7½" x 3½"	McCoy	Chartreuse Gloss	$30.00 – 40.00
	1961	Harmony Line Planter	12"	McCoy	Lime	$40.00 – 50.00

Gold-decorated football paperweight, no mark, 1940s. Hard to find. $125.00 – 175.00.

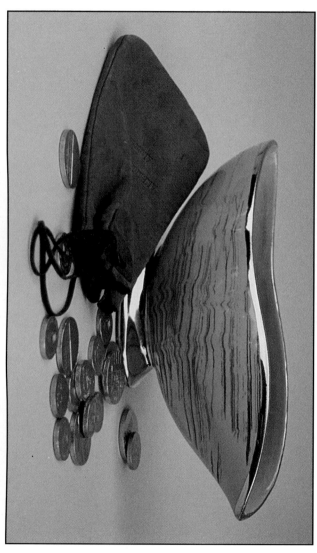

1961 Harmony Line, 12" planter with gold trim, yellow/brown. Pictured with leather gold bank pouch and yummy chocolate gold coins just for fun. $40.00 – 50.00.

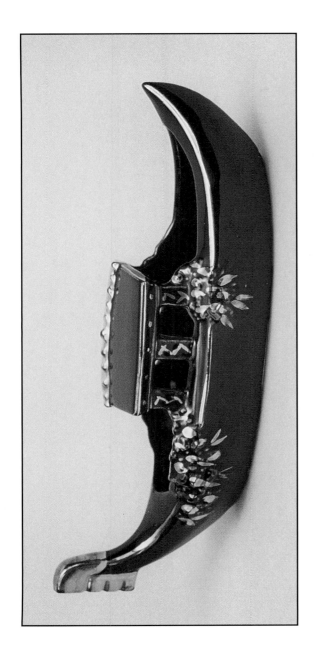

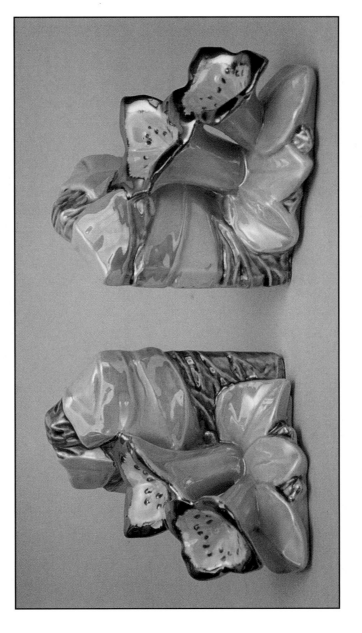

GRECIAN LINE

Introduced in 1956 and described as ivory with green spray and decorated in 24K gold marbleizing, the Grecian line was certainly one of the most elegant lines produced by the Nelson McCoy Pottery Company. Cost of the gold used in production was much higher than originally estimated. In fact, Nelson McCoy told us that they actually lost money on each piece sold. A necessary price increase caused the sales

to drop enough so that they abandoned the gold process and attempted to sell the line without the gold. An example of the non-gold line is on page 194. It did not sell and the line was dropped in 1958.

The following pages contain all the Grecian shapes and sizes produced in 1956.

Large Grecian centerpiece with 4" matching candleholders displayed with a lovely holiday bouquet. The candleholders are not marked. Centerpiece, $50.00 – 60.00. Candleholders, $75.00 – 100.00 pair.

PAGE 193

	Year	Description	Size	Mark	Value
Top					
Row 1:	1956	Tall Urn Vase	9½"	McCoy	$100.00 – 150.00
	1956	Bud Vase	7¼"	McCoy	$30.00 – 40.00
	1956	Winged Flower Dish	9"	McCoy	$50.00 – 70.00
Row 2:	1956	Small Centerpiece	8"	McCoy	$30.00 – 40.00
	1956	Long Planting Dish	12"	McCoy	$40.00 – 50.00
Bottom					
	1956	Large Centerpiece	12"	McCoy	$50.00 – 60.00
	1956	Square Planter	3½"	McCoy	$40.00 – 50.00
	1956	Covered Teapot	7½"	McCoy	$75.00 – 100.00

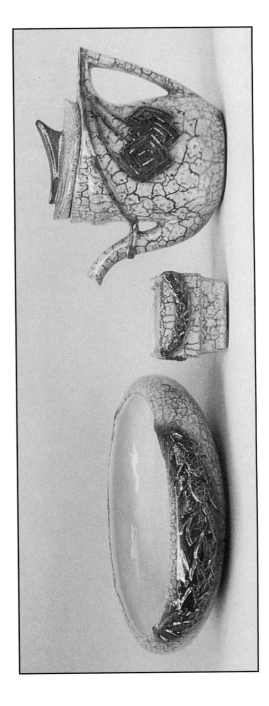

A Grecian line, 8" pedestal dish, 1958, without its elegant gold marbleizing. Since Grecian did not sell too well without its special look, these nonmarbleized pieces are hard to find. *$50.00 – 55.00.*

PAGE 195

	Year	Description	Size	Mark	Value
Top					
	1956	Covered Sugar Bowl	4½"	McCoy	$35.00 – 45.00
	1956	Coffee Server	10½"	McCoy	$100.00 – 125.00
	1956	Creamer	4¼"	McCoy	$30.00 – 35.00
Bottom					
Row 1:	1956	Pedestal Dish	8"	McCoy	$35.00 – 45.00
	1956	Pedestal Bowl	6½" x 5½"	McCoy	$40.00 – 50.00
	1956	Small Pedestal Dish	5½"	McCoy	$30.00 – 35.00
Row 2:	1956	Large Jardiniere	6½" x 5½"	McCoy	$40.00 – 50.00
	1956	Jardiniere	5½" x 5½"	McCoy	$45.00 – 55.00
	1956	Small Jardiniere	5½" x 4¼"	McCoy	$35.00 – 40.00

The middle Jardiniere is the hardest to find.

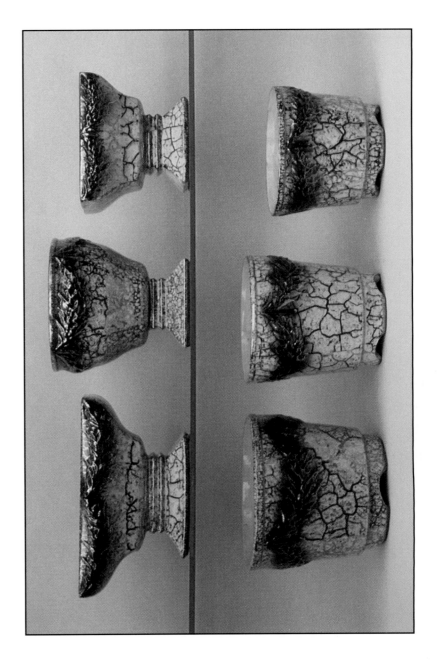

Sunburst Gold was another of the better selling lines, first manufactured in 1957. Production had to be stopped because of the high cost of the gold. McCoy simply could not sell them at a competitive cost and make a profit. All pieces are marked with a small circle containing "24k gold" in the center. Later on, they sold the Gold Brocade line, Sunburst glaze.

attempting to duplicate the Sunburst look without the gold content. The gold effect easily washed off the Brocade Line and could not compare to the glitter found on Sunburst. The entire line produced in 1957, is shown on this and the facing page; however, other items have been found with the Gold

	Description	Size	Mark	Value
Top				
Row 1:	Gondola Candy Boat	11½" x 3½"	McCoy	$50.00 – 65.00
	Swan	4½" x 3½"	No Mark	$40.00 – 50.00
	Square Vase	6¼"	Mccoy	$35.00 – 45.00
Row 2:	Covered Sugar Dish	2¾" x 5"	McCoy	$30.00 – 40.00
	Creamer	2¾" x 5½"	McCoy	$25.00 – 30.00
	36 ounce Teapot	5¾"	McCoy	$60.00 – 85.00
Bottom				
Row 1:	Beverage Server	11"	McCoy	$60.00 – 80.00
	Bud Vase	6¼"	McCoy	$25.00 – 30.00
	Small Pitcher	3½" x 3¾"	No Mark	$30.00 – 40.00
Row 2:	Covered Candy Dish	5" x 5"	McCoy	$40.00 – 50.00
	Fan Wall Pocket	8½" x 8"	McCoy	$75.00 – 90.00
	Cornucopia Vase	3½" x 3½"	No Mark	$30.00 – 40.00
	Umbrella Wall Pocket	8¾" x 6"	McCoy	$75.00 – 85.00

Swan planter, 6" x 4½", McCoy mark. Usually found with white interior. Wall pockets have been found with pink inside, but more commonly found with the standard white interior. McCoy mark, $50.00 – 65.00.

Coffee server, 7½" high with McCoy mark. Pictured on reverse painted serving tray with the covered candy dish as described above. $85.00 – 100.00.

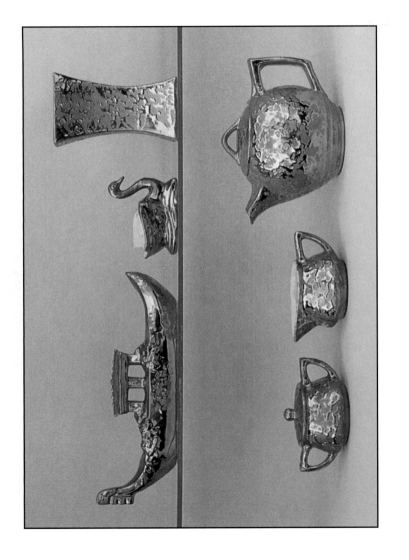

The Lost Glaze line was produced before the factory was destroyed by fire in 1950. It was not originally called the lost glaze, but the formula was lost during the fire and they were unable to duplicate this exact effect. Because of the mystique behind the line, it has become very collectible. *All the pieces, with the exception of the two-piece relish tray, were marked McCoy. The tray has no mark.*

Covered casserole, $75.00 – 100.00; beverage server, $80.00 – 100.00; creamer, $40.00 – 50.00; sugar dish, $45.00 – 55.00.

32 oz. teapot, $85.00 – 95.00; two-piece relish dish, $95.00 – 125.00; sugar dish, $45.00 – 55.00; creamer, $40.00 – 50.00.

LIBERTY BELL PLANTERS

There have been Liberty Bell planters found with a white bell. We believe these may have been sold with the bell painted black, but the cold paint has washed off.

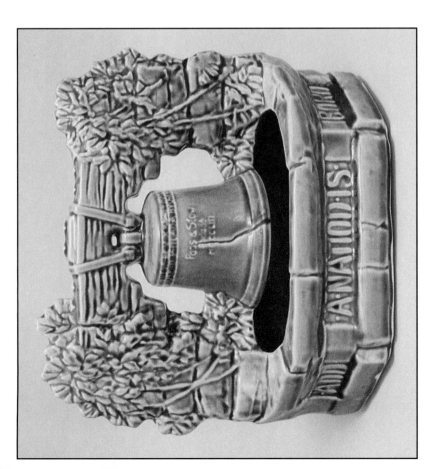

Unusual green glazed undecorated Liberty Bell planter, 10" x 8¼", McCoy mark. $225.00 – 350.00.

Standard color, ivory/green decorated, Liberty Bell planter with cold painted black bell, McCoy mark. $200.00 – 300.00.

The fish planters were not produced for very long. The top fins, because of their design, are easily broken. Because of these facts they're an extremely hard find.

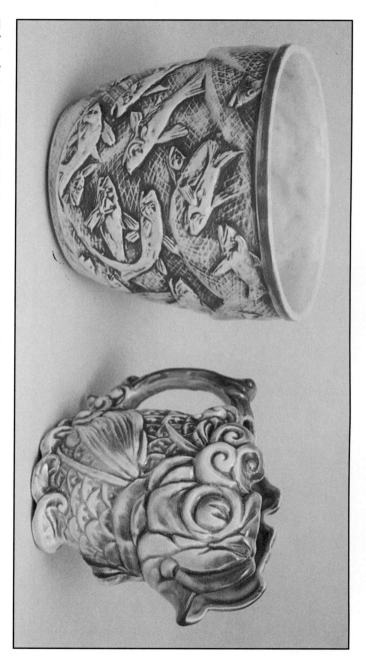

Fish jardiniere, 7½", 1958, McCoy mark, brown spray; also available in green spray, rare. $350.00 – 400.00. Fish pitcher, 1949, McCoy mark, rare. $350.00 – 400.00.

Fish planter, 1955, 12" x 7", McCoy mark, green glaze with great hand-painted eyes, rare. $700.00 – 1,000.00.

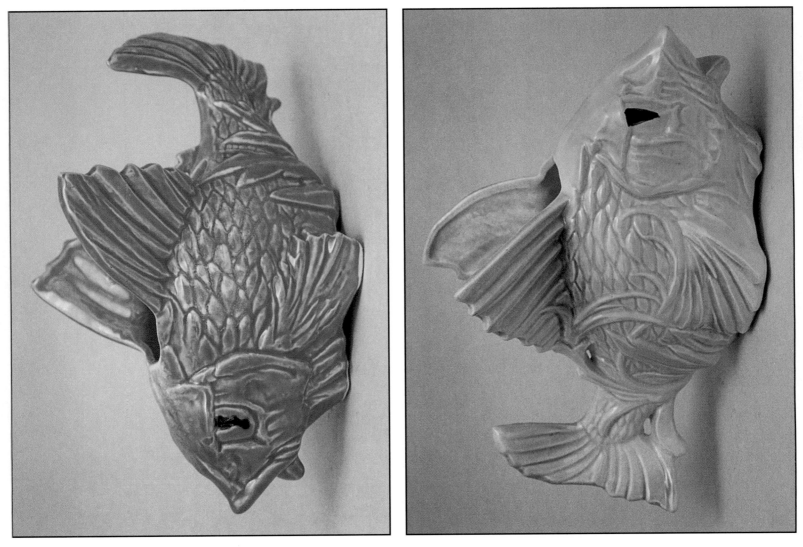

Fish planters, 1955, 12" x 7", McCoy mark, green, pink, and pink and green decorated. $700.00 – 1,000.00.

Flying duck planter, 1955, chartreuse with pink ducks. $125.00 – 175.00.

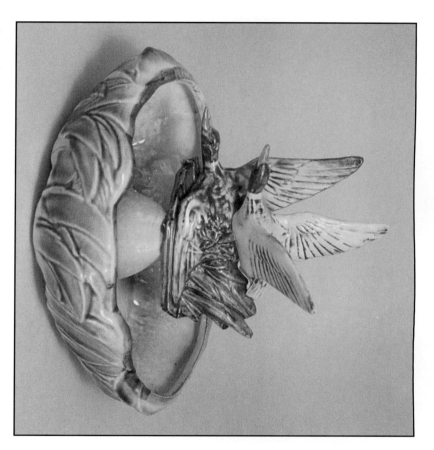

Flying duck planter, 1955, 10¾" x 8½", hard to find in mint condition; check wings and beak for damage. Chartreuse with pink ducks or ivory with brown ducks. $125.00 – 175.00.

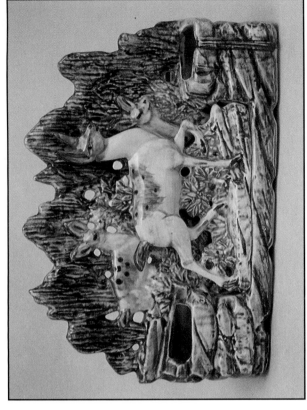

Fawn planter, 1954, 12" x 8", McCoy mark, natural hand decorated. $250.00 – 300.00.

These planters are all becoming scarce. The green bird dog planter is the most rare.

Bird dog planter, 1954, 12½" x 8½", McCoy mark, natural hand decorated. $200.00 – 250.00.

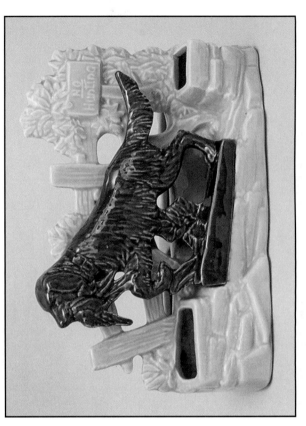

Bird dog planter, 1954, 12½" x 8½", McCoy mark, green with brown dog. Also found in same green with black dog. $225.00 – 300.00.

Left: Fawn planter, 5" x 3½", 1957, McCoy mark, brown with green or tan decoration. *$25.00 – 30.00 Right:* Doe and fawn planter, 7"x 6¼", 1940, McCoy mark, ivory with green & brown spray decoration. This piece was introduced in 1940 with the NM mark in matte pastel colors, see page 82, later decorated as shown. *$50.00 – 60.00.*

Swallow bookends, 1956, 6" x 5½", available in ivory with hand decoration, McCoy marked. *$200.00 – 250.00.*

PAGE 205

	Year	Description	Size	Mark	Available colors	Value
Top	1955	Bird Dog Planter Bookends	6" x 5¾"	McCoy	Green or Yellow/Brown Dog Black Base with White Dog	$150.00 – 200.00
Middle	1959	Bird Dog Planter	7¾"	McCoy	Brown or White w/ Spray Dec.	$125.00 – 175.00
Bottom	1955	Quail Planter	9" x 7"	McCoy	Ivory or Tan Blend Decorated	$60.00 – 75.00
	1959	Pheasant Planter	7½" x 6"	McCoy	Brown & Green Spray Dec.	$50.00 – 75.00

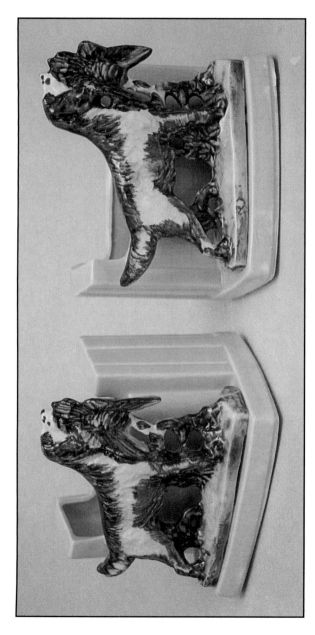

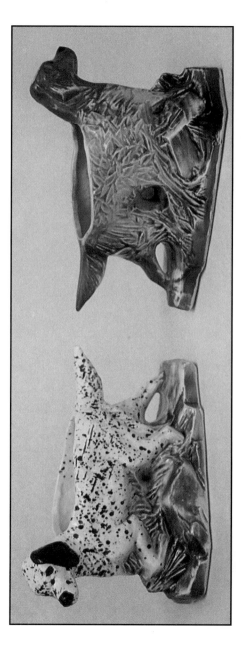

McCoy made quite a number of lamps although many were never cataloged. A significant portion of them were not sold under the McCoy name, were not marked and were actually produced for other companies to sell as their prod-

ucts. Several of the floral vases were made into lamps. Blossomtime, Wild Rose and Hyacinth style vases have been found as lamps. These were not sold directly by McCoy.

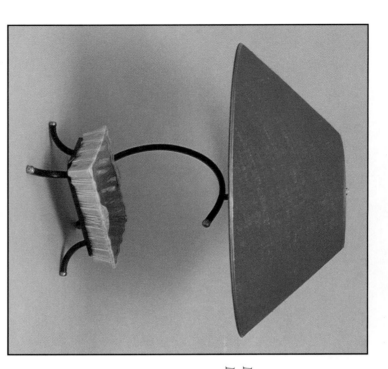

McCoy lamp with shade, 5" x 8", 1960s, McCoy mark on dish. *$60.00 – 85.00*.

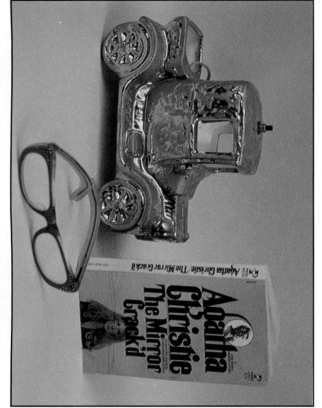

Colorful shot of the Model A pick-up, 1956. *$85.00 – 100.00*.

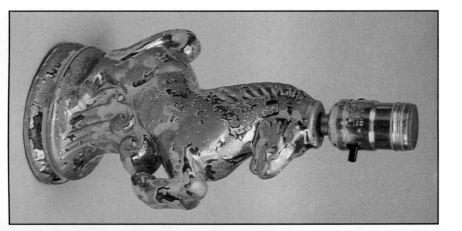

Horse lamp shown in the Sunburst glaze. The horse lamps are available and not marked, so they are not generally known to be McCoy. In that event, they can be found at reasonable prices. *$65.00 – 95.00*.

Left: Gondola candy boat lamp, 1955, 11½" x 3½", McCoy mark, green black, yellow. $75.00 – 100.00. *Right:* Sunburst gold planter lamp, 1957, 6½" x 4", no mark, gold. $50.00 – 75.00.

Left: Horse lamp, 1950s, 8¼" x 6", no mark, black, white, maroon. $65.00 – 95.00. *Middle:* Sunflower lamp, 1954, 9", no mark, yellow, green, and chartreuse, purple and burgundy also produced $65.00 – 85.00. *Right:* Horse lamp, 1950s, same as left but, different colors available turquoise, lime, and sunburst gold. $65.00 – 95.00.

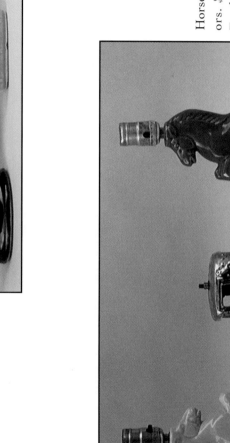

Horse lamps shown in different colors. $65.00 – 95.00. 1956, Model A Truck lamp, 1956, 9"x 4½", no mark, sunburst gold. $85.00 – 100.00.

Bird dog planter TV lamp, 12½" x 8½" x 5", chartreuse with brown decorated dog, no mark. $200.00 – 250.00.

Mermaid lamp, 9¾" x 6", no mark, chartreuse/green, black/white, or gray/burgundy mermaid. $200.00 – 300.00.

Fireplace lamp, 6" x 9", 1950s, chartreuse, black, and dark green, no mark. $75.00 – 100.00.

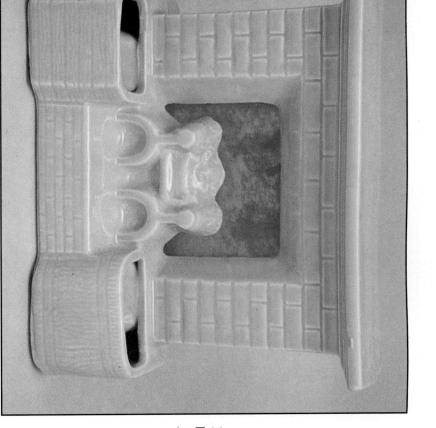

Arcature lamp with bird, no mark, 9" x 6", 1951, black with white bird. $125.00 – 150.00.

Wagon wheel lamp, 8", no mark, 1954, green or black. $60.00 – 75.00.

Cowboy boots lamp with original shade, 1956, McCoy mark, black or brown decorated. $150.00 – 200.00.

Panther lamp, 9½" x 7½", 1950s, no mark, maroon, black, and lime. $65.00 – 80.00.

Art pottery lamps, 1930s. *Left:* 6", no mark. $90.00 – 110.00. *Middle:* 6", no mark, different finish on glaze. $125.00 – 175.00. *Right:* 7", no mark. $100.00 – 125.00.

Art pottery lamp, 1930s, 9", no mark, matte glazed. 18" high to the top of the harp. $125.00 – 175.00. Lamp, 5½", no mark, matte glaze. $125.00 – 175.00.

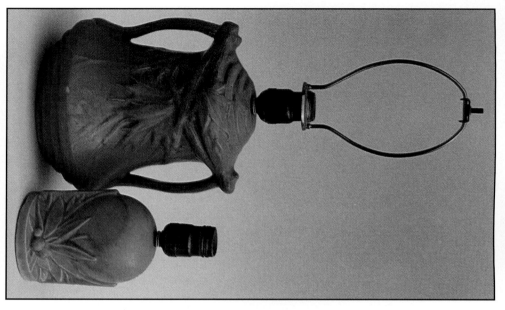

Many of these hard-to-find pieces were only produced for one or two years.

Flower with bird vase, 6½" x 5", 1948, McCoy mark. $100.00 – 125.00. Glaze is more vibrant than similar wall pocket. Very rare.

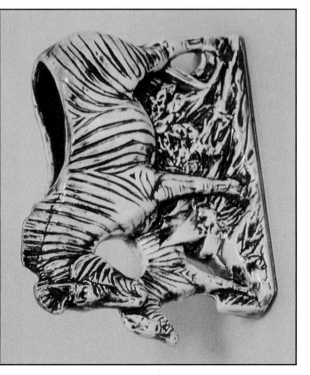

Zebra planter, 8½" x 6½", 1956, McCoy mark. A prize for the serious collector. $550.00 – 700.00.

Antelope centerpiece, 12" x 8½", 1955, no mark, black or green with tan antelope. $250.00 – 550.00.

CASCADE LINE

The Cascade line has wonderful Art Deco flair to it. It is described in the catalog pages as being decorated with iridescent colors coordinated to harmonize with any color theme. There were seven shapes available when it was first produced in 1961; these are all shown on the opposite page. More items were made later because of the widespread popularity of the glazes. More shapes are shown below.

Page 213

	Year	Description	Size	Mark	Value
Row 1	1961	Flower Bowl	5"	McCoy	$30.00 – 35.00
	1961	Bud Vase	6¼"	McCoy	$30.00 – 35.00
Row 2	1961	Large Vase	9"	McCoy	$60.00 – 75.00
	1961	Small Vase	7½"	McCoy	$45.00 – 60.00
Row 3	1961	Low Centerpiece	9" x 7"	McCoy	$50.00 – 65.00
	1961	Large Flower Bowl	7"	McCoy	$45.00 – 55.00
Row 4	1961	Centerpiece	10½" x 7½"	McCoy	$50.00 – 65.00

Left: Napkin holder, 5¼", McCoy, $40.00 – 50.00. *Middle:* Pitcher, 9", McCoy, $45.00 – 65.00. *Right:* Salt and pepper, 4", McCoy, $40.00 – 50.00. The bottom photo depicts the four colors, blue with green, mother of pearl, black with scarlet, and scarlet.

First produced in 1945, the Rustic line was made for many years at McCoy Pottery. It has an antique look to both color and glaze. They are ivory in color with turquoise and brown spray. Some shapes were produced in plain colors, like the two blue vases below, but the more popular shades were the rustic look of the main line.

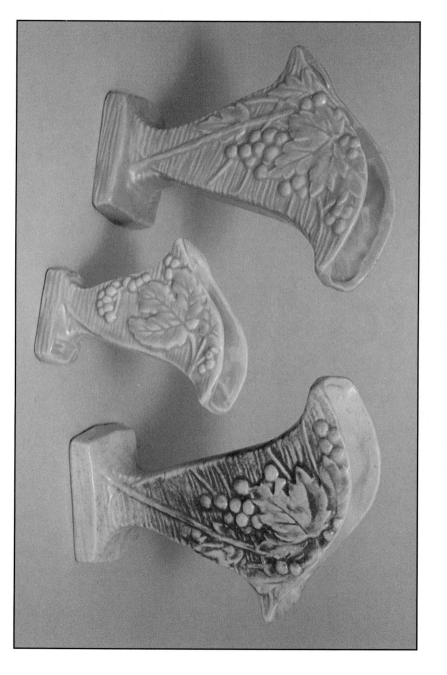

Rustic vase, 8" and 5". Glaze and color distinctive to Rustic vase, line shown on right. Also in blue, turquoise, coral, and yellow. 8", $35.00 – 55.00; 5", $40.00 – 60.00.

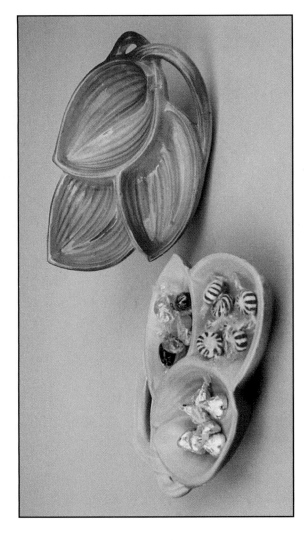

Three-piece snack dish, 1952, 11" x 8", McCoy mark. $35.00 – 45.00. Shown in Rustic and Rose glazes.

Hanging basket, 6½". $30.00 – 40.00. Vase, 10". $75.00 – 100.00. Both marked McCoy.

PAGE 217

	Year	Description	Size	Mark	Value
Top					
Row 1:	1945	Window Box	7½"	McCoy	$20.00 – 30.00
	1945	Large Vase	8"	McCoy	$25.00 – 35.00
	1945	Soap Dish	2" x 4½"	McCoy	$30.00 – 40.00
Row 2:	1945	Small Jardiniere	5"	McCoy	$15.00 – 25.00
	1945	Large Jardiniere	6" x 6"	McCoy	$50.00 – 75.00
	1945	Soap Dish	2" x 4¼"	McCoy	$30.00 – 40.00
Bottom					
Row 1:	1945	Pitcher Vase	9"	McCoy	$25.00 – 35.00
	1945	Handled Vase	9"	McCoy	$70.00 – 90.00
	1945	Flower Basket	6" x 8½"	McCoy	$40.00 – 50.00
Row 2:	1945	Round Jardiniere	7¼"	McCoy	$35.00 – 50.00
	1945	Wall Pocket	6"	McCoy	$30.00 – 35.00
	1945	Candy Dish	8½" x 2½"	McCoy	$35.00 – 45.00

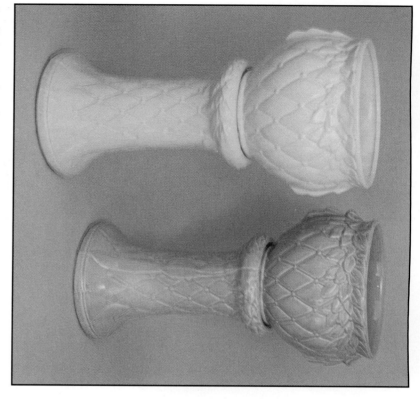

Jardiniere and pedestal set, 8½" jardiniere, 12½" pedestal, 1955, green or white. $200.00 – 250.00.

Vine design planter, 8½", 1956, McCoy mark. $40.00 – 50.00. Jeweled planter, 3 shapes w/jewels, all marked McCoy, 7½" or 8½", 1956. $85.00 – 125.00. Difficult to find, but very rewarding.

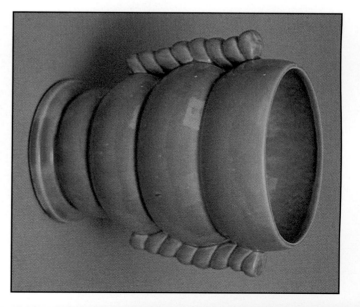

Large vase, 9" x 8½", 1957, white, yellow, or green. $80.00 – 100.00. This vase is hard to find, but worth looking for.

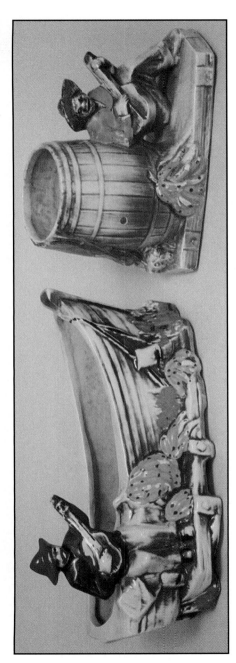

Banana boat planter, 11", 1959, brown spray with decorated features, marked McCoy. $125.00 – 175.00. Barrel planter 7½" x 5", 1959, brown spray with decorated features, marked McCoy. $100.00 – 140.00.

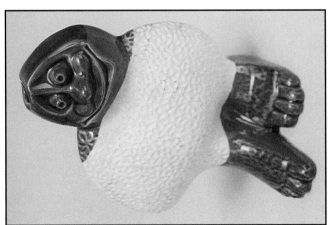

Grass Growing Gleep, 1970s, 8" x 6½", McCoy mark on back of foot. $70.00 – 90.00.

Baseball glove paperweight, $75.00 – 100.00; basketball paperweight, $125.00 – 175.00; football paperweight, $125.00 – 175.00; all from 1940s.

PAGE 221

	Year	Description	Size	Mark	Colors	Value
Top						
Row 1	1950	Ripple Ware Vase	7"	McCoy	Yellow/Green Drip	$35.00 – 45.00
	1950	Ripple Ware Vase	7"	McCoy	Green/Red Drip	$35.00 – 45.00
	1950	Ripple Ware Jardiniere	4"	McCoy	Yellow/Black Drip	$20.00 – 25.00
	1950	Lotus Leaf Pot	4"	McCoy	Green, Yellow or Turquoise	$20.00 – 25.00
Row 2	1950	Ripple Planting Dish	8¾ x 5¼"	McCoy	Yellow/Green Drip	$25.00 – 35.00
	1950	Novelty Dish with Bird	10" x 7½"	McCoy	Turq/Pink & Yellow/Green	$25.00 – 35.00
Bottom						
Row 1	1950	Fancy Lotus Leaf Pot	5"	McCoy	Ivory/Hand Decorated	$30.00 – 40.00
	1956	Console Bowl	14½"	McCoy	Yellow, White & Green	$35.00 – 45.00
Row 2	1951	Arcature Vase	8" x 6"	McCoy	Yellow/Green – Black/White	$40.00 – 50.00
	1951	Arcature Vase	9" x 6"	McCoy	Also found: Burgundy/Gray	$40.00 – 50.00
	1951	Arcature Vase	6¾" x 6"	McCoy	Also found: Green/Green	$40.00 – 50.00

Strawberry jar with bird, 1950, ivory/brown or green/brown, 8", marked McCoy. $40.00 – 50.00. Arcature vase, 8" x 6". $40.00 – 50.00.

Arcature vase, 1951, burgundy and gray color. $40.00 – 50.00.

1950 Ripple Ware display with reverse painted tray.

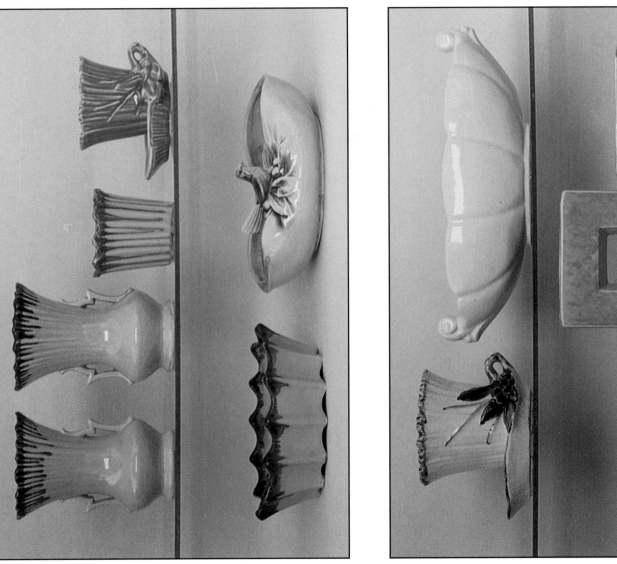

BROCADE LINE

First produced in 1956, the Brocade line was one of the most colorful lines produced during this period. The color combinations on the glazes were really in tune with the '50s – '60s. The available colors were black and pink, cherry and green, chartreuse and green, pink and lime, and black and blue. These combinations made for very interesting and colorful retail trade displays.

Creamer and covered sugar on stand. McCoy mark. $60.00 – 80.00. Covered casserole on stand, 3 pint, McCoy mark. $60.00 – 80.00.

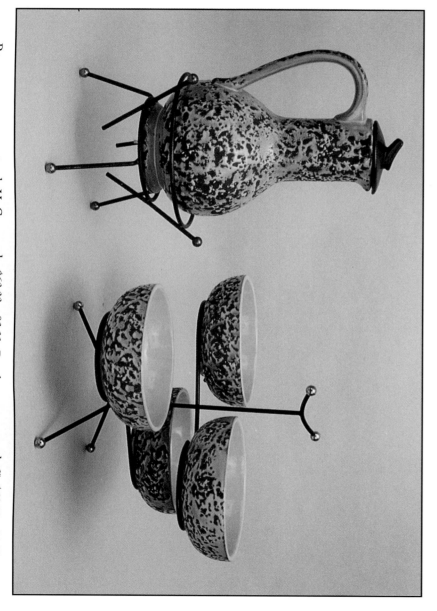

Beverage server on stand, McCoy mark. $60.00 – 80.00. Bowls on tree stand, 6". $60.00 – 80.00.

The complete Brocade line as found in 1956 is shown on pages 222 through 225.

Square jardiniere, 6½", McCoy mark, cherry and green. $25.00 – 30.00. Vase in black and pink, McCoy mark. $25.00 – 30.00.

PAGE 225

	Year	Description	Size	Mark	Colors	Value
Top						
Row 1:	1956	Planter Bowl	5½" x 4"	McCoy	See below*	$15.00 – 20.00
	1956	Beverage Server	11"	McCoy		$40.00 – 50.00
	1956	Planter Bowls shown in different colors – information & pricing above.				
Row 2:	1956	Planter	5½" x 3½"	McCoy		$15.00 – 20.00
	1956	Planter	9¾" x 3½"	McCoy		$20.00 – 25.00
	1956	Planter Bowl	See above			
Bottom						
Row 1:	1956	Planting Dish	14¼"	McCoy		$45.00 – 60.00
	1956	Planting Dish	7¾"	McCoy		$25.00 – 30.00
Row 2:	1956	Vase – Two examples	9½"	McCoy		$35.00 – 45.00
	1956	Bud Vase – Two examples	7¼"	McCoy		$20.00 – 30.00

* The available colors were black and pink, cherry and green, chartreuse and green, pink and lime, and black and blue.

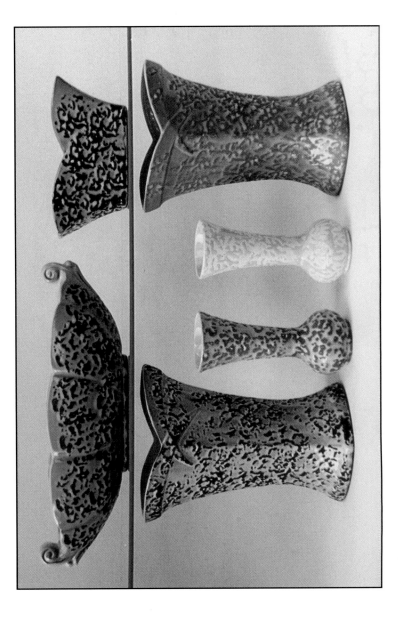

Black panther, 16"x 5½", 1950, McCoy mark. $40.00–50.00.

Black panther, 16"x 5½", 1950, McCoy mark. $125.00 – 175.00. Panther planters, 1950, no mark. $40.00–50.00.

Lion figurine, 14½", 1950s, green, yellow, black, and burgundy, no mark. $50.00–65.00.

Bud vases, McCoy mark, 1958, 6½", yellow/green with brown base or pink/green leaves with black base or pink/green leaves with black base. $65.00–80.00.

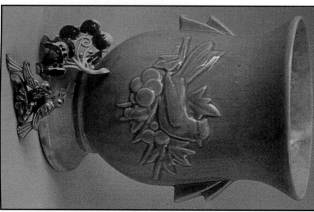

Vase with bird, 8"x 6", 1940s, green, pink and yellow, McCoy mark. $35.00–45.00.

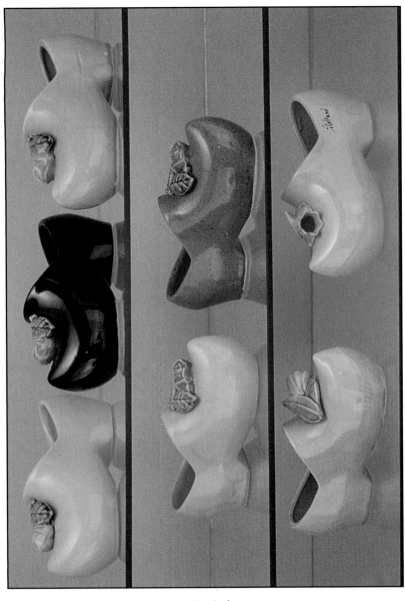

Dutch shoe planter, 7½", 1947, McCoy mark. $25.00 – 50.00. Shoes on third shelf are 1953 with different variety of flower on toe. $30.00 – 35.00.

Pansy ring, 1950, McCoy mark, hard to find. $65.00 – 75.00.

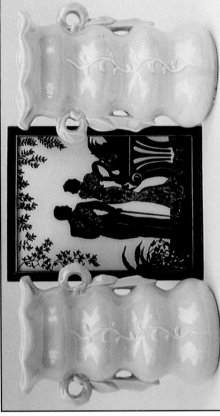

Fancy vase, 9", 1953, McCoy mark, turquoise, pink, and yellow. $40.00 – 50.00.

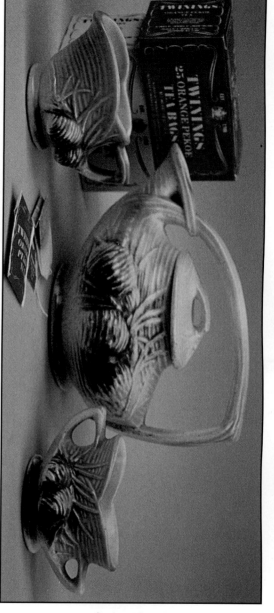

Pine cone tea set, 1946, green and brown sprayed, McCoy mark. *$75.00 – 100.00.*

Scottie dog dish, 8", 1949, McCoy mark, green or ivory/brown spray. Pictured with plastic pins. *$40.00 – 50.00.*

PAGE 229

	Year	Description	Size	Mark	Colors	Value
Top Left	1954	Sunflower Vases	9"	No Mark	Yellow, Green & Chartreuse	$40.00 – 60.00
Middle Left						
Row 1:	1955	Shell Planter	5" x 4"	No Mark	Yellow or Green	$15.00 – 20.00
	1955	Turtle Planter	12½" x 9"	McCoy	Green or Chartreuse/over Drip	$150.00 – 200.00
Row 2:	1955	Fish Planter	12" x 7"	McCoy	Difficult to Find	$700.00 – 1,000.00
	1955	Stump Planter	5" x 4"	McCoy	Yellow, Green, or Brown	$15.00 – 20.00
Top Right	1950s	Whaling Man	16¾"	No Mark	Brown & Tan	$200.00 – 350.00

Not many of these were produced so avid collectors have paid a lot to get one.

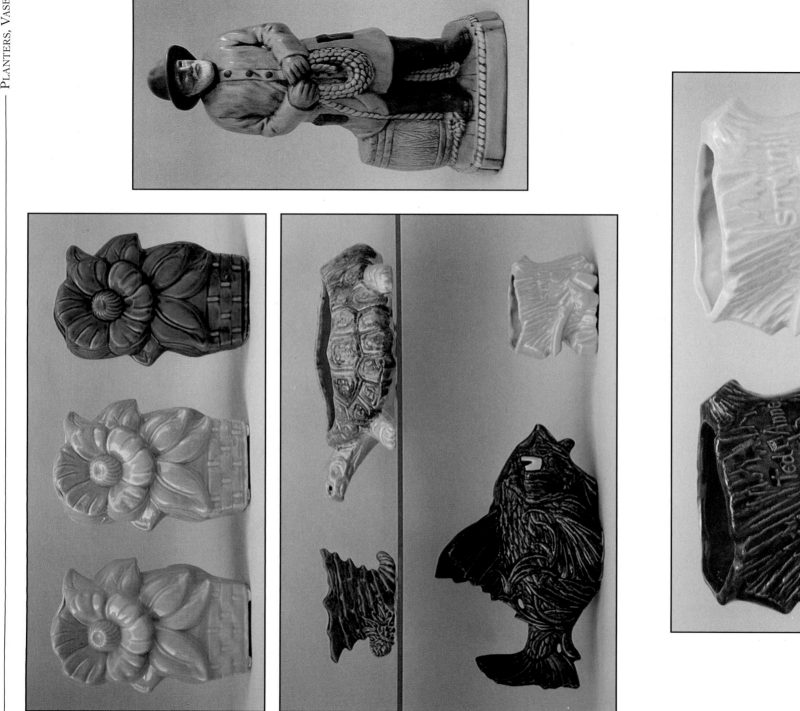

Uncommon brown stump planter, shown with more common yellow one, has "Ted & Ann" inscription. Valued at $40.00 – 50.00.

Dripolator coffee maker (3 pieces), 1943, McCoy marked, 7". $50.00 – 60.00. Coffee makers have improved with time!

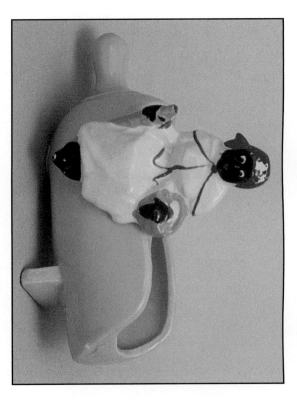

Scoop with mammy planter, 7½", 1953, McCoy mark, green or yellow decorated. $150.00 – 200.00.

Old mill planter, 7½" x 6½", McCoy mark. $35.00 – 50.00. Pussy at the well planter, 7" x 7", 1957, McCoy mark. $125.00 – 175.00.

PAGE 233

	Year	Description	Size	Color	Value
Top					
Row 1:	1953	Strawberry Jar/chain	6" x 7"	Maroon, Brown, Green	$35.00 – 40.00
		Two examples shown.			
	1950	Hanging Basket	6"	Green or Yellow	$30.00 – 40.00
Row 2:	1953	Village Smithy Planter	7½" x 6½"		$45.00 – 65.00
	1949	Ivy Bowl	7½" x 4"		$30.00 – 40.00
	1953	Village Smithy Planter	7½" x 6½"		$50.00 – 75.00
Bottom					
Row 1:	1953	Spinning Wheel Planter	7¼" x 7¼"		$30.00 – 40.00
		Three colors of the spinning wheel planter, gray/green, ivory/brown & brown/green. Animal colors vary.			
Row 2:	1954	Flower Bowl w/Grapes	10½" x 8"		$60.00 – 75.00
	1954	Liberty Bell Planter	10" x 8¼"		$200.00 – 300.00
		All the above pieces are marked McCoy			

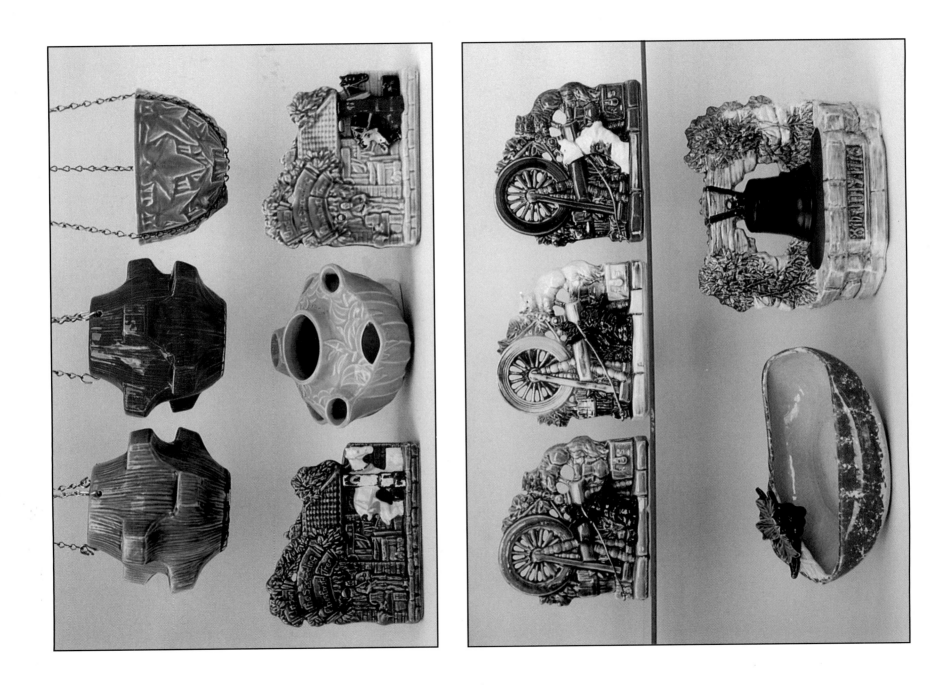

	Year	Description	Size	Mark	Colors	Value
Top	1950s	Frog Planter	5" x 7½"	No Mark	Green Decorated	$30.00 – 40.00
	1951	Frog with Leaf Planter	7½"	McCoy	Green Decorated	$30.00 – 40.00
Middle	1950	Frog Planter	8" x 5"	McCoy	Green Decorated	$30.00 – 40.00
	1950	Frog Planter	8" x 5"	McCoy	Green Decorated	$30.00 – 40.00
		These frogs are the same except for the leaf clusters on the back as shown				
Bottom	1967	Frog Planter (reissue)	6" x 5"	McCoy	Various Green Tones	$20.00 – 30.00
	1954	Frog with Umbrella	6½" x 7½"	McCoy	Gray, Green & Black	$125.00 – 175.00

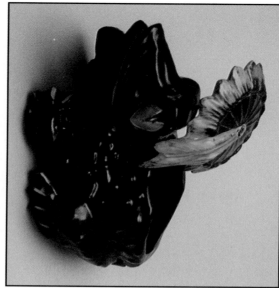

Black frog with umbrella, 1954, McCoy mark. $125.00 – 175.00. Hard color to find.

Carriage planter, McCoy mark, 8" x 9", 1955, green or black/yellow. $150.00 – 200.00.

Umbrella pieces, all marked McCoy, 1955 carriage, 1954 frog, 1954 duck. Carriage and frog priced above. Duck with umbrella, 7½" x 7¼", yellow or white with decorated umbrella. $100.00 – 150.00.

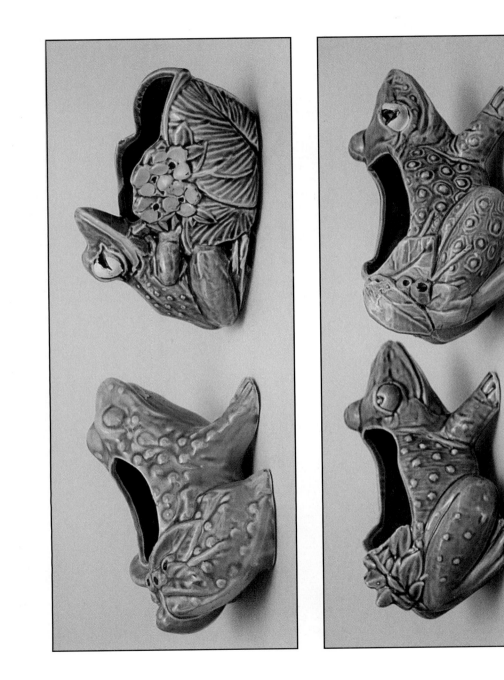

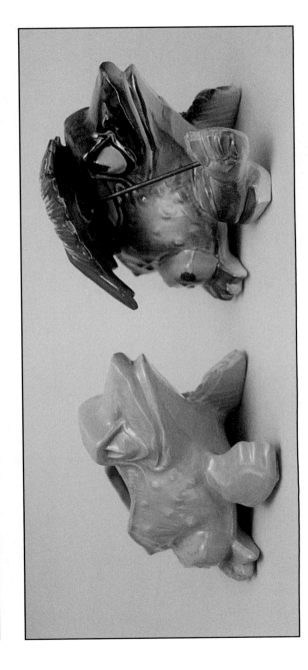

PAGE 237

	Year	Description	Size	Mark	Colors	Value
Top	1950	Alligator Planter	10" x 4¾"	McCoy	Green Decorated	$40.00 – 60.00
	1951	Frog Planter	3" x 5"	No Mark	Green or Yellow	$25.00 – 30.00
Middle	1960s	Turtle Planter	7" x 5"	McCoy	Green & Various	$30.00 – 35.00
	1950	Turtle Planter	8" x 5"	McCoy	Green & Various	$35.00 – 45.00
Bottom	1950	Turtle Sprinkler	10" x 5½"	McCoy	Green Decorated	$60.00 – 80.00
	1943	Frog with Lotus	5" x 4"	No Mark	Various Colors	$15.00 – 20.00

Bottom of Turtle sprinkler, paper SPRIN-KLER label.

McCoy mark on back of cabbage salt and pepper shakers.

Cabbage salt and pepper, 4½", 1954, McCoy mark. $75.00 – 100.00. Cucumber and mango salt and pepper, 5", 1954, McCoy mark. $75.00 – 100.00.

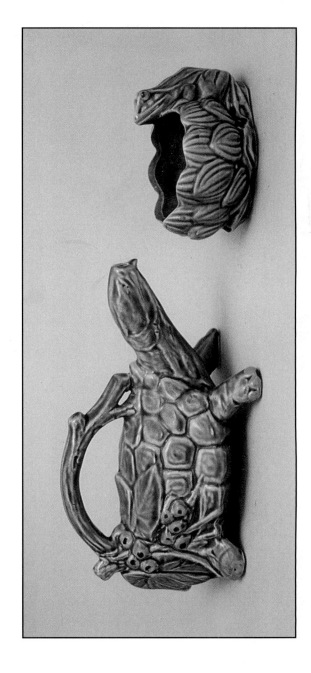

PAGE 259

	Year	Description	Size	Mark	Colors	Value
Top						
Row 1:	1956	6-cup Beverage Server	11"	McCoy	Pink & Black, Black & White	$40.00 – 50.00
	1956	Covered Sugar	4½"	McCoy	Pink & Black, Black & White	$15.00 – 20.00
	1956	Creamer	4½"	McCoy	Pink & Black, Black & White	$15.00 – 20.00
		The above three pieces were also sold as a 5-piece set counting lid.				
Row 2:	1956	3-pint Covered Casserole	7½"	McCoy	Pink & Black, Black & White	$30.00 – 35.00
	1956	10 oz. French Casserole	5½"	McCoy	Pink & Black, Black & White	$20.00 – 30.00
	1945	Stick Handled Creamer	3½"	McCoy	Various Color Combinations	$20.00 – 25.00
Bottom						
Row 1:	1956	Mixing Bowl	6"	McCoy	Pink, Yellow, White & Aqua	$15.00 – 20.00
	1956	Mixing Bowl	7"	McCoy	Pink, Yellow, White & Aqua	$18.00 – 25.00
	1956	Mixing Bowl	8"	McCoy	Pink, Yellow, White & Aqua	$20.00 – 30.00
		McCoy also made this bowl in a 5" size.				
Row 2:	1953	Wheat Vase	8" x 5"	McCoy	Ivory & Yellow with Brown Tint	$40.00 – 50.00
	1948	48 oz. Ice Jug	6"	McCoy	Green, Yellow & Maroon	$40.00 – 50.00
	1953	Large Vase	9½" x 5½"	McCoy	Yellow or Gray/Brown Foot	$25.00 – 35.00

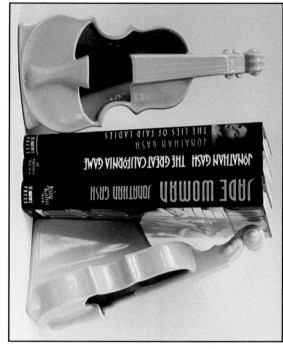

Violin planter bookends, 1959, 10", white, turquoise fleck, or black matte, McCoy mark and felted. $100.00 – 150.00.

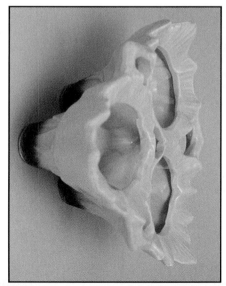

Triple bulb bowl, 1950s, McCoy mark, yellow, pink with darker base spray, hard to find. $60.00 – 75.00.

Chinese with wheelbarrow planter, 5½" x 5", 1950. Chinese Planter, 5½", 1950, McCoy mark. Both these planters have bisque face and hands and are available in yellow, green, or black and decorated with cold paint. $20.00 – 30.00 each.

PAGE 241

Year	Description	Size	Mark	Colors	Value
Top					
Row 1: 1952	Parrot Pitcher Vase	7"	McCoy	Green or Brown Spray Decorated	$150.00 – 200.00
1948	Planting Dish	6½"	McCoy	Green, Coral & Yellow	$15.00 – 20.00
1952	Second color combination of the Parrot Pitcher Vase.				$150.00 – 200.00
Row 2: 1953*	Flower Pot/Saucer	4½" & 6"	McCoy	Yellow with Brown	$30.00 – 40.00
1953	Centerpiece	9" x 6"	McCoy	Green or Yellow	$20.00 – 25.00
1953	Described as Flower Pot with decorative Saucer in Gray/Green & Green & also available in 5½."				
Bottom					
Row 1: 1953	Centerpiece	11" x 8"	McCoy	Chartreuse, Gray & Pink	$25.00 – 35.00
1953	Window Box	6¾" x 4½"	McCoy	Gray, Green, & Ruby w/ Spray	$15.00 – 20.00
Row 2: 1948	Basket	9" x 7"	McCoy	Sprayed Green & Brown	$40.00 – 50.00
1951	Modern Vase	9"	McCoy	Green, Pink & Yellow	$40.00 – 50.00

The Pot & Saucer on this row is the only know piece known where McCoy is misspelled "Mcoy" on the bottom; also produced in gray/green and pink/black.

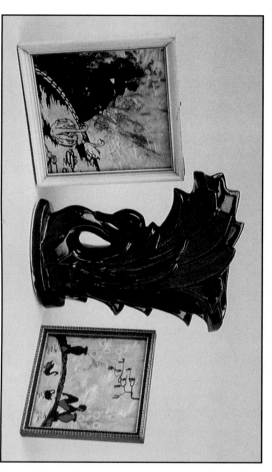

Swan vase, 1956, white, yellow or black, McCoy mark, $40.00 – 60.00. Pictured with Milkweed silhouettes. The more common Swan Vase, pictured on the cover, was first produced in 1948 in various colors. It has softer lines and a smaller opening than the vase pictured above, but is very similar. The Swan Vase pictured above is marked McCoy USA. The cover vase is simply marked McCoy and is valued at $35.00 – 45.00.

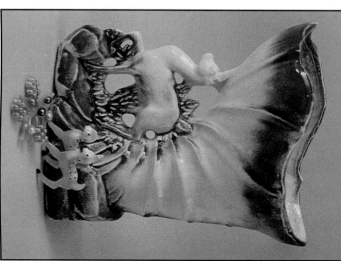

Fawn vase, 9", 1954, McCoy mark, birchwood, chartreuse/green, and white and pink. $100.00 – 120.00.

Jardiniere, 7½", 1955, McCoy mark, pink, ivory or chartreuse with decorated leaf. Harder to find! $100.00 – 125.00. Fan planting dish, 1956, 9" x 4¾", McCoy mark, chartreuse, lime, and pink. $55.00 – 45.00.

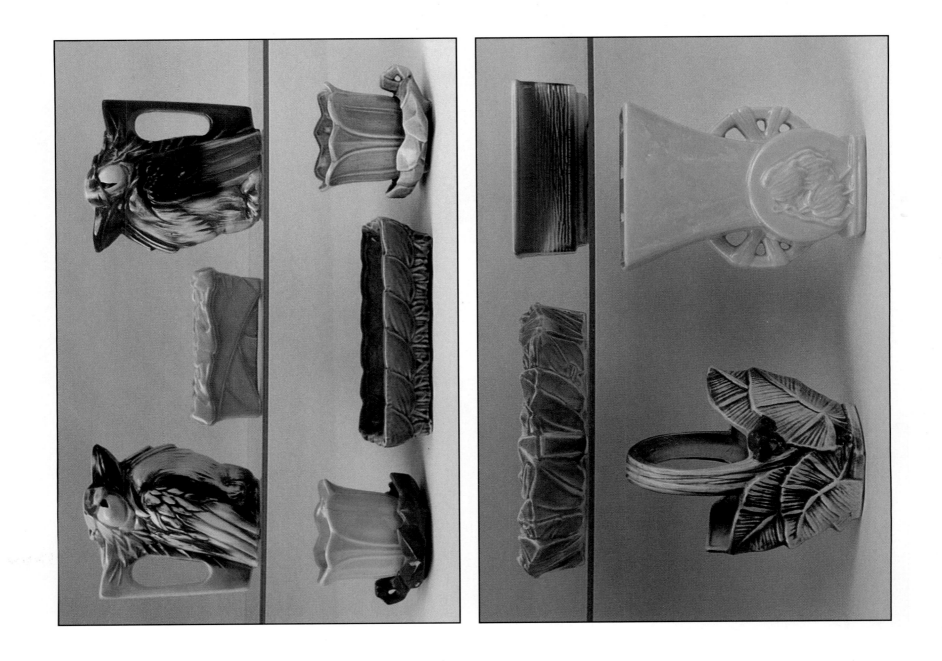

	Year	Description	Size	Mark	Colors	Value
Top						
Row 1:	1954	Basket Vase	9" x 5½"	McCoy	Ivory w/Two-tone Green Spray	$90.00 – 110.00
		Color further described as ruby & green tint on ivory brown blended handle.				
	1953	Planter	6", 8", or 9"	McCoy	Green or White	$12.00 – 18.00
	1953	Pot & Saucer	6½"	McCoy	Dark Green, Brown, or Wine	$20.00 – 30.00
		Was also produced in 3½", 4½" & 5½" sizes.				
Row 2:	1954	Console Bowl	9½" x 8" x 6¾"	McCoy	Gray or Chartreuse w/ Red Drip	$30.00 – 40.00
	1954	Stone Planter	6¾"	McCoy	Birchwood, Gray, or Chartreuse	$15.00 – 20.00
		Same as first console bowl, different color.				
Bottom						
Row 1:	1950	Wishing Well Planter	6¾" x 6"	McCoy	Brown or Gray Blend	$20.00 – 25.00
	1950	Wishing Well Planter	7¾" x 7"	McCoy	Same as above	$20.00 – 30.00
	1950	Same as first Well Planter, different glaze. Produced in various colors over the years.				
Row 2:	1954	Flower Pot	6½"	McCoy	Green, Maroon, or Yellow	$20.00 – 40.00
		This pot also produced in 4½", 5½", 7½" & 8½" sizes.				
	1953	Double Basketweave Planter	8¼"	McCoy	Green, Yellow, or White	$30.00 – 35.00
	1954	Rocking Chair Planter	8½" x 5½"	McCoy	Black, Brown, Chartreuse	$35.00 – 45.00

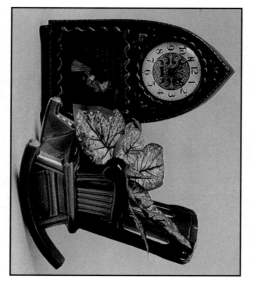

Rocking chair planter, 1954, sprayed birchwood. $35.00 – 45.00. Pictured with novelty clock.

Trivet planter, 8¾" x 5", 1953, green, yellow, or maroon with metallic base, McCoy mark, $50.00 – 60.00.

Trolley car planter, 7" x 3¾" no mark, 1954, green or birchwood. $80.00 – 100.00.

Wishing well planter, 1950, rare, pink spray color. $40.00 – 50.00.

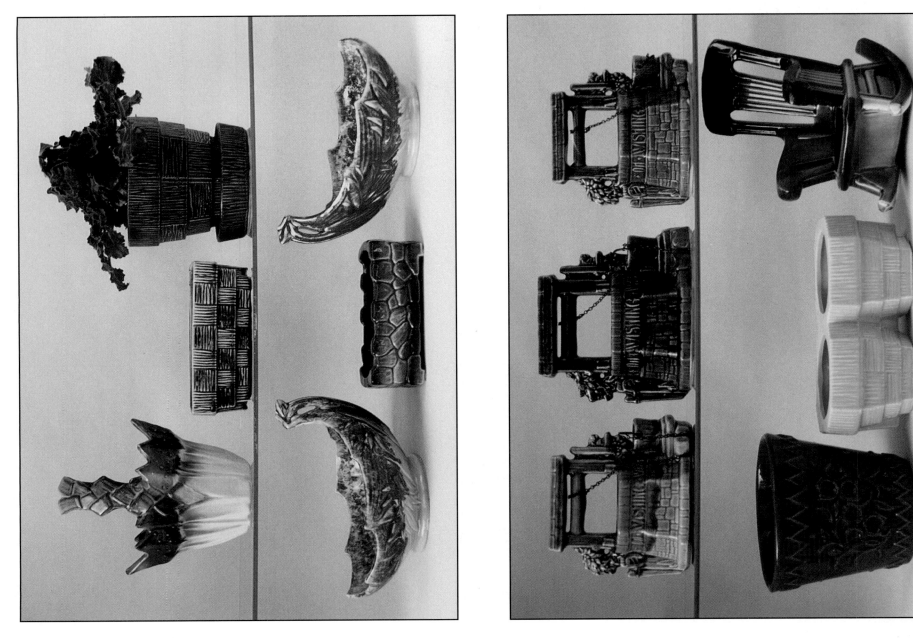

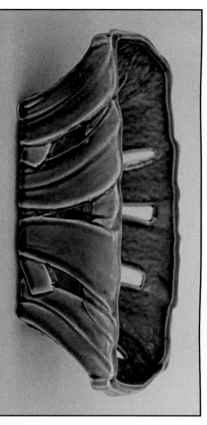

Filigree planting dish, McCoy mark, 8¾" x 5", 1953, sold with liner; not pictured forest green with chartreuse liner, brown with yellow liner. $60.00 – 75.00. Great looking planter!

McCoy rooster platter, 1974, 16" x 11", McCoy mark. $50.00 – 65.00. *Left:* Aqua rooster planter, 7"x 6", 1943, pastel colors, NM mark. $35.00 – 45.00. *Right:* Rooster planters, 7"x 6", 1957, ivory, brown, gray decorated, McCoy mark. $35.00 – 45.00.

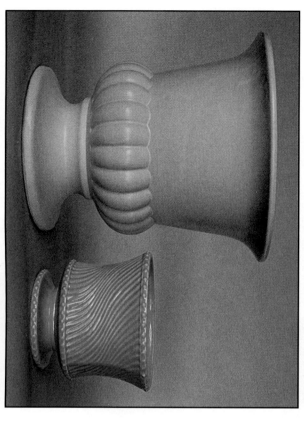

Left: Large urn, 15"x15", McCoy mark, 1961, green or white matte also was produced in 12"x12" size, $75.00 – 100.00. *Right:* Swirl jardiniere, 7", in aqua, McCoy mark. This shape also available in 6" and 5" sizes. $25.00 – 35.00.

Baseball boy paperweight, 6", 1978, no mark. $40.00 – 50.00. This is the same figure found on the McCoy baseball cookie jar. Another great find!

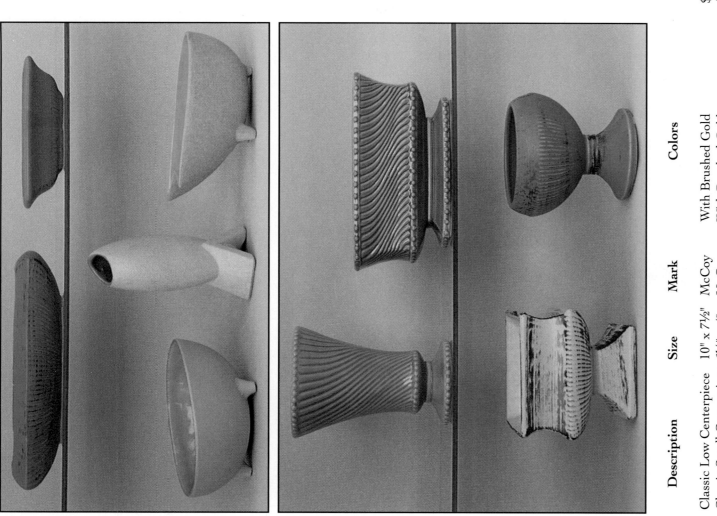

	Year	Description	Size	Mark	Colors	Value
Top						
Row 1:	1962	Classic Low Centerpiece	10" x 7½"	McCoy	With Brushed Gold	$20.00 – 30.00
	1962	Classic Small Centerpiece	6½" x 4"	McCoy	With Brushed Gold	$15.00 – 25.00
	The Classic Line consisted of ten shapes or sizes.					
Row 2:	1957	Round Capri Bowl	6½"	McCoy	Blue, Pink, White, Yellow, or Lime	$25.00 – 35.00
	1957	Capri Bud Vase	7"	McCoy	Interiors Glazed in Contrasting Colors	$30.00 – 40.00
	1957	Capri Planting Dish	7"	McCoy	Same as Above	$20.00 – 25.00
Bottom						
Row 1:	1962	Swirl Vase	7"	McCoy	White, Orchid, Tangerine, or Yellow	$15.00 – 25.00
	1962	Swirl Planting Dish	8"	McCoy	White, Orchid, Green, or Aqua	$20.00 – 25.00
	The Swirl line was produced in three shapes with various sizes & six colors. The third shape, a jardiniere, is shown on the previous page.					
Row 2:	1962	Classic Line Pedestal	5½"	McCoy	White, Black, or Turquoise	$20.00 – 30.00
	1962	Classic Line Pedestal	5½"	McCoy	With Brushed Gold	$20.00 – 30.00

The contemporary Capri line is described as modernistic shapes with permanent fired-on colors, semi-gloss textured pastel glazes of blue, pink, white, yellow, and lime outside with interiors glazed in contrasting complementary hues. There were eleven shapes in the Capri line.

Auto planters, 1954, 9"x 4½", USA mark, black, maroon, chartreuse, or birchwood. Note: wire windshield. $35.00 – 50.00.

"EXCUSE MY DUST," painted on the spare tire of the convertible pictured below.

Black convertible planter, with wire windshield, USA mark, produced with pride in 1954. $35.00 – 50.00. Piece is incomplete if wire is missing from windshield holes. Pictured with vintage gas station novelty clock.

Antique rose swan planter, 1959, 7½" x 5½", McCoy mark. $50.00 – 60.00. Antique rose flower bowl, 1959, 9½" x 6½", McCoy mark. $40.00 – 50.00.

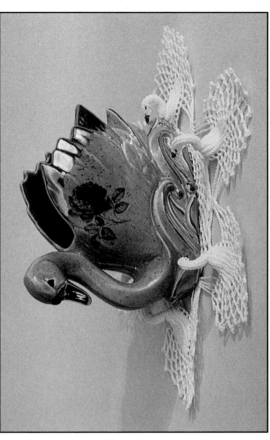

Antique rose swan planter in two-tone blue w/flecked brown. Also in white, brown or flecked blue, red rose decoration and gold trim. $50.00 – 60.00. One of the only lines that had gold trim painted on at the factory.

Conch shell planters, 1954, 7" x 5¼", no mark, gray with ruby spray, ivory with green spray or white with pink spray. $35.00 – 50.00. Hard to find.

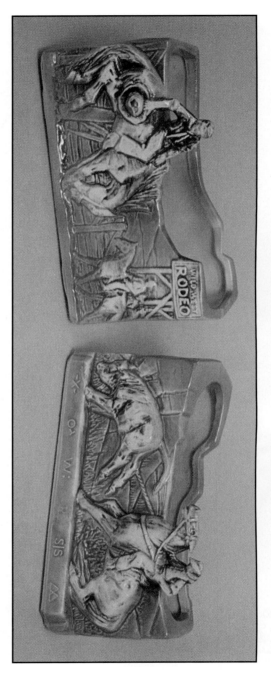

Left: Rodeo cowboy planter, 7¾" x 4", 1956, bucking bronco motif, McCoy (in mold) reads backwards. *$150.00 – 200.00. Right:* Rodeo cowboy planter, 7¾"x 4", 1956, calf roping motif, McCoy mark. *$150.00 – 200.00.* Orange tan with brown spray and ivory with green and brown spray. Also found in ivory with blue spray. These are collectible for both McCoy collectors and western memorabilia collectors.

PAGE 249

Year	Description	Size	Mark	Colors	Value
Top					
Row 1:					
1956	Cowboy Boots Vase	7" x 6"	McCoy	Black Decoration & Ivory/Brown Spray	$40.00 – 50.00
1956	Second color of the Boots Vase.				
Row 2:					
1956	Cowboy Hat Planter	8" x 3"	McCoy	Black, Ivory or Brown Sprayed	$35.00 – 50.00
1956	Log Planter	12¼" x 4"	McCoy	Ivory with Green or Brown Spray	$60.00 – 75.00
1956	Same hat planter as above, different color.				
Bottom					
Row 1:					
1953	Anvil Planter	9"	McCoy	Green or Metallic with Chartreuse	$35.00 – 50.00
	Anvil planter has applied chains & hammer:				
Row 2:					
1954	Cobbler's Bench Planter	8¾"	McCoy	Brown or Green	$30.00 – 40.00
1954	Wagon Wheel Planter	8" x 6¾"	No Mark	Birchwood, Green, or Yellow	$30.00 – 40.00
1954	Wagon Wheel Vase	8" x 6¾"	No Mark	Birchwood, Green, Yellow & Gray	$30.00 – 40.00
	Back of Wheel Vase, different color.				

Page 251

Year	Description	Size	Mark	Colors	Value
Top					
Row 1: 1948	Vase with Applied Bud	5¾"	McCoy	White, Pink, or Yellow Decorated	$30.00 – 45.00
Row 2: 1955	Pot & Saucer	4", 5" or 6"	McCoy	Yellow, Green, White, or Pink	$20.00 – 30.00
1948	Vase with Applied Bud	5¾"	McCoy	Pink, White, or Yellow Decorated	$30.00 – 45.00
1955	Same as first pot, different color.				
Bottom					
Row 1: 1954	Violet Pot & Saucer	6"	McCoy	Green, Yellow, White, or Pink	$20.00 – 25.00
1954	Violet Pot & Saucer	5"	McCoy	Green, Yellow, White, or Pink	$15.00 – 20.00
1954	Violet Pot & Saucer	4"	McCoy	Green, Yellow, White, or Pink	$10.00 – 15.00
Row 2: 1957	Ribbed Vase	10", 12" or 14" McCoy		Green or White	$40.00 – 90.00
1955	Pot & Saucer	6"	McCoy	Rare Two-tone Color Combination	$25.00 – 30.00
Same as first ribbed vase.					$40.00 – 90.00

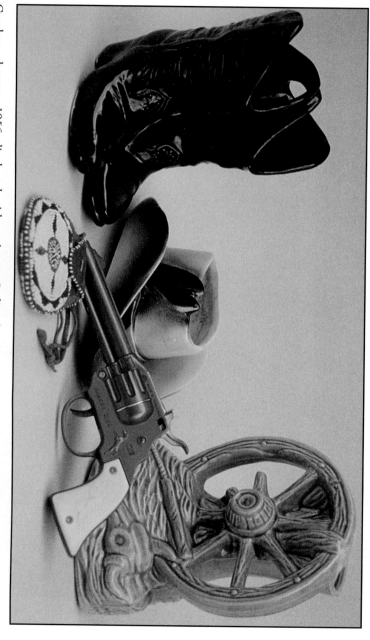

Cowboy planters, 1956, displayed with a vintage Indian bead purse and a toy cowboy cap gun. Wagon Wheel planter. $30.00 – 40.00. Cowboy Boots vase. $40.00 – 50.00. Cowboy Hat planter. $35.00 – 50.00. Details on page 248.

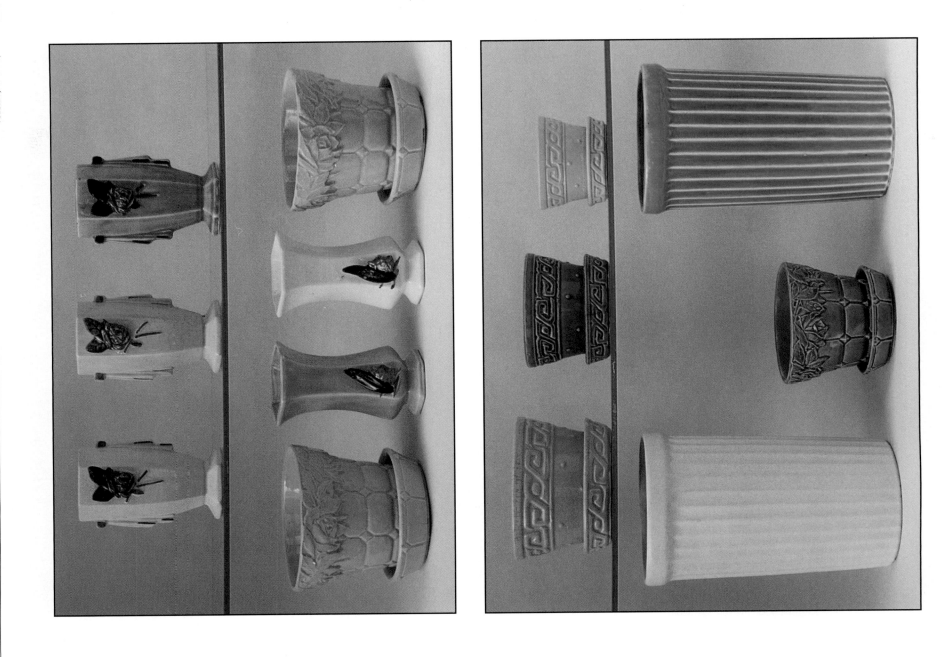

PAGE 253

Top

	Year	Description	Size	Mark	Colors	Value
Row 1:	1961	Silhouette Centerpiece	12" x 6¾"	McCoy	White, Mint Green, or Yellow Matte	$25.00 – 30.00
	1961	Silhouette Low Dish	6"	McCoy	White, Dark Green, or Yellow Matte	$20.00 – 25.00
Row 2:	1957	Pot & Saucer	4¼, 5¼ & 6¼"	McCoy	Green, Yellow & Turquoise Decorated	$15.00 – 25.00
	1957	Same as above, larger size, different color.				$15.00 – 25.00
	1974	Green Thumb Pot & Saucer	7½"	McCoy	Exotic Green, Gloss White & Yellow	$10.00 – 25.00

Green thumb pot also available in 4½", 5½" & 6½" sizes & exotic brown color.

Bottom

	Year	Description	Size	Mark	Colors	Value
Row 1:	1965	Tonecraft Pedestal Planter	6 x 3¾"	McCoy	Frosted White, Nile Green	$20.00 – 25.00
	1965	Tonecraft Scalloped Bowl	8½" x 3"	McCoy	Oriental Orange	$20.00 – 30.00
	1965	Tonecraft Planter same as above, copper black.				$18.00 – 28.00
Row 2:	1965	Artisan Pedestal Planter	7½"	McCoy	White, Green, Yellow & Blue	$20.00 – 30.00
	1965	Artisan Vase	7½"	McCoy	White, Green, Yellow & Blue	$30.00 – 40.00
	1965	Artisan Jardiniere	5"	McCoy	White, Green, Yellow & Blue	$15.00 – 25.00

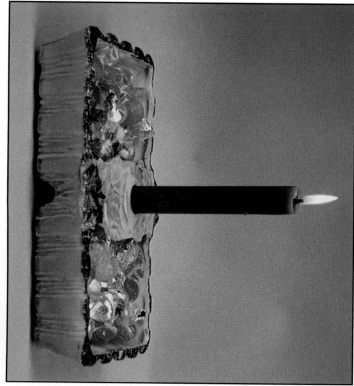

Centerpiece with candleholder, 1960s, green or ivory spray. $30.00 – 35.00.

Artisan vase, 1965, McCoy mark 9½", green glaze. $35.00 – 50.00. Artisan Jardiniere, 5", in green glaze. $30.00 – 40.00. Vase was also sold in a 12" size. $50.00 – 60.00.

GARDEN CLUB LINE

The Garden Club Line was introduced in 1958 and consisted of sixteen different shapes. The glaze is a matte satin finish and is sometimes thought to be older than it is. Flowers and plants look very nice displayed in this pottery and the subdued colors are pleasing in any decor.

	Year	Description	Size	Mark	Colors	Value
Top						
Row 1:	1958	Vase	7" x 6"	McCoy	White, Green, or Yellow	$20.00 – 25.00
	1958	Bud Vase	6½"	McCoy	Peach, Yellow & White	$25.00 – 35.00
Row 2:	1958	Pedestal Bowl	5½" x 4"	McCoy	Green, Black, or Yellow	$15.00 – 25.00
	1958	Planting Dish	8", 10", or 15½"	McCoy	White, Yellow, Peach, or Black	$20.00 – 45.00
Bottom						
Row 1:	1958	Pillow Vase	5½" x 4"	McCoy	Same as above or Gray & Green	$20.00 – 25.00
	1958	Planting Dish	8", 10", or 15½"	McCoy	White, Yellow, Peach, or Black	$20.00 – 45.00
		Same as first pillow vase, different color.				
Row 2:	1958	Pitcher Vase	8"	McCoy	Yellow, Peach, or Gray	$20.00 – 30.00
	1958	Centerpiece	8" x 10"	McCoy	Yellow, Peach, or Gray	$20.00 – 30.00

These pieces look lavender, but are referred to as gray.

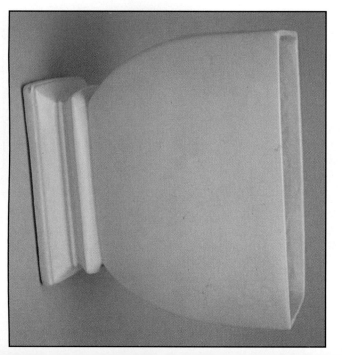

Yellow Garden Club, 8", pitcher vase, 1958. $20.00 – 30.00. 10" beverage server. $25.00 – 40.00.

White Garden Club large vase, 9½" x 11", 1958, McCoy mark, white, green, or yellow. $80.00 – 100.00.

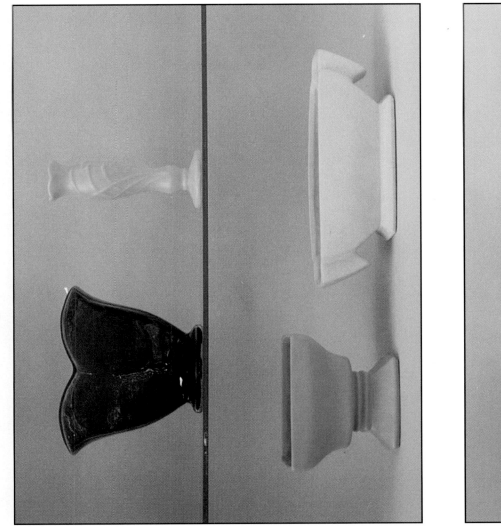

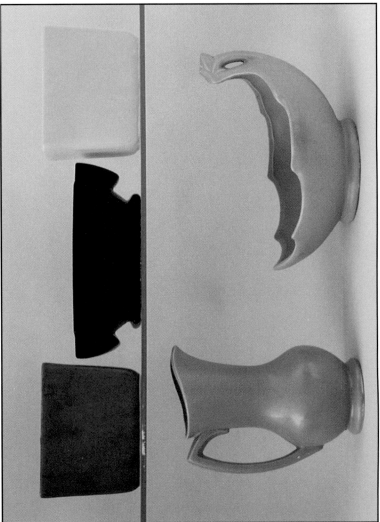

Garden Club pillow vase, 5½" x 4", McCoy mark, $20.00 – 25.00. Garden Club bud vase, 6½", 1958, McCoy mark, $25.00 – 35.00. Garden Club bud vase, 6½", 1958, McCoy mark, $25.00 – 35.00. The line contained 16 different shapes in white, peach, black, gray, green, and yellow. Pictured with garden hat and tool.

BASKET LINE – PEDESTAL LINE

PAGE 257

	Year	Description	Size	Mark	Colors	Value
Top						
Row 1:	1959	Basket Line Planting Dish	11½"	McCoy	Brown Bisque /Dark Green Interior	$30.00 – 40.00
	1959	Pedestal Line Hanging Pot	6½"	McCoy	Green, Yellow or Pink/Decorated Ft.	$30.00 – 40.00
	1959	Basket Line Dish	6½"	McCoy	Yellow Bisque/White Interior	$30.00 – 40.00
Row 2:	1959	Basket Line Planting Dish	9½"	McCoy	Green Bisque/Yellow Interior	$25.00 – 30.00
	1959	Basket Line Planter	6½"	McCoy	Shown in Green/Yellow	$25.00 – 30.00
Bottom						
Row 1:	1959	Pedestal Line Planting Dish	7"	McCoy	Shown in Yellow /Decorated Foot	$20.00 – 30.00
	1959	Pedestal Line Planting Dish	11"	McCoy	Green/ Decorated Foot	$25.00 – 30.00
Row 2:	1959	Basket Line Cart Planter	10"	McCoy	Same as above for Basket Line	$30.00 – 45.00
	1959	Pedestal Line Planter Bowl	5"	McCoy	Shown in Green	$15.00 – 20.00
	1959	Pedestal Line Planter Bowl	6"	Mccoy	Shown in Yellow	$20.00 – 25.00

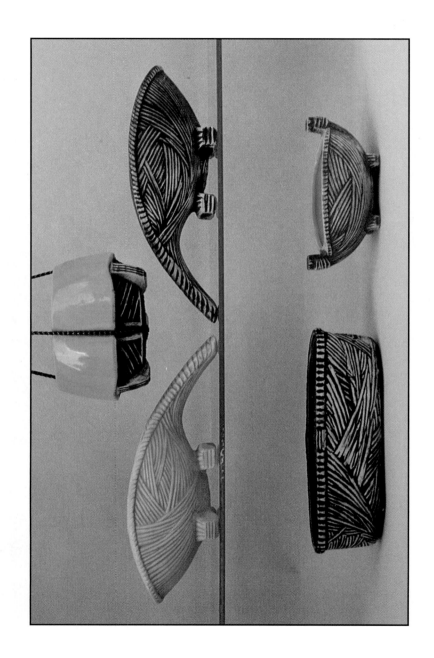

PAGE 259

Year	Description	Size	Mark	Colors	Value
Top					
Row 1:					
1966	Dish Garden	3½" x 6"	McCoy	Green, Yellow, or White	$12.00 – 18.00
1972	Pitcher Vase	5"	Mccoy	Matte White	$10.00 – 15.00
1966	Artificial Flower Dish	7" x 4"	McCoy	White, Brown, Yellow	$10.00 – 15.00
Row 2:					
1972	Pitcher Vase	9"	McCoy	Black, Green, or Red/White	$15.00 – 25.00
1972	Vase	9"	McCoy	Gold/White & Above Colors	$15.00 – 25.00
1972	Pitcher vase same as vase to the far left, different color combination				$15.00 – 25.00
Bottom					
Row 1:					
1967	Dish Garden Pebble Planter	8" x 4"	McCoy	Chartruese, Dark Green & White	$10.00 – 20.00
1967	Small Pebble Planter	6" x 3"	McCoy	Chartruese, Dark Green & White	$10.00 – 15.00
1967	Dish Garden Pebble Planter	8" x 4"	McCoy	Chartruese, Dark Green & White	$10.00 – 20.00
Row 2:					
1959	Tall Vase	12"	McCoy	Green, Yellow, or White	$40.00 – 50.00
1962	Vesta Vase	9"	McCoy	Green, Yellow, or White	$15.00 – 25.00
1957	Vase	10"	McCoy	Green, White, or Maroon	$25.00 – 35.00

Pedestal vase, Vesta line, 8", 1962, green, McCoy mark. $25.00 – 35.00.

Salad bowl, 1958, 5", McCoy mark. $20.00 – 25.00. Pedestal salad bowl, 11½", 1958, McCoy mark. $40.00 – 50.00. Color combinations: white inside, aqua outside with a smoke pearl base; amethyst inside, pink outside with a black base; yellow inside, mustard outside with white base.

Introduced in 1960, McCoy described the Spring Wood line as hand decorated Dogwood pattern finished in satin glazes of pink, white, and mint green. There were eight shapes and sizes to choose from, all pictured on the facing page. Also introduced were brass stands to hold the three sizes of jardinieres; one is pictured below.

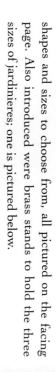

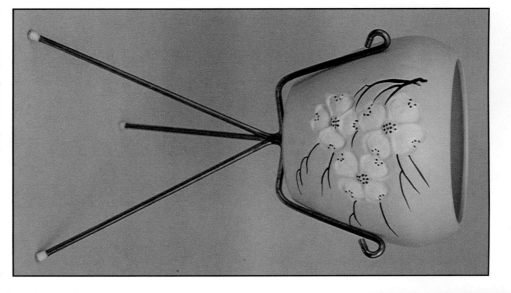

Spring Wood 10" jardiniere sitting on original brass stand. Stand adds $20.00 – 30.00 to value.

Three available colors of Spring Wood, white, pink, or mint green. 10", jardinieres displayed on iron stand. $50.00 – 60.00.

PAGE 261

	Year	Description	Size	Mark	Colors	Value
Top						
Row 1:	1960	Round Planter	6½"	McCoy	Pink, White, or Mint Green	$25.00 – 35.00
	1960	Planting Dish	8"	McCoy	Pink, White, or Mint Green	$30.00 – 40.00
Row 2:	1960	Jardiniere	7"	McCoy	Pink, White, or Mint Green	$40.00 – 50.00
	1960	Planting Dish	10½"	McCoy	Pink, White, or Mint Green	$30.00 – 45.00
Bottom						
Row 1:	1960	Jardiniere	8½"	McCoy	Pink, White, or Mint Green	$50.00 – 60.00
	1960	Vase	7½"	McCoy	Pink, White, or Mint Green	$25.00 – 35.00
Row 2:	1960	Jardiniere	10"	McCoy	Pink, White, or Mint Green	$50.00 – 60.00
	1960	Large Vase	9½" x 6¼"	McCoy	Pink, White, or Mint Green	$30.00 – 40.00

Page 265

	Year	Description	Size	Mark	Colors	Value
Top						
Row 1:	1961	Pot & Saucer	4", 5" & 6"	McCoy	White, Tangerine or Green	$12.00 – 20.00
	1961	Pot & Saucer	4", 5" & 6"	McCoy	Lemon Yellow & Mist Blue	$12.00 – 20.00
	1959	Long Planting Dish	10" & 14"	McCoy	White, Green, or Yellow	$15.00 – 30.00
Row 2:	1970	Low Planter	10" x 2½"	McCoy	Tangerine, White, or Yellow	$20.00 – 30.00
	1966	Irrestables Pedestal Bowl	4¼"	McCoy	White, Green, or Yellow	$10.00 – 20.00
	1967	Planting Dish	5" x 5"	McCoy	White, Green, or Yellow	$30.00 – 40.00
Bottom						
Row 1:	1957	Bulb Bowl	6½" x 8"	McCoy	White, Green, or Yellow	$10.00 – 15.00
	1940s	Planting Dish	7" x 3"	NM	Pastel Matte Colors	$15.00 – 25.00
		This NM planter looks modern, but is older than it looks.				
	1959	Flower Pot	4", 5" & 6"	McCoy	Yellow, Pink, Turquoise & Oatmeal Flecked	$10.00 – 15.00
Row 2:	1960s	Fern Box	8" x 3"	McCoy	Green, White, or Yellow	$25.00 – 35.00
	1959	Flower Bowl	7½" x 5½"	McCoy	Ivory or Green	$15.00 – 25.00

Jardinieres, 1960, white, green, or tangerine. Available sizes: 4½", 5½", 6½", 7½" 8½", 9½", or 10½". Pictured are the 3½" green and 9½" white. *$10.00 – 50.00.*

PAGE 265

	Year	Description	Size	Mark	Colors	Value
Top						
Row 1:	1956	Vase	5" x 5¾"	McCoy	Pink/Black or Chartreuse/Brown	$20.00 – 30.00
	1956	Basketweave Vase	4¼" x 5¾"	McCoy	Lime with Green Bisque	$20.00 – 25.00
	1956	Basketweave Vase	6½" x 5¾"	McCoy	Pink with Brow Bisque	$25.00 – 35.00
Row 2:	1961	Harmony Planter Vase	7"	McCoy	*White/Green and Yellow/Brown	$15.00 – 20.00
	1961	Harmony Planter	9¼"	McCoy	*Tangerine and Yellow	$20.00 – 25.00
Bottom						
Row 1:	1961	Harmony Round Planter	6"	McCoy	*Yellow and Brown	$15.00 – 20.00
	1961	Harmony Large Planter	12"	McCoy	*Mist Blue and Brown	$25.00 – 35.00
Row 2:	1961	Harmony Vase	9¼"	McCoy	*Yellow and Brown	$20.00 – 25.00
	1961	Harmony Vase	12"	McCoy		$30.00 – 40.00

*The Harmony line was available in these color combinations.

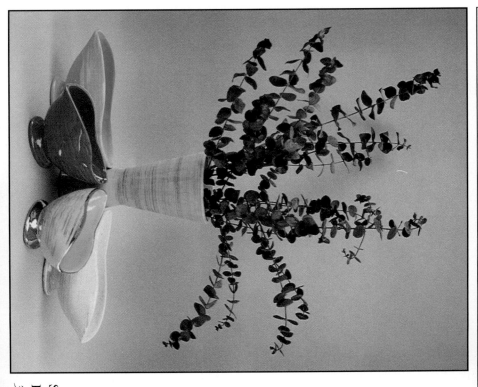

Simple lines accent the floral arrangement. Display of the Harmony line 12" planters and 12" large vase. Planter, $25.00 – 35.00. Vase, $30.00 – 40.00.

Paper label from the Modern Cope Originals candy dishes.

Modern Cope Originals described as hand-decorated modernistic designs. Modern Cope Originals candy dishes. $20.00 – 35.00.

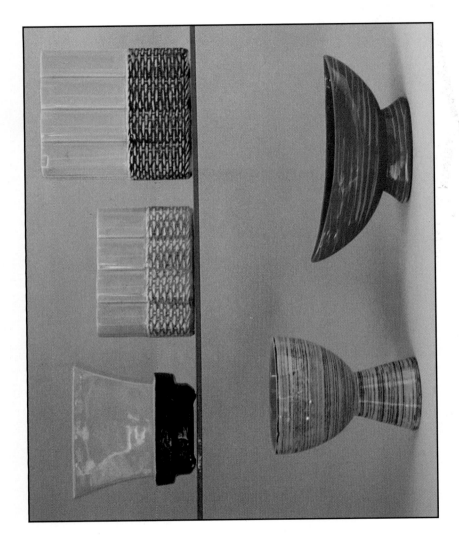

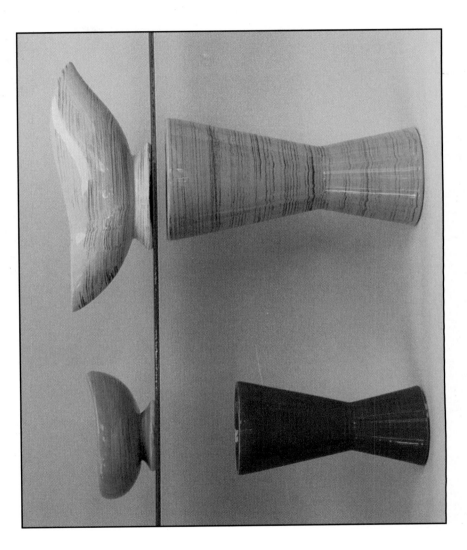

The 1962 Antique Curio line consisted of nine different shapes in three color combinations. The grapes and leaves pattern was hand decorated in beautiful lifelike colors. This was a very popular line for McCoy and is a favorite for many collectors. All shapes were available in matte white, gloss green, or gloss brown with hand-decorated grape pattern.

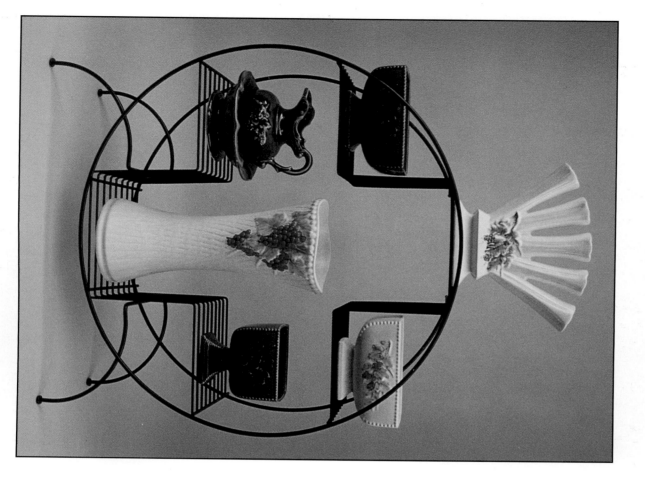

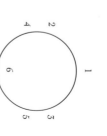

1. Finger vase, 10" x 8", McCoy mark. $60.00 – 75.00. The finger vase has been found as a lamp. It's beautiful! $100.00 – 125.00.

2. Pedestal planter, 7x 4½", McCoy mark. $25.00 – 35.00.

3. Pedestal planter, 7" x 4½", McCoy mark. $25.00 – 35.00.

4. Pitcher and bowl, one piece, no mark. $25.00 – 40.00.

5. Pedestal planter, 5" x 4", McCoy mark. $20.00 – 50.00.

6. White tall vase, 14", McCoy mark. $75.00 – 100.00.

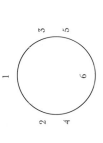

1. Pitcher and bowl, 7" x 6½", no mark. $25.00 – 40.00.

2. Round pedestal planter, 6" x 5½", no mark. $25.00 – 35.00.

3. Round pedestal planter, 6" x 5½", no mark. $25.00 – 35.00.

4. Pedestal vase, 7", McCoy mark. $30.00 – 40.00.

5. Pedestal vase, 7", McCoy mark. $30.00 – 40.00.

6. Green tall vase, 14", McCoy mark. $75.00 – 100.00.

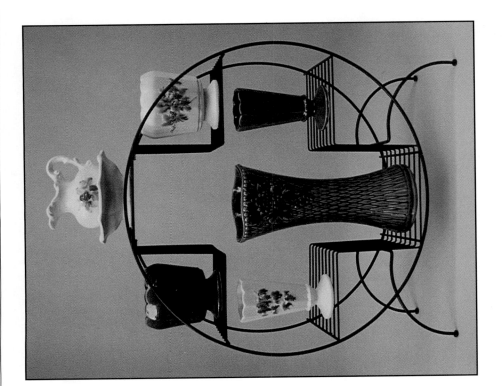

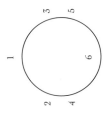

1. White centerpiece, 10", McCoy mark. $35.00 – 45.00.

2. Jardiniere, 7½", McCoy mark, yellow, maroon and turquoise. Same shape, but not part of the Antique Curio line. $40.00 – 50.00.

3. Green jardiniere, McCoy mark, 7½". $45.00 – 60.00.

4. Green finger vase, 10" x 8", McCoy mark. $60.00 – 75.00.

5. White jardiniere, 7½", McCoy mark. $45.00 – 60.00.

6. Brown tall vase, 14", McCoy mark. $75.00 – 100.00.

Floraline was introduced by McCoy in 1960 for the sole purpose of selling exclusively to the floral industry. Large customers such as Teleflora, FTD and Smith Bottle of Atlanta supported the Floraline program. The colors were mostly green or white and the molds were kept simple in order to keep the costs down. Floraline was a very successful part of the McCoy factory with annual sales reaching $1,000,000. The simplicity of production made Floraline pottery very profitable to McCoy Pottery. Floraline pottery is marked FLORALINE.

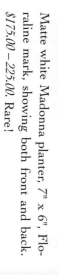

Floraline vase, 8¾", matte white. Valentine for that someone special!
$12.00 – 20.00.

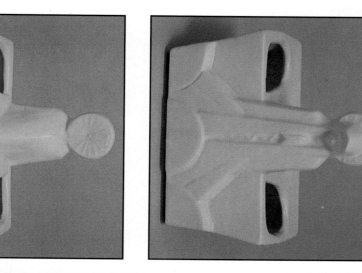

Matte white Madonna planter, 7" x 6", Floraline mark, showing both front and back.
$175.00 – 225.00. Rare!

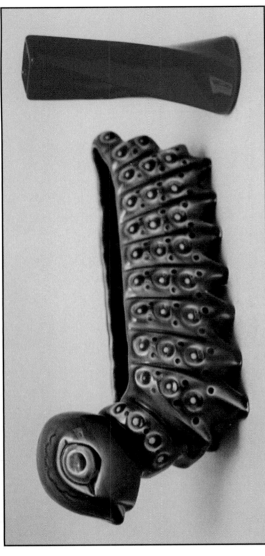

Caterpillar planter, 13½".
$35.00 – 50.00. Twist vase, 6½".
$20.00 – 25.00.

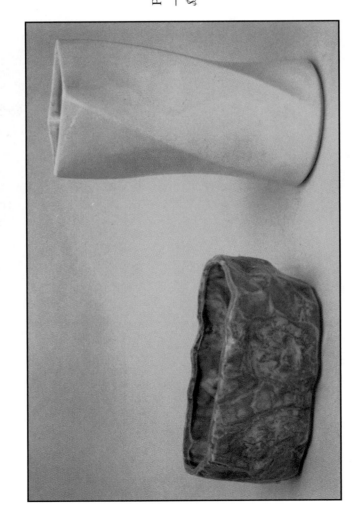

Pebble planter, 8" x 4". $15.00
– 20.00. Large twist vase, 9".
$25.00 – 50.00.

Jardiniere, 9". $30.00 – 40.00.

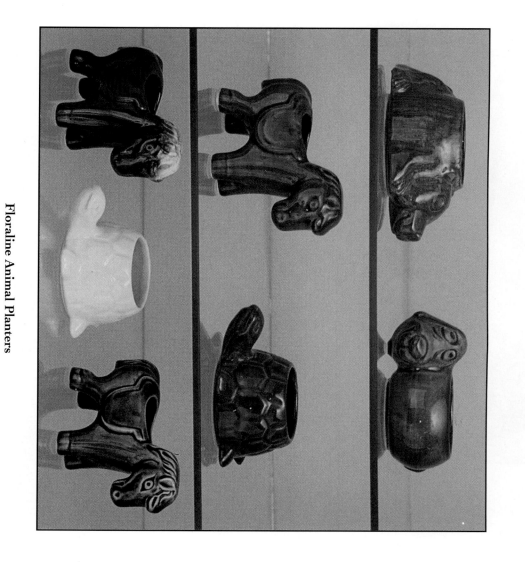

Floraline Animal Planters

	Description	Size	Value
Row 1:	Bear	5" x 3½"	$10.00 – 15.00
	Brown Dog	4½" x 3"	$10.00 – 15.00
Row 2:	Brown Horse	5" x 3¾"	$15.00 – 20.00
	Brown Turtle	5¼" x 3¼"	$12.00 – 18.00
Row 3:	Decorated Horse	5" x 3¾"	$18.00 – 25.00
	White Turtle	5¼" x 3¼"	$12.00 – 18.00
	Green Horse	5" x 3¾"	$15.00 – 20.00

These animals are all marked Floraline with the exception of the horse. The horses are all marked USA. Many of these animals have also been found with the McCoy mark.

	Description	Size	Value
Row 1:	Pedestal Urn	7½"	$15.00 – 25.00
	Round Footed Vase	9¼"	$15.00 – 20.00
	Dozen Rose Vase	9½"	$20.00 – 25.00
Row 2:	Auto Planter	8" x 3½"	$25.00 – 35.00
	Green Dog	4½" x 3"	$10.00 – 15.00
	Turtle	5¼" x 3¾"	$12.00 – 18.00

All of these pieces are marked Floraline.

Large vase, 10¼". $25.00 – 35.00. Tall vase, 12½". $20.00 – 50.00.

Goblet style vase, 6½" x 4½". $15.00 – 25.00.

Child's block and baby planter, 3" x 5". Planter, $25.00 – 30.00. Block, $20.00 – 30.00.

Child's teddy bear planter, 5" x 4". $75.00 – 100.00.

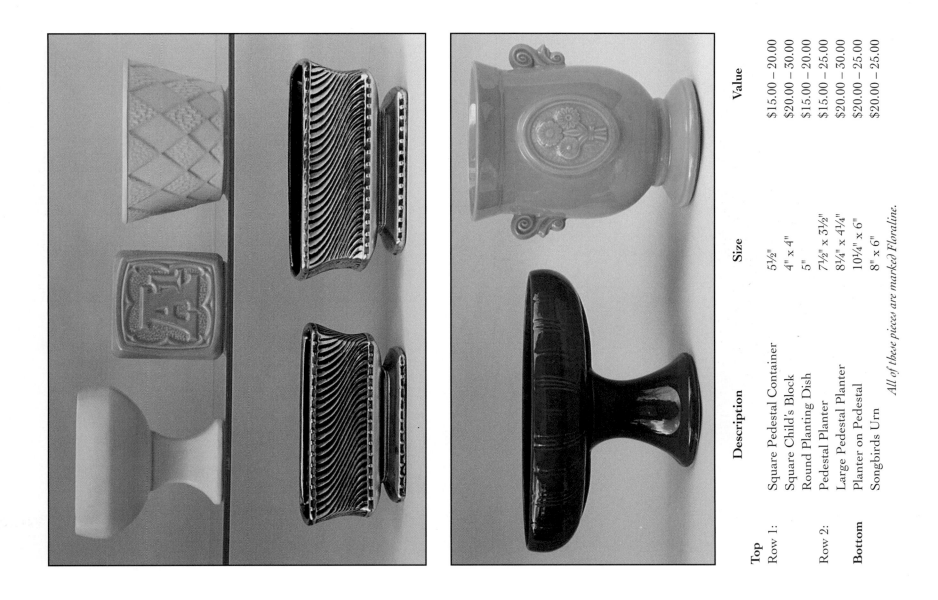

	Description	Size	Value
Top			
Row 1:	Square Pedestal Container	5½"	$15.00 – 20.00
	Square Child's Block	4" x 4"	$20.00 – 30.00
	Round Planting Dish	5"	$15.00 – 20.00
Row 2:	Pedestal Planter	7½" x 3½"	$15.00 – 25.00
	Large Pedestal Planter	8¼" x 4¼"	$20.00 – 30.00
	Planter on Pedestal	10¼" x 6"	$20.00 – 25.00
Bottom	Songbirds Urn	8" x 6"	$20.00 – 25.00

All of these pieces are marked Floraline.

Corinthian Garden Line planter, 1966, 4½" x 4½", McCoy mark. *$12.00 – 18.00.* The Corinthian Garden Line consisted of six different shapes and was available in the following colors: carnation green, avocado, terra cotta, and matte white.

ANTIQUA LINE

PAGE 275

	Year	Description	Size	Mark	Colors	Value
Top						
Row 1:	1973	Antiqua Pitcher Vase	9½"	McCoy	Gold or Silver	$25.00 – 35.00
	1973	Reds & Oranges Basket	7" x 9"	McCoy	Red/Orange with Green Interior	$35.00 – 45.00
	1973	Reds & Oranges Vase	9"	McCoy	Red/Orange with Green Interior	$30.00 – 40.00
Row 2:	1973	Antiqua Vase	9"	MCP	Silver or Gold	$30.00 – 40.00
	1973	Antiqua Pedestal Vase	8½"	MCP	Silver or Gold	$25.00 – 35.00
Bottom						
Row 1:	1973	Covered Compote	8"	MCP	Silver or Gold	$30.00 – 40.00
	1973	Round Antiqua Dish	7" x 3½"	McCoy	Gold & Silver	$20.00 – 30.00
Row 2:	1973	Reds & Oranges Strap Vase	12"	McCoy	Red/Orange with Green Interior	$75.00 – 100.00
	1974	Antiqua Strap Vase	12"	McCoy	Gold or silver	$75.00 – 100.00

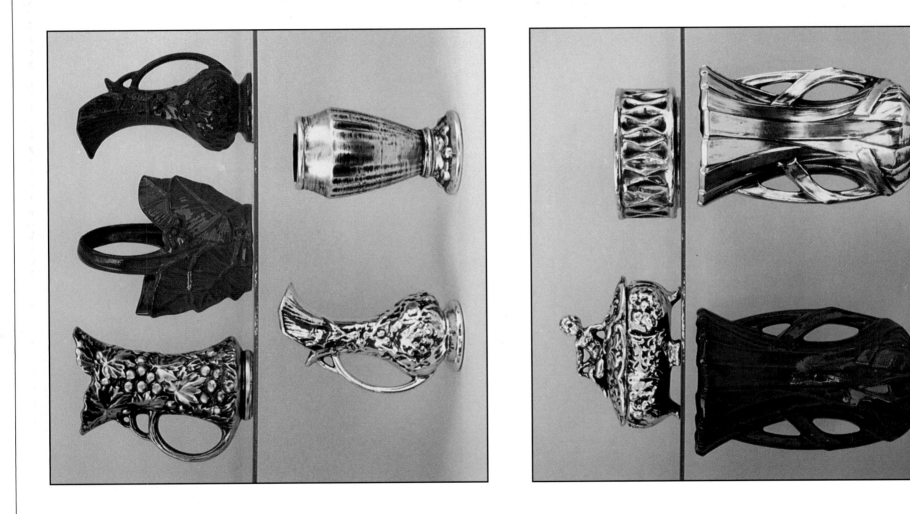

PAGE 277

	Year	Description	Size	Mark	Colors	Value
Top						
Row 1:	1950	Planting Dish	8"	McCoy	Green, Maroon & Turquoise	$15.00 – 20.00
	1970	Bud Vase	6"	McCoy	White, Yellow Tan & Green	$12.00 – 18.00
	1950	Planting Dish	8"	McCoy	Green, Maroon & Turquoise	$15.00 – 20.00
Row 2:	1966	Planting Dish	7"	McCoy	Green or White	$10.00 – 15.00
	1966	Planter	6"	McCoy	Green or White	$10.00 – 15.00
	1966	Planter	6"	McCoy	Green or White	$15.00 – 20.00
Bottom						
Row 1:	1966	Planting Dish	7"	McCoy	Green or White	$10.00 – 15.00
	1953	Planting Dish	8"	McCoy	Green, Yellow & Turquoise	$15.00 – 20.00
	1952	Planting Dish	6½"	McCoy	Green, Yellow or Turquoise	$12.00 – 18.00
	1960	Jardiniere	8¾"	McCoy	Green, White, or Yellow	$50.00 – 75.00
	This jardiniere was sold with a brass, three-legged stand.					
Row 2:	1958	Planting Dish	6½" x 7½"	McCoy	Pink, Yellow, or Green	$20.00 – 25.00

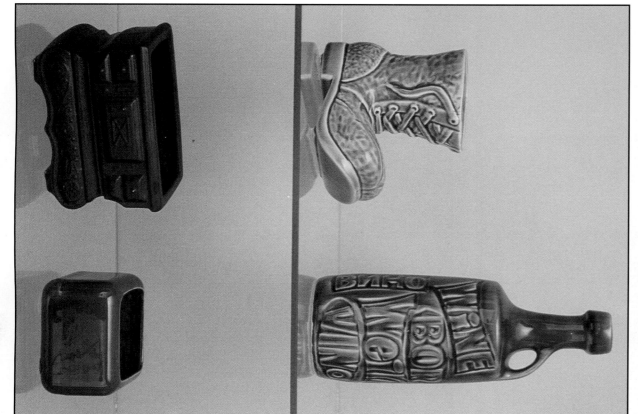

Row 1: Brown shoe planter, 5", no mark, 1970s. $30.00 – 40.00. Wine bottle decanter, 10", McCoy mark, 1972. $25.00 – 35.00. *Row 2:* Black stove planter, 4", McCoy mark, 1970s. $30.00 – 40.00. Brown planter, square, 3", McCoy mark, 1970s. $10.00 – 15.00.

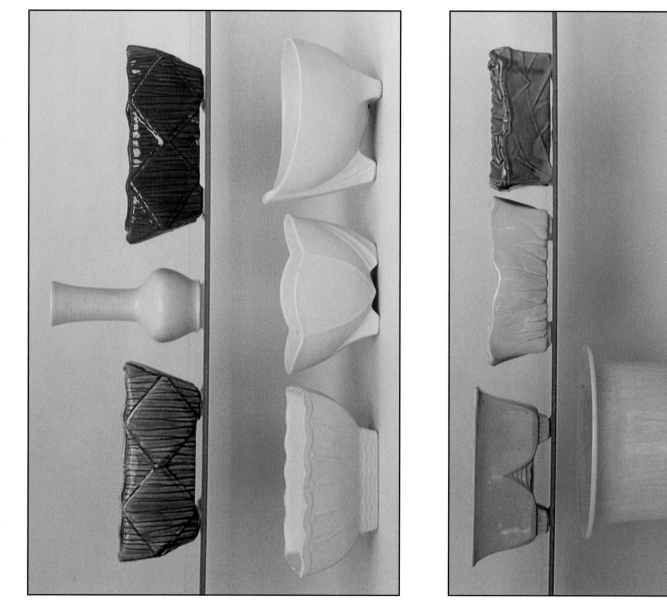

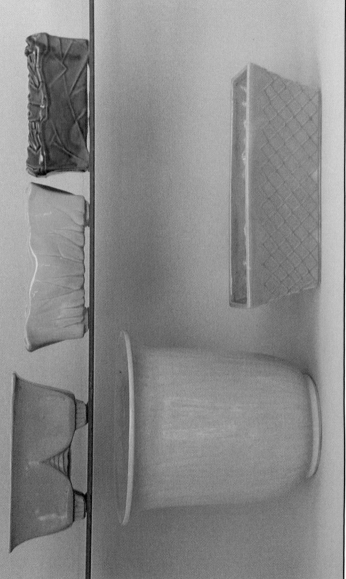

PAGE 279

	Year	Description	Size	Mark	Color	Value
Top						
Row 1:	1971	Happy Face Mug	4"	McCoy	White, Yellow & Tan	$12.00 – 18.00
	1971	Happy Face Planter	4"	McCoy	Yellow & White	$15.00 – 20.00
	1971	Happy Face Mug	4"	McCoy	Pictured in Most Common Yellow	$12.00 – 18.00
Row 2:	1971	Happy Face Mug	4"	McCoy	Tan, Yellow, or White	$15.00 – 20.00
	1971	Smile America Mug	4"	McCoy	White, Yellow, or Tan	$15.00 – 20.00
	1971	Happy Face Mug	4"	McCoy	Tan, Yellow, or White	$12.00 – 18.00
Bottom						
Row 1:	1971	Happy Face Cookie Jar	11½"	McCoy	Yellow	$75.00 – 100.00
	1971	Happy Face Bank	6"	USA	Yellow	$40.00 – 60.00

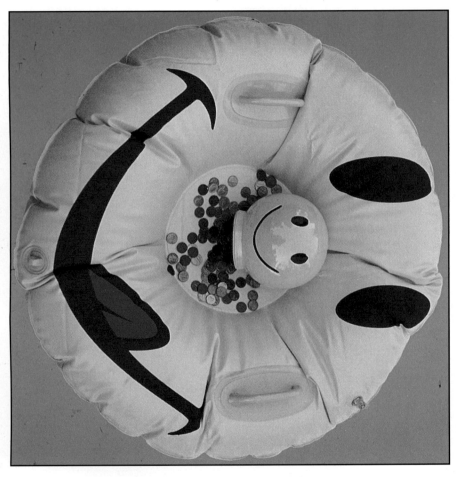

McCoy Happy Face bank floating on Happy Face pool float. For many McCoy collectors, it doesn't get any better than this.

STARBURST – GREEN THUMB – SPICE DELIGHT

Introduced in 1970, the Starburst line was available in a number of very pleasing color combinations. The modern distinctive design of the ten shapes make this line somewhat expensive when found. Available colors: matte orange with yellow flake interior and gold spray outside; matte green with gloss avocado gold spray outside; gloss white with gloss white and black highlights outside, matte white with gloss blue gold spray outside; gloss yellow interior with gloss yellow interior and gold spray outside; gloss yellow outside and white with white highlights.

PAGE 281

	Year	Description	Size	Mark	Color	Value
Top						
Row 1:	1970	Candlesticks	5"	MCP	Shown in Three Colors	$25.00 – 30.00
Row 2:	1970	Vase	9"	MCP	Shown in Two Colors	$30.00 – 40.00
	1970	Planter	6" x 3"	MCP	Matte White/Blue Shown	$30.00 – 35.00
Bottom						
Row 1:	1970	Planter	6" x 3"	MCP	Gloss White/White Shown	$30.00 – 35.00
	1970	Large Planter	9" x 3"	MCP	Gloss White/White Shown	$35.00 – 45.00
Row 2:	1970	Cherub Centerpiece	11"	No Mark	Silver with Gloss Black	$40.00 – 50.00

Lazy Susan, 1966, 14", McCoy mark, $40.00 – 50.00.

Lazy Susan, McCoy mark, 12", 1966, $35.00 – 45.00.

Iron hanging basket planter, Green Thumb line, 6½" x 6½", 1975, McCoy mark. $35.00 – 45.00. Spice Delight pitcher, 5", 1975, McCoy mark. There were over 30 pieces in this line. $10.00 – 15.00.

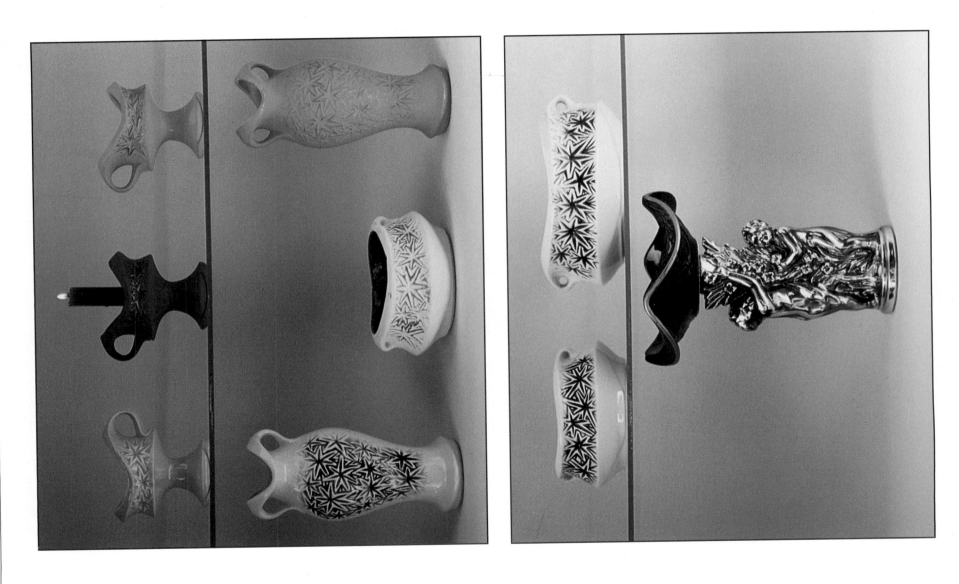

Year	Description	Size	Mark	Colors	Value
Top					
Row 1: 1968	Artificial Flower Dish	7" x 4"	McCoy	Matte White, Burnt Orange	$15.00 – 25.00
1968	Artificial Flower Dish	10" x 4"	McCoy	Carnation Green	$20.00 – 30.00
Row 2: 1968	Early American Pedestal	8½"	McCoy	Antique Crackle & Blue-Green	$30.00 – 40.00
1968	Low Flower Dish	7" x 4"	McCoy	White, Yellow & Green	$15.00 – 20.00
1968	Early American Vase	8"	McCoy	White, Yellow & Green	$25.00 – 30.00
Bottom					
Row 1: 1968	Tierra Line Planter	8" x 4"	McCoy	Various Colors	$10.00 – 20.00
1968	Flower Dish	7" x 4"	McCoy	White, Yellow & Green	$10.00 – 15.00
1968	Tierra Line Planter	5" x 5"	McCoy	Various Colors	$12.00 – 18.00
Row 2: 1968	Jardiniere	8½"	McCoy	White, Green & Brown	$35.00 – 45.00
1968	Jardiniere	10½"	McCoy	White, Green & Brown	$50.00 – 75.00

1968 Tierra line planter. All dressed up and ready to go. $12.00 – 18.00.

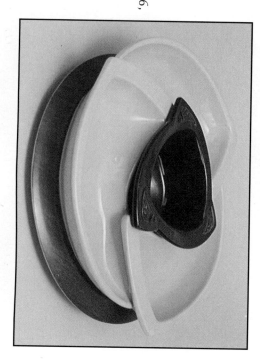

Lazy Susan, 14", 1966, McCoy mark. $40.00 – 50.00.

Page 285

	Year	Description	Size	Mark	Colors	Value
Top						
Row 1:	1971	7-League Boot Stein	8¼"	McCoy	Black/Gray & Ivory/Brown	$35.00 – 50.00
		7-League Boot has original tag attached telling the German fairy tale and giving the origin of the 7-League Boot.				
	1978	Beer Stein	7"	McCoy	Ivory with Brown Spray	$30.00 – 40.00
	1971	German Theme Stein	8¾"	USA	Various	$40.00 – 60.00
Row 2:	1971	Brightly Colored Mug	3" x 5"	McCoy	Orange, Green & Yellow (Bright)	$10.00 – 15.00
	1971	Mug	3" x 5"	McCoy	These were sold with a saucer	$10.00 – 15.00
	1979	Western Line Mug	4"	McCoy	Brown & Tan	$30.00 – 35.00
	1978	Western Theme Mug	6"	McCoy	Brown & Tan	$30.00 – 35.00
Bottom	1974	Coal Bucket Planter	8" x 10"	McCoy	Black with Gold Decoration	$35.00 – 75.00
	1959	Coffee Server	7"	USA	Turquoise, Yellow, Pink & Brown	$30.00 – 40.00
	1959	Creamer	2½"	USA	Turquoise, Yellow, Pink & Brown	$10.00 – 15.00

Western line mug pictured with vintage Western theme plastic pins, 4", 1979, McCoy mark. $50.00 – 55.00. Mug information above.

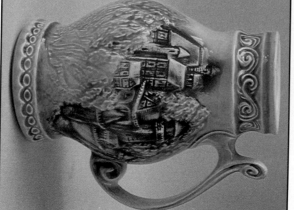

Detail both sides of the German stein described above. The bottom is marked "Hand Decorated USA."

7-league boot beer stein shown in both colors, 8¼", 1971, McCoy mark. $35.00 – 50.00. 7-league boot pencil holder, 5", 1973, matte brown spray. $50.00 – 60.00.

Islander collection ashtray, 4¼", 1979, pineapple & shell shapes, McCoy mark. $10.00 – 15.00. Novelty fish ashtray, 4", honey glazed brown. McCoy mark. $10.00 – 15.00.

Western Ware line, 1979. Popular Western theme pottery double collectible – Designed by: Billie McCoy & Al Klubert. The "JR" brand incorporated is from Billie's father's ranch. Besides those shown here, McCoy made three more items in the line: cookie jar called grub box; smaller mug; 10 oz.; and a 2½ qt. milk pitcher. Honey glazed or taupe brown, all McCoy marked. Mug, 16 oz., $30.00 – 35.00; boots vase, 7", $40.00 – 60.00; snack bowl, 4", $15.00 – 25.00; ashtray, 10", $40.00 – 60.00.

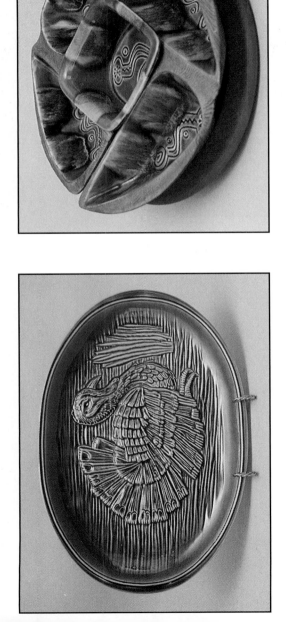

	Year	Description	Size	Mark	Colors	Value
Top photo left:	1973	Turkey Platter	16" x 11"	McCoy	Brown Glazed & Decorated	$50.00 – 65.00
Top photo right:	1970s	Lazy Susan	12"	McCoy	Green & Brown	$40.00 – 50.00
Bottom photo:	1971	Beer Stein, 68 oz.	9¾"	Hand Decorated, USA	Exotic Green, Brown & Gray	$35.00 – 50.00
	1971	German Theme Stein	8¾"	Hand Decorated, USA	Blue & Brown, Hand Decorated	$40.00 – 60.00

Introduced in 1972 to commemorate the 200th anniversary of America, the Spirit of '76 was a very successful line as seen by its availability. There were seventeen items produced for sale during 1972. Besides the pieces shown on the facing page, there were a smaller candle holder, a four-piece canister set, two sizes of bean pots and a covered bowl. All

pieces have the Eagle & Flag decal that says "The Spirit of '76." They are brown and white gloss and have the following information stamped on the bottom: "Carved Wooden Eagle, Artist unknown, National Gallery of Art, Washington, D.C."

Left and above: 1995 photographs of the murals painted in 1972 on the outside wall at the McCoy Pottery factory in Roseville, Ohio. This line, and its introduction in 1972, meant a great deal to McCoy and the hundreds of employees at McCoy Pottery.

PAGE 289

	Year	Description	Size	Mark	Value
Top					
Row 1:	1972	Large Pitcher	8"	USA	$25.00 – 35.00
	1972	Small Pitcher	5½"	McCoy	$12.00 – 18.00
	1972	Bean Pot	6½" x 10"	McCoy	$25.00 – 40.00
Row 2:	1972	Coffee Mugs	4"	McCoy	$10.00 – 15.00
	1972	Bell	5¼"	No Mark	$30.00 – 40.00
Bottom					
Row 1:	1972	Salt & Pepper Shakers	3¾"	USA	$15.00 – 30.00
	1972	Creamer	4¼"	McCoy	$15.00 – 20.00
	1972	Large Candleholder	3" x 7"	McCoy	$20.00 – 35.00
Row 2:	1972	Cookie Jar	10½"	USA	$50.00 – 75.00
	1972	Tall Vase	9"	McCoy	$25.00 – 35.00
		This vase has been found with the FLORALINE mark.			
	1972	Jug	10"	USA	$25.00 – 40.00

1975 Green Thumb planters pictured with a burlap bunny. Both pieces have the McCoy mark. Wooden bucket jardiniere, 8" x 6½", $25.00 – 50.00. Turtle planter, 8" x 6", $20.00 – 50.00.

Verse on Happytime water can:
"The happiest time I ever had
Was when I made another glad."

PAGE 291

	Year	Description	Size	Mark	Colors	Value
Top						
Row 1:	1973	Fish Platter	18" x 8¼"	USA Ovenproof	White, Brown & Rose	$40.00 – 55.00
Row 2:	1973	Small Fish Platter	5½" x 4½"	USA	Rose, White & Brown	$25.00 – 30.00
Bottom						
Row 1:	1973	Happytime Water Can	5½" x 9½"	McCoy	White Matte	$20.00 – 30.00
	1973	Happytime Pitcher	5½" x 4½"	McCoy	White Matte	$10.00 – 15.00
	1973	Snack Bowl	5" x 8"	McCoy	Brown, White & Green	$25.00 – 35.00
Row 2:	1971	Soup Kettle w/Cover	7" x 7"	McCoy	Metallic Brown	$20.00 – 35.00
	1971	Soup Pots	3" x 4"	McCoy	Metallic Brown	$5.00 – 10.00

The 2 qt. soup kettle was sold with a copper handle as shown.

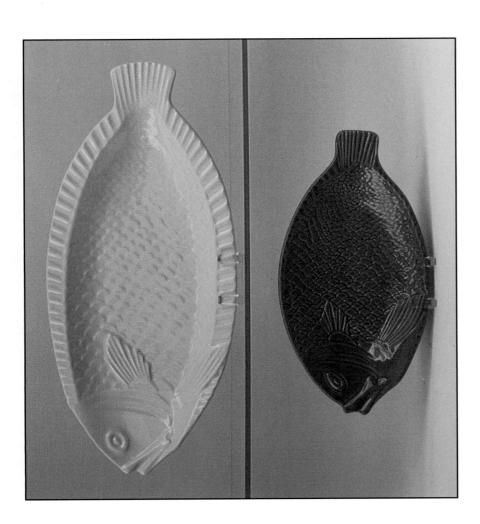

From left:	Year	Description	Size	Mark	Value
	Early '70s	Kitten with ball of yarn planter	7" x 5½"	McCoy Mark & Mold #3026	$80.00 – 100.00
	Early '70s	Dog Planter	7½" x 5"	Factory Mold #3027	$80.00 – 100.00
	Early '70s	Deer Planter	6¾" x 6"	Factory Mold #3028	$70.00 – 90.00

Available colors: Black, Blue, White, or Brown with an over wash glaze as shown. These three animal planters are very much McCoy and very collectible. Look for mold numbers.

The Pottery Shop sign by McCoy. This plaque was made for the J.C. Penney Co. in the early 1980s shortly following the departure of Nelson McCoy. However, the company lost the account before the plaques could be shipped. No one knows for sure how many were produced, but best estimate puts the number at between 125 – 150 pieces. There are no marks on the back. 4" x 5". $350.00 – 500.00. Very desirable

Page 293

	Year	Description	Size	Mark	Colors	Value
Top						
Row 1:	1974	Small Pitcher & Saucer	5"	McCoy	Various	$10.00 – 20.00
	1974	Same pitcher, different color and decal.				
Row 2:	1974	Pitcher & Saucer	5" x 7"	McCoy	Various	$15.00 – 25.00
	1972	Large Pitcher & Bowl	11" x 12"	MCP	Brown, Blue, Green & White	$50.00 – 70.00
Bottom						
Row 1:	1970s	Fish Hanging Basket	5¼" x 10½"	McCoy	Various Matte Colors	$25.00 – 35.00
	1970s	With Love Vase	7¼"	McCoy	Various	$25.00 – 30.00
Row 2:	1970s	Love Planting Dish	6" x 3"	McCoy	Various	$25.00 – 30.00
	1970s	Turtle Planter	5" x 9½"	McCoy	Various	$30.00 – 40.00

Cat face planter, also produced in gray, 1978, 5" x 6", McCoy mark. $35.00 – 50.00. Long necked cat, 1950s, no mark, 15½" x 5" base. $50.00 – 65.00.

Scary gorilla mug, 1978, McCoy mark. $30.00 – 40.00.

PASTA CORNER LINE

Introduced in 1979, the Pasta Corner line was a favorite dishware line for the '80s pasta craze. Like the Spirit of '76 line, Nelson McCoy hit the nail on the head for timing with this introduction. The line sold very well and is readily avail-

able today. Many collectors use these pieces for entertaining dinner guests because there are over twenty-five different pieces. The line is described as almond with brown stripe and decal.

PAGE 295	Year	Description	Size	Mark	Value
Top					
Row 1:	1979	Salt & Pepper Shakers	3¾"	No Mark	$15.00 – 25.00
	1979	Wine Carafe	7½"	McCoy	$30.00 – 40.00
	1979	Two Wine Cups	3½"	McCoy	3-piece set
Row 2:	1979	Parmesan Shaker	5"	No Mark	$15.00 – 25.00
	1979	Bread Tray	13"	McCoy	$20.00 – 30.00
Bottom					
Row 1:	1979	Salad Bowl	12½"	McCoy	$25.00 – 35.00
	1979	Antipasto Platter	9½"	McCoy	$15.00 – 25.00
Row 2:	1979	Lasagna Platter	12½"	McCoy	$25.00 – 35.00
	1979	Soup Pot w/Ladle	7"	McCoy	$30.00 – 45.00

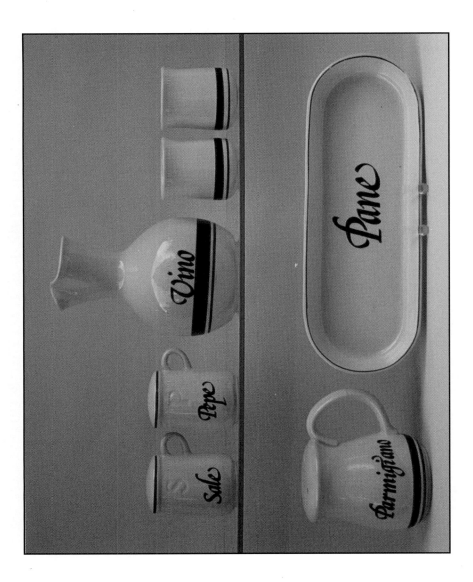

The two most prevalent lines shown here are Graystone and Canyon. Graystone is described as elegant country casual ware, from freezer to oven. The Canyon line which has a textured tan finish is dark brown with a darker rim. Only the coffee mugs and some of the serving pieces are marked McCoy.

Brown drip salt and pepper shaker set, 1968, original Nelson McCoy box. $25.00 – 35.00.

Morano line relish tray and shell serving bowl, 1968. Tray, $20.00 – 25.00. Bowl, $25.00 – 35.00.

PAGE 297

	Year	Description	Size	Mark	Colors	Value
Top						
Row 1:	1977	Creamer	4"	McCoy	Brown Drip	$8.00 – 10.00
	1977	Coffee Mug	5"	McCoy	Brown Drip	$6.00 – 10.00
	1977	Coffee Mug	4"	McCoy	Brown Drip	$5.00 – 10.00
	1977	Coffee Mug	4"	McCoy	Brown Drip	$5.00 – 10.00
Row 2:	1977	Graystone Dinner Plate	10½"	NM	Speckled Tan & Brown	$10.00 – 15.00
	1977	Graystone Salad Plate	7½"	NM	Speckled Tan & Brown	$7.00 – 10.00
	1977	Graystone Cup & Saucer	4" x 6"	McCoy	Speckled Tan & Brown	$8.00 – 12.00
Bottom						
Row 1:	1977	Canyon Serving Bowl	3" x 8"	NM	Textured Tan/Brown	$20.00 – 25.00
	1977	Canyon Mug & Saucer	4" x 6"	McCoy on mug	Same as Above	$8.00 – 12.00
	1977	Canyon Salad Plate	7½"	NM	Textured Tan/Brown	$7.00 – 10.00
Row 2:	1977	Canyon Dinner Plate	10½"	NM	Textured Tan/Brown	$10.00 – 15.00
	1977	Graystone Milk Pitcher	7¼"	NM	Textured Tan/Brown	$20.00 – 30.00
	1977	Canyon Covered Casserole	8" x 4"	NM	Textured Tan/Brown	$20.00 – 30.00

	Year	Description	Size	Mark	Colors	Value
Top						
Row 1:	1975	Stone Craft Creamer	4"	McCoy	Almond w/ Brown Stripes	$10.00 – 15.00
	1975	Stone Craft Pitcher	5¾"	McCoy	Same as above	$20.00 – 30.00
	1975	Stone Craft Covered Sugar	4"	McCoy	Same as above	$12.00 – 18.00
Row 2:	1975	Stone Craft Coffee Mug	4"	McCoy	Almond w/ Pink & Blue Stripes	$8.00 – 10.00
	1975	Stone Craft Coffee Mug	6"	McCoy	Almond w/ Pink & Blue Stripes	$8.00 – 10.00
	1975	Stone Craft Bowl	6"	McCoy	Almond w/ Brown Stripes	$7.00 – 10.00
	1975	Stone Craft Bowl	7"	McCoy	Almond w/ Brown Stripes	$7.00 – 10.00
Bottom						
Row 1:	1975	Stone Craft Teapot	5"	McCoy	Almond w/ Blue & Pink Stripes	$20.00 – 30.00
	1975	Stone Craft Dog Dish	6"	McCoy	Same as above	$20.00 – 30.00
	1975	Stone Craft Mixing Bowl	3½ qt.	McCoy	Almond w/ Blue & Pink Stripes	$15.00 – 20.00
Row 2:	1975	Stone Craft Mixing Bowl	6 qt.	McCoy	Same as above	$20.00 – 30.00
	1975	Stone Coffee Mug	4"	McCoy	Same as above	$6.00 – 10.00
	1975	Stone Craft Mixing Bowl	10 qt.	McCoy	Same as above	$25.00 – 35.00

There is a bridge in Zanesville, Ohio, that is shaped like a "Y" where two roads come together on the bridge to form one. $35.00 – 45.00.

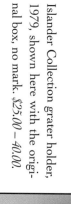

Wine Cellar line decanter, 13¾" tall, 1973, USA mark. $40.00 – 50.00.

Islander Collection grater holder, 1979, shown here with the original box, no mark. $25.00 – 40.00.

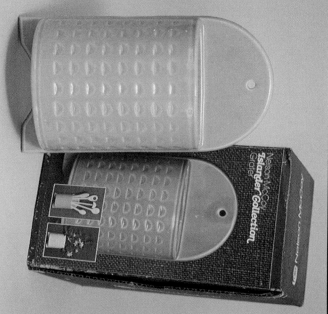

Islander Collection grater, 1979, shown here with the original box. $25.00 – 40.00.

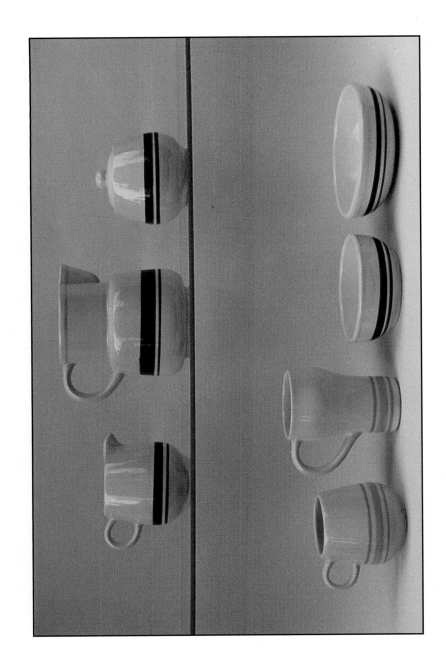

J.C. Penney sold this collection during the late 1970s and early '80s. This is the Oriental flower design pattern that was moderately successful. The pottery is perfect for the powder room where the large floor vase can be used as a wastepaper basket. Empty basket with adult supervision. All are marked McCoy and have a floral decal under the glaze.

Wall Pocket	9"	$40.00 – 75.00
Covered Temple Jar	11"	$60.00 – 75.00
Large Floor Vase	15"	$90.00 – 110.00
Small Ginger Jar	5¼"	$30.00 – 40.00
Bud Vase	6"	$20.00 – 30.00

SCANDIA LINE

Introduced in 1972, the Scandia line looks attractive with flowers as shown below. The line was produced in matte red, matte green, and matte tan with gloss white interiors. The matte finish was sprayed with a contrasting color for depth.

From Left:			
Scandia Line Planting Dish	6¼" x 4¼"	McCoy Mark	$20.00 – 25.00
Scandia Line Low Planting Dish	5¼" x 3¼"	McCoy Mark	$15.00 – 20.00
Scandia Line Floor Vase	14½" x 6½"	McCoy Mark	$40.00 – 50.00
Scandia Line Large Planter	10¾" x 4¼"	McCoy Mark	$25.00 – 35.00

The 1975 Fruit Festival line offered many kitchen accessories with the fruit motif decal under the glaze. They have the McCoy mark on the bottom.

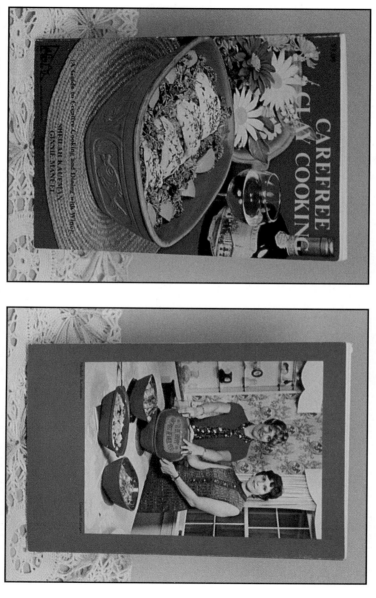

Front and back cover pages of the 1974, *Carefree Clay Cooking, A Guide to Creative Cooking and Dining with Wine* by Sheilah Kaueman & Ginnie Manuel. *$40.00 – 50.00.* The book has the McCoy logo in the front cover page and features the Islander Collection line.

Four piece canister set, 12", 10", 8", 6", with lids. $75.00 – 100.00. During the 1970s McCoy offered a large variety of canister sets and dishware accessories with decals under the glaze. Following is a partial line list:

Flower Burst with yellow decal
Spirit of '76 with eagle decal
Happytime with verse decal
Pagoda with sunflower decal
Yorkville Milk Can with rooster decal

Strawberry Country with strawberry decal
Antique Dutchland with windmill decal
Spice Delight with vegetable decal
Pasta Corner with italian decal

Canisters were also produced as part of the dishware lines without decals and in the same designs and glazes that were offered within the line. Following is a partial list: Gray Stone, Sand Stone, Brown Drip, Canyon.

Brown Drip corn dishes, 1966, 9" x 3¼", McCoy mark. $10.00 – 15.00 ea. These corn dishes still have the price tag on the bottom and sold for 88¢ retail in 1966.

Described as "The Gift Ware for Gracious Living"

Heart-shaped covered dish, MCP mark. The MCP mark was used at McCoy during the Mount Clemens Pottery ownership. 8" across, $30.00 – 40.00.

Golden Brocade jewel pedestal centerpiece, 8¾" x 4", paper label, no mark. $30.00 – 40.00. Golden Brocade jewel candleholder, USA mark, 9" tall. $25.00 – 35.00.

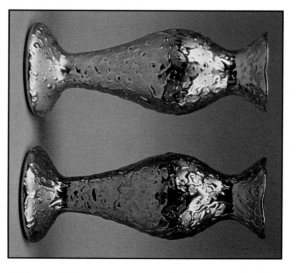

Golden Brocade bud vases, 6", 1972. $10.00 – 15.00. Both of these vases were made to be gold in color, but as you can see the gold has washed off the vase on the left leaving it silver in color. These bud vases were sold in colorful two-pack boxes. No mark.

Brocade paper labels. The paper labels were used on the bottoms of the Brocade line and instructed the owner to: "Wash in Lukewarm Soap Water."

McCoy Ashtrays

During the '60s and '70s McCoy produced a wide array of ashtrays in different shapes, sizes, and glazes. Enough ash-trays were produced during this period that there are McCoy collectors of ashtrays only.

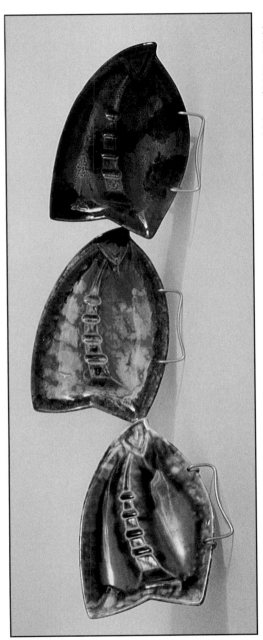

Arrowhead-shape ashtrays, 1965, McCoy mark, 9¾" x 6¾", bronze, green, tangerine, and blue. $20.00 – 50.00.

Modern shape ashtray, 1965, McCoy mark, 10⅛" x 8¾", fiesta red, white speck, blue and brown. $20.00 – 50.00. These were sold in assortment to dealers. "Party Group" ashtrays, 1965, McCoy mark, 3½" x 2½", stackable individuals, brown, white, bronze and yellow holder with assorted individual colors. $25.00 – 35.00, set. Fancy design ashtray, 1965, McCoy mark, 9¼" x 6¾", white speck and bronze. $20.00 – 50.00.

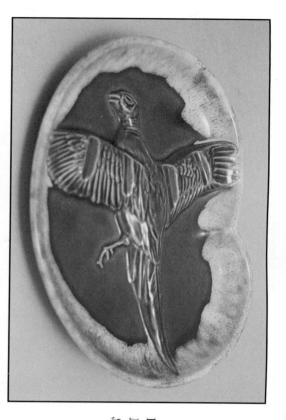

Pheasant ashtray, 9", McCoy mark. Great find! $50.00 – 60.00.

Square ashtray, 8" x 8", McCoy mark. $20.00 – 30.00. Sun Face round ashtray, McCoy mark. $25.00 – 35.00. Seagram's round ashtray, no mark. $20.00 – 30.00.

Page 307

Year	Description	Size	Mark	Value
Top:				
1970s	Seagram's Ashtray with Cup Holder Attached	9¾" x 7½"	No Mark	$25.00 – 35.00
1960	50th Anniversary Ashray	4" x 4" x 4"	McCoy	$60.00 – 80.00
1960s	Weightlifter Spoof Ashtray	8¼"	McCoy	$35.00 – 50.00
1965	Square Shape Ashtray	7" x 7"	McCoy	$10.00 – 20.00
	Bronze, Yellow & Green			
Middle:	Bottom of 50th Anniversary ashtray.			
Bottom:	1965 Figure-8 Shape Ashtray (two colors shown)	10¾" x 7"	McCoy	$20.00 – 30.00
	Avocado & Blue with Satin Speck Finish			
	1970s Schering Advertising Ashtray	8¾" x 5"	No Mark	$40.00 – 50.00
	Under the footprint is the following slogan: "Your Feet Must Last a Lifetime."			
	1970s Hydroplane Shape Ashtray Various Colors	7¼" x 7½"	McCoy	$20.00 – 30.00
	1957 Sunburst Gold Ashtray, Gold Color	6¾" x 8½"	McCoy	$25.00 – 35.00

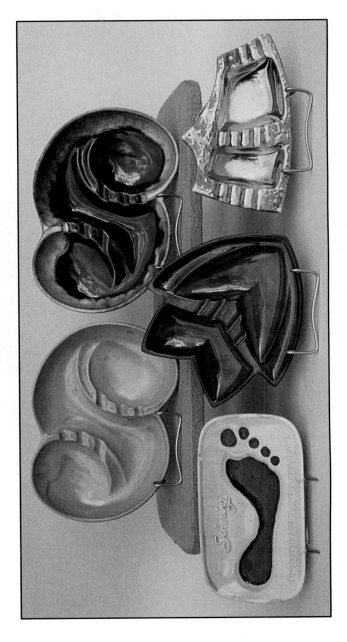

EL RANCHO BARBECUE SERVICE

Introduced in 1960, the El Rancho Barbecue Service pieces have become one of McCoy Pottery prized collectors' possessions. The value has risen greatly over the past decade due to its Western theme and the increasing popularity of McCoy pottery. The following excerpt is from a 1960 magazine advertisement: "EL RANCHO will serve equally well when you sit down at home on the patio, den or living room.

Beautifully hand decorated in ivory and saddle brown oven-proof pottery, the muted tones blend artfully with any decor, indoors or outdoors."

"THE IDEAL SERVICE TO RUSTLE UP THE GRUB FOR CHILDREN, TEENAGERS AND GROWN-UPS."

Sombrero serve all, no mark, 1960, 12" x 13", five-quart bowl, ice tub or chips bowl. (*The El Rancho sombrero cover doubles as an hors d'oeuvre tray.*) With Sombrero sitting on bowl, $350.00 – 400.00.

Row 1: 1960 El Rancho chuck wagon food warmer with brass wagon wheels/candleholder, 3-quart capacity, no mark. $225.00 – 250.00. 10 oz. coffee mugs, no mark, both sides shown. $35.00 – 45.00. *Row 2:* Ice tea server, USA mark, 11½" x 7½". $250.00 – 300.00. Coffee server, no mark, 12 – 14 cup capacity. $200.00 – 250.00.

Bowery savings bank, no mark, 3" x 6¼" x 4". $40.00 – 50.00. National Bank of Dayton eagle bank, 7½", no mark. $45.00 – 60.00. The Howard Savings Institution, N.J., 1857, 9", no mark. $40.00 – 50.00.

Bottom of the Bowery Saving bank shown to the right. It says "Replica, First Money Chest, 1834."

Page 311

	Description	Size	Mark	Colors	Value
Top					
Row 1:	Unipet Bowl with Lid	5"	No Mark	Green or Tan, as shown	$25.00 – 35.00
	There is a bell in the lid to call your pet for a treat. Pet vitamins were sold in this container.				
Row 2:	The Williamsburg Savings Bank	7"	No Mark	Various	$25.00 – 35.00
	Drydock Saving Bank	5"	No Mark	Various	$25.00 – 30.00
Bottom					
Row 1:	Immigrant Industrial Savings Bank	7½"	No Mark	Natural Eagle	$40.00 – 50.00
	Victory Depends on You, political figure	5½"	No Mark	Gray/Black	$40.00 – 50.00
	Seaman's Bank	5¾"	No Mark	White/Hand Decorated	$50.00 – 75.00
Row 2:	Large Metz Brewing Co. Bank	8¼"	No Mark	Tan w/Black, Red & White	$50.00 – 60.00
	Small Metz Brewing Co. Bank	6¼"	No Mark	Tan w/Black, Red & White	$35.00 – 45.00

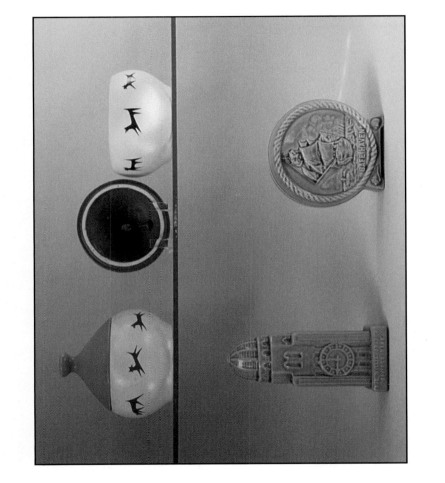

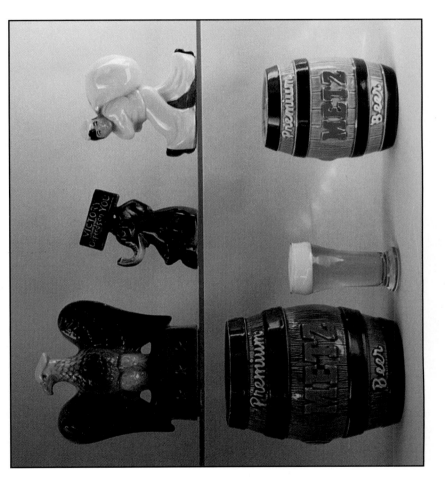

Nice display of American patriotic memorabilia. Statue of Liberty lighted clock with: McCoy-produced eagle theme Immigrant Industrial Savings bank and the Swank American Eagle dresser caddy.

ACCESSORIES FOR SWANK

McCoy produced pottery dresser caddies and accessories for the Swank Company. Swank sold these items through their network of men's apparel retailers and department stores. None of these pieces are marked McCoy.

PAGE 313

	Description	Size	Mark	Colors	Value
Top:	American Eagle Dresser Caddy	12" x 4½"	No Mark	Various	$40.00 – 55.00
	Lion Dresser Caddy	11" x 6"	No Mark	Black & White w/Red Felt	$50.00 – 60.00
Middle:	Dog with Shoehorn Tail	11" x 4½"	No Mark	Black or Brown Dog	$35.00 – 50.00
	Smiling Horse Dresser Caddy with Brush Tail	8" x 9"	No Mark	Green or Blue Blanket	$50.00 – 60.00
Bottom:	Hung-over Dog Bank	6" x 8"	No Mark	Various	$35.00 – 45.00
	Buffalo Dresser Caddy	10" x 5½"	No Mark	Black or Brown Decorated	$40.00 – 50.00

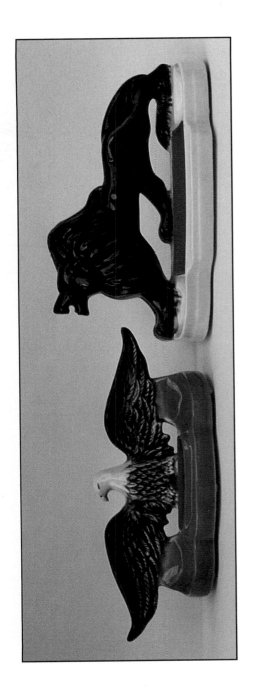

Hall of Education commemorative ashtray, 1965, NEWF, 5" round, no mark. $25.00 – 35.00. Pictured with school kid's vintage plastic pin.

Botton of the Lorena paddlewheeler, row one, facing page. It says: "BICENTENNIAL PROJECT OF ZANESVILLE AREA CHAMBER OF COMMERCE 1976 USA."

PAGE 315

	Description	Size	Mark	Colors	Value
Top					
Row 1:	Primo Beer Stein	6½"	No Mark	White with Primo Decal	$25.00 – 30.00
	Mirth is King Whiskey Decanter	9½"	No Mark	Gold Glaze with Black Base	$50.00 – 75.00
	The Mirth has green rhinestone eyes and a red rhinestone belly button.				
Row 2:	Lorena Bicentennial Project 1976	8½"	USA	White & Black Decorated	$50.00 – 75.00
	Vat 69 Pitcher	5½"	No Mark	Black/White	$40.00 – 50.00
	W.C. Fields Pitcher	7¾"	No Mark	Tan	$50.00 – 60.00
	Pitcher has Kentucky 86 proof whiskey printed in the mold on his shoulder				
	W.C. Fields Whiskey Decanter	8½"	No Mark	Tan & Black	$50.00 – 60.00
Bottom					
Row 1:	1932 Pierce Arrow Auto Decanter	11"	McCoy	Black/White with Gold Trim	$60.00 – 75.00
	Barcardi Rum Pitcher	5½"	No Mark	Black	$40.00 – 50.00
Row 2:	Apollo Missile Decanter	10"	MCP	Ivory/Brown Decorated	$40.00 – 75.00
	Apollo Astronaut Decanter	12"	USA	Ivory/Brown with Gold Face Mask	$100.00 – 125.00
	Miller Brewing Co. 1977 Stein	6¾"	No Mark	Ivory/Brown	$30.00 – 40.00

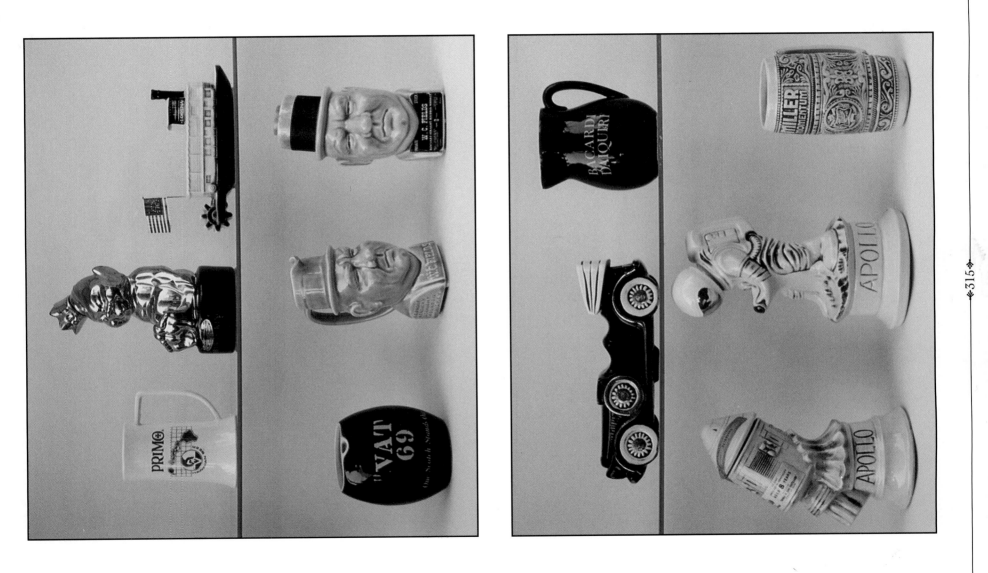

Retirement coffee mug from Nelson and Billie McCoy's retirement party. $100.00 – 150.00. It says: "Thanks for a wonderful 33 years. Good health and much happiness September 1981."

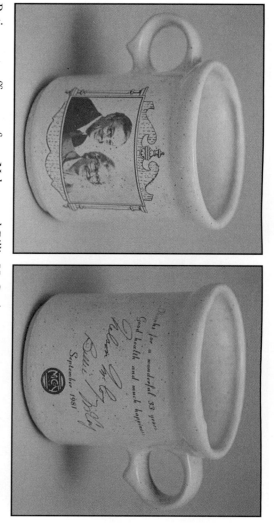

Child's planter for newborn, 4¼" x 5", McCoy mark, pink, blue, or yellow. $30.00 – 40.00.

Late '60s centerpiece, 10¾" across, McCoy mark, green and pink. Also produced in green/yellow combination. Also found without mark or with stamped letter "T" on bottom. $50.00 – 75.00.

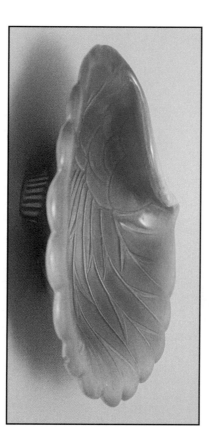

PAGE 317

	Description	Size	Mark	Value
Top:	Clown TV Bank	10"	McCoy	$65.00 – 80.00
	Lion TV Bank	9½"	McCoy	$65.00 – 80.00
	Bunny TV Bank	10½"	McCoy	$65.00 – 80.00

These banks have escalated in value rather quickly because they are good pieces both for McCoy collectors and for bank collectors.

Bottom:	Cats at the Barrel Bank	6½"		$65.00 – 80.00

The glaze on this piece is chalklike, and finished like the sports planters.

	The Lion TV Bank shown in the original box.		MCP	$80.00 – 100.00

Hard-to-find pottery pieces in their original package raise their value.

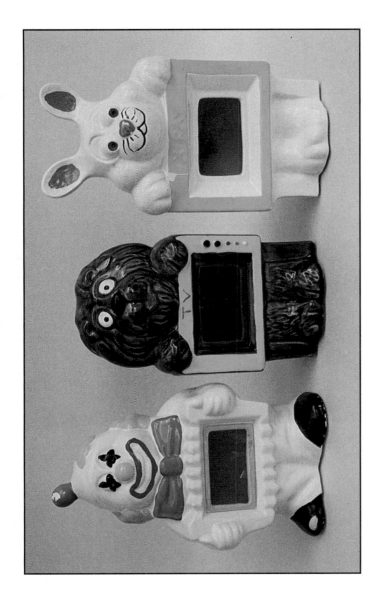

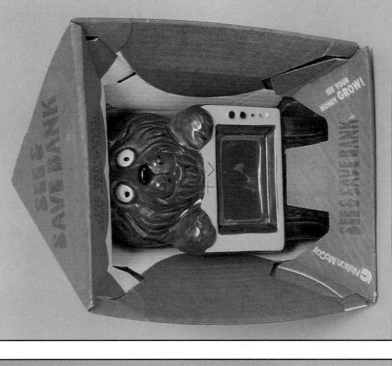

PAGE 319

	Description	Size	Mark	Value
Top				
Row 1:	Hunting Dog Mug	5"	McCoy	$20.00 – 25.00
	Your Father's Mustache Mugs	5"	MCP/USA	ea. $25.00 – 30.00
	There are many different advertisements found on these mugs. These mugs read: "Greenwich Village, NY, 426			
Row 2:	*Bourbon St., New Orleans, and Latimer Square, Denver."*			
	Coricidin Galen 131-201 AD	3½"	Schering	$20.00 – 25.00
	Three colors of the coffee mugs are shown.			
	DOM Coffee Mug	3½"	USA	$15.00 – 20.00
Bottom				
Row 1:	Secundum Artem	5"	Schering	$25.00 – 30.00
	Maimonides 1135-1204	5"	Schering	$25.00 – 35.00
	U.S.P 150th Anniversary	5"	No Mark	$35.00 – 45.00
Row 2:	Nassau County G.O.P. Pitcher	6¼"	McCoy	$30.00 – 40.00
	Old Crow Distillery Pitcher	7"	No Mark	$30.00 – 40.00
	Beer Stein/Vintage Auto Decal	5½"	McCoy	$25.00 – 30.00

DOM coffee mugs, USA mark. 3½", $15.00 – 20.00. 4" covered mug. $35.00 – 50.00.

Coffee mug from GM's introduction of the Pontiac Fiero automobile. McCoy mark, black and gold. $35.00 – 45.00.

Old Milwaukee beer stein with the original box. McCoy mark. $30.00 – 40.00.

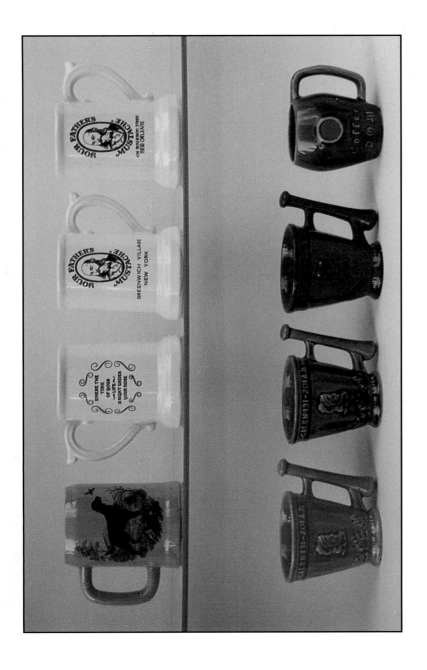

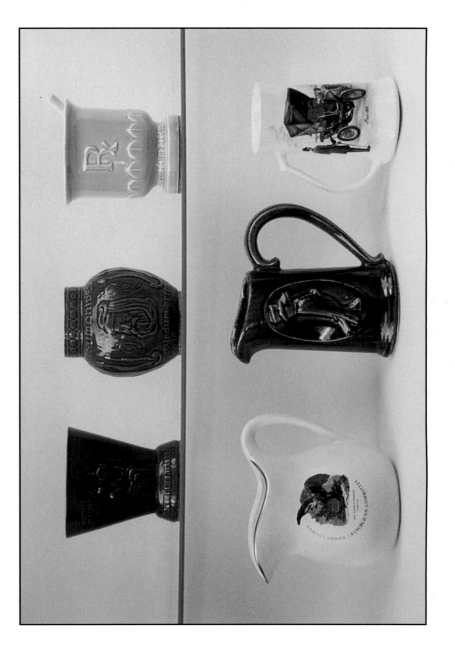

McCormick Iron Horse "Jupiter 60"

Introduced in 1969, the "Jupiter 60" train decanter set consists of a locomotive, wood tender, mail car, and a passenger car. This collection was first introduced at the Golden Spike Centennial at Promontory, Utah, and was an instant success with collectors. The locomotive is a replica of Central Pacific's #60 engine called Juniper. Central Pacific's Juniper 60 was built in New York and shipped west to help build the railroads. In 1869 the Juniper 60, going east, met Number 119 going west to complete the railroad. A golden spike was driven into the crosstie at that spot in the Promontory Valley.

"Jupiter 60" Iron Horse Locomotive in the original box, no mark. $75.00 – 100.00.

Entire set with locomotive, wood tender, mail car, and passenger car. $250.00 – 550.00.